Research in Dance IV: 1900-1990

Judith A. Gray, Editor

National Dance Association
an association of the
American Alliance for Health,
Physical Education, Recreation and Dance

This book is dedicated to my father,
Owen George Morgan,
who passed away July 4, 1991.

© 1992
American Alliance for Health,
Physical Education, Recreation and Dance
1900 Association Drive
Reston, Virginia 22091

ISBN: 0-88314-528-6

Purposes of the American Alliance for Health, Physical Education, Recreation and Dance

The American Alliance is an educational organization, structured for the purposes of supporting, encouraging, and providing assistance to member groups and their personnel throughout the nation as they seek to initiate, develop, and conduct programs in health, leisure, and movement-related activities for the enrichment of human life.

Alliance objectives include:

1. Professional growth and development—to support, encourage, and provide guidance in the development and conduct of programs in health, leisure, and movement-related activities which are based on the needs, interests, and inherent capacities of the individual in today's society.

2. Communication—to facilitate public and professional understanding and appreciation of the importance and value of health, leisure, and movement-related activities as they contribute toward human well-being.

3. Research—to encourage and facilitate research which will enrich the depth and scope of health, leisure, and movement-related activities; and to disseminate the findings to the profession and other interested and concerned publics.

4. Standards and guidelines—to further the continuous development and evaluation of standards within the profession for personnel and programs in health, leisure, and movement-related activities.

5. Public affairs—to coordinate and administer a planned program of professional, public, and governmental relations that will improve education in areas of health, leisure, and movement-related activities.

6. To conduct such other activities as shall be approved by the Board of Governors and the Alliance Assembly, provided that the Alliance shall not engage in any activity which would be inconsistent with the status of an educational and charitable organization as defined in Section 501(c)(3) of the Internal Revenue Code of 1954 or any successor provision thereto, and none of the said purposes shall at any time be deemed or construed to be purposes other than the public benefit purposes and objectives consistent with such educational and charitable status.

Bylaws, Article III

ACKNOWLEDGEMENTS

The following people made direct contributions to the production of this book:

Buff Brennan: I would like to thank Buff for her willingness to help me get started and for her valuable support and understanding in the early stages. Her *Research in Dance III* was an invaluable document and proved to be the solid foundation on which this book is based.

Patricia Rowe: I own much gratitude to Pat, my mentor, who vigorously took it upon herself to become involved in the data collection process. Through her generous efforts, many hard-to-find dissertations have been included in the final draft. I would also like to thank her for her provocative ideas and constant support.

Daneen Morgan: I'd like to acknowledge my indebtedness to Daneen who was responsible for entering the data into the computer's database. Her familiarity with the Macintosh computer and the database software was remarkable. I wish also to thank her for accessing and utilizing the UC network and thereby making the abstracting much more efficient.

Ellen Meyer: I wish to thank Ellen for her role as my developmental editor and as my publication sounding board. She kept the writing project running smoothly and coordinated the final production of this book.

Finally, I would especially like to thank those dance researchers who sent personal photos for inclusion in the book. The photos have greatly enhanced the content and the appearance of the finished product.

TABLE OF CONTENTS

PREFACE, *Judith A. Gray*   vi

CATALOG BY CATEGORY   1

    Administration   1
    Biography   3
    Children   8
    Choreography and Performance   10
    Education   20
    Ethnology and Anthropology   34
    History   46
    Music and Rhythm   54
    Notation and Movement Analysis   61
    Psychology and Therapy   63
    Related Arts:
        Literature   72
        Opera   75
        Painting   76
        Theatre   76
        Visual   78
    Science   78
    Styles:
        Ballet   81
        Jazz   85
        Modern   86
        Social   87
        Social (Square)   88
        Tap   89
    Technology and Film   89
    Theory and Philosophy   91

INDEX BY AUTHOR   99

INDEX BY ABSTRACT TITLE   105

PREFACE

Research in Dance IV is the latest and largest publication reflecting the impressive growth of doctoral-level research in dance and dance-related areas. It is actually the fifth published anthology of dance research and the fourth in a continuing series begun in 1968 with *Research in Dance I*, published by AAHPERD. The impressive volume of studies represented in this book is due in part to recent technological advances, particularly in the areas of computerized searches and retrieval of research documents and to sophisticated database management software.

The collection and organization of the approximately 550 doctoral dissertations that comprise this book began with an enormous challenge and a box of forms and materials from Buff Brennan, editor of *Research in Dance III*. It was argued that if it was important to publish the latest and largest compilation of dance research then it was equally important that each piece of research be available, as far as feasible, to the reader. Hence, a decision was made to limit the book to doctoral research which meant that the readers could be assured of access to the primary documents.

This decision had other ramifications. First, by eliminating the master's theses, the sheer size of the database was reduced to a more manageable and printable size. Second, most of the doctoral research had already been submitted to *Dissertation Abstracts International*, an internationally recognized institution which monitors and standardizes doctoral research across all disciplines. This meant that there was in existence an umbrella database which could provide a frame of reference and also verify the dance information. Third and finally, it was granted that doctoral research in dance was of the highest calibre and hence the book could be regarded by researchers as a valid and reliable authority.

HOW THE INFORMATION WAS GATHERED:
Accumulating all the doctoral research from 1990 was no small task. Indeed, the task is not complete, and may never be complete. As this book goes to press, more dissertations will undoubtedly come to light as a result of deeper and better computer search capabilities. Fortunately, this new information is neither discarded nor disregarded. It is simply added to the database to be retrieved on demand or readied for a published update. In the meantime, additions can be accessed by using the computerized database itself and then can be printed out individually.

The data gathering process began with an assessment of the contents of *Research in Dance III*, compiled and edited by Buff Brennan of the University of Wisconsin at Madison. 305 reports of doctoral dissertations were extracted from this document and subsequently formed the base of the current collection. Next, letters were sent to prominent universities and colleges to apprise them of the project and to solicit abstracts from their own archives. The remainder of the search was conducted electronically. Using key words such as "dance," "rhythm," "movement," "arts," and "labanotation," it was possible to retrieve over 600 titles from computerized bibliographic sources. The University of California computer network provided the necessary access.

The network search not only provided important elements of the database such as author, title, year, and institution, but it also included the 350 words-or-less abstracts for dissertations submitted after 1980. For abstracts prior to this time, a foot search was undertaken, typically within the confines of a university library reference section. Notwithstanding, most of the abstracts were found by these two methods, approximately 85% of the total. An additional 7% were located by individual dance department chairs and in particular Dr. Patricia Rowe of New York University. The result is that an overwhelming 92% of the dance dissertation references include brief abstracts. As a consequence, readers using this book will not only have bibliographic information at their fingertips, but they will also get a summary description of the research itself in the form of a 50-100 word abstract which will enable them to identify, review, compare, and evaluate trends and directions in dance research.

DATA DESCRIPTION AND ENTRY:
Once the information was located it required formatting and massaging to fit the published page. The data was formatted according to 14 descriptors or "fields." These were:
- Author's name
- Title
- Degree
- Advisor
- Institution
- Year
- Number of pages
- Category
- Availability
- Volume and page in *Dissertation Abstracts International*
- Order number
- Abstract
- Related category
- Author photo

The contents of these fields can be found and sorted using special features of the software. For example, it is possible to find and list all the dissertations from a specific institution and then sort them by advisor or category or year or any of the other field descriptors. The series charts that are found in this Preface were generated using these features and then converting the results into graphic form.

Data entry was accomplished by keyboarding the information in each field per dissertation into the open-ended files of the computer's database. The original abstracts were condensed and summarized and entered into the pertinent field. Formats or layouts for the arrangement of the information once it was entered could take many forms. This proved to be a very useful feature and greatly assisted the search and analysis procedures. Data entry is ongoing and when a doctoral reference is submitted, the details are quickly and easily added to the master file. The overall product is a new device for taming and managing the mass of information generated by hundreds of doctoral dissertations in dance and dance-related areas.

HOW TO ORDER: To place an order for a dissertation listed in this book, call or write:

University Microfilms International
300 North Zeeb Road
Ann Arbor, MI 48106
U.S.A.
or call toll free: 1-800-521-3042

Have the following information ready:
   Order number
   Author's last name
   Complete dissertation title
   Choice of format (microform or paper)
   Billing name and address
   Shipping name and address if different from above
   Credit card name, number, and expiration date
   From Canada, call toll-free: 1-800-343-5299

If you have access to a university library, it may prove more efficient to simply locate the reference by its *Dissertation Abstracts International* volume and page number.

ANALYSIS OF DATA:

Research in Dance IV: 1900-1990 presents, organizes, and synthesizes information needed to review or conduct dance research. The database on which it is founded can do much more. It allows researchers to experiment with different ways to organize information and to use the computer's ingenuity to take advantage of new ideas and hypotheses. The database has the graphical power to transform data into valuable and visual information. This book mirrors some of the versatility of the database and in it you will find the information organized according to category, alphabetically by author, and indexed. It is possible, for example, by activating the database to analyze the data by a number of research questions and issues relating to the following perspectives:

   1. **Historical**: Discussing the first published dissertations in dance and posing relationships between their content and the onset of the first dance major program in 1926 at the University of Wisconsin at Madison. Tracing dance research by way of historical events and conditions, particularly from the 1930s to the 1980s and making connections between dissertation categories and dance history.

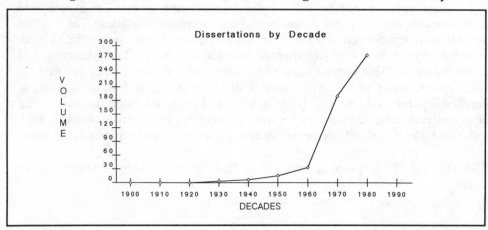

2. **Institutional**: Calculating the volume of dissertation output by university. Identifying those institution with the significant incidence and duration of dance research. Which advisors tended to have the greatest influence? What geographic parts of the country are most highly represented?

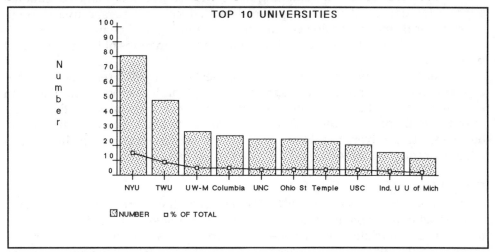

3. **Stylistic:** Overviewing the range of dance styles represented in the doctoral research. Attempting to explain why ballet studies dominate the research. Demonstrating trends in styles over time and identifying the emergence of one style over another. Focusing on unusual approaches to studying dance style. Which styles lend themselves to scientific research?

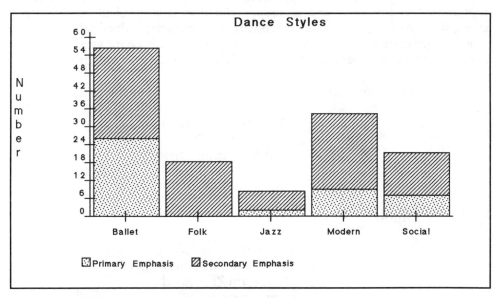

4. **Theoretical**: Describing a number of theoretical approaches to studying dance—philosophy, criticism, history, aesthetics, etc., and analyzing accordingly.

Identifying nonperformance based research and suggesting relationships between this research and performance-based research. How many theoretical studies have a basis in dance performance as opposed to dance education?

5. **Educational**: Differentiating between levels of education and educational settings for dance. Approaching the dance educational perspective through psychological and physiological dissertation findings. Tracing the research methodology trends from mid-century to the present in terms of instruments and populations.

6. **Ethnographic**: Describing a cross-section of studies representing other cultures and geographic areas. Summarizing the anthropological studies from ancient to modern times pointing out the strengths and weaknesses. Explaining how dance ethnographic research can play a role in embracing cultural diversity in our schools and universities. How many studies were conducted in the field and in other countries outside America?

CONCLUSION:

Although *Research in Dance IV: 1900-1990* represents a vast array of dance research and surpasses all previous attempts to gather and collate doctoral dissertations in dance and dance-related areas, it nonetheless serves another very important purpose. It preserves for all time the remarkable efforts of over 500 women and men who sought to expand the knowledge base of the dance field by dedicating months and months of their lives to the pursuit of greater understanding. This book then recognizes these creative, committed researchers and commends them for their perseverance and will to succeed. A doctoral dissertation is a landmark accomplishment in the lives of those who take on this awesome task and complete it. I would like to take this opportunity to congratulate all of you who are represented in this book and to assure you that your level of scholarship is exemplary. And for those readers who are contemplating a doctoral program or who are interested in conducting research related to dance, I hope you are inspired and encouraged by what you are about to discover in the following pages.

If your doctoral research is not listed in this book, please contact:

National Dance Association
AAHPERD
1900 Association Drive
Reston, VA 22091
U.S.A.

Or write to:

Dissertation Publishing
University Microfilms International
300 North Zeeb Road
Ann Arbor, MI 48106
U.S.A.

Catalog by Category

Administration

Bible-Federbush, Deborah Ann, Ed.D. (1983)
University of Cincinnati, Ohio
Performance requirements held by artistic directors of professional modern dance companies
158 pp. 44/06-A, 1611   ORDER NO. 832,3190
Available from: Diss. Abstracts International
This study analyzes the opinions held by twentysix artistic directors of professional modern dance companies on the performance requirements for modern dancers. The results describe the values they hold in terms of importance of specific qualities for a modern dance performance.
See also: Choreography and Performance

Bushey, Richard James, Ph. D. (1976)
University of Southern California, California.
Societal influences on the programmes of modern dance in American colleges and universities: 1918–1945
37/11-A, 7019   ORDER NO. Not Available
Available from: Diss. Abstract International
This study indentifies important developments occurring in the growth of modern dance programmes in higher education and determines which societal changes have the greatest influence. The chief influences are found to be the philosophies of the various educational components and the developments in the arts.
See also: Styles: Modern

Casten, Carole M. Sokolow, Ph. D. (1983)
University of Southern California, California
The differences between dance programs allied with physical education departments and fine arts departments in American colleges and universities
45/05-A, 1307   ORDER NO. 0554323

Available from: Diss. Abstracts International Micrography, Doheny Library USC
This study identifies the differences between dance programs allied with physical education departments and fine arts departments in American colleges and universities. Selected findings reveal many differences and similarities, but also program autonomy. The program focus of the fine arts is performance preparation while the focus is split between teacher preparation and performance in the physical education programs. It is concluded however, that dance flourishes in both alliances.
See also: Education

Clemente, Karen, Ed. D. (1990)
Temple University, Pennsylvania
Dance in the public schools: Implementing state policies and curricular guidelines for dance in education—a nationwide study
203 pp. 51/09-A, 2902   ORDER NO. 91-03565
Available from: Diss. Abstracts International
An investigation of statewide policies regarding dance programs in public education. The study considers national trends in arts education reform in the 1980's. Certain nationwide concerns are revealed including lack of dance teacher certification, the need for dance as a graduation requirement, and the lack of regular dance instruction in public schools.
See also: Education

Hagood, Thomas Kerry, Ph. D. (1990)
University of Wisconsin at Madison, Wisconsin
The organizational sociology of dance: An analysis, comparison and environmental description of primary organizations advocating dance in higher education.
205 pp. 51/04-A, 1156   ORDER NO. 902,5720
Available from: Diss. Abstracts International
This study presents an analysis, comparison, and environmental description of three pri-

mary organizations advocating dance in higher education: the National Dance Association, the Council of Dance Administrators, and the National Association of Schools of Dance. The organizational network these groups create among themselves is also analyzed for cohesiveness and goal direction.

Hearth, Dale Lynn, Ph. D. (1984)
Texas Technical University, Texas
Marketing the performance arts: The Joffrey Ballet's twenty-fifth anniversary season.
347 pp. 45/08-A, 2591   ORDER NO. 8419864
Available from: Diss. Abstracts International
This study identifies differences between marketing business products and performing arts products, analyzes which marketing practices may or may not work for performing arts organizations, and proposes specific techniques for building a total marketing plan for the performing arts. It also examines ways in which the Joffrey Ballet successfully applied specific marketing practices to compile a total marketing plan, analyzes and evaluates the effectiveness of that plan, and outlines ways in which performing arts managers can learn from the Joffrey Ballet's marketing experimentations.
See also: Styles: Ballet

Lally, Kathleen Ann, Ph. D. (1978)
Texas Woman's University, Texas.
A history of the Federal Dance Theatre of the Works Progress Administration, 1935–1939
110 pp. 41/01-A, 06   ORDER NO. 791,5877
Available from: Diss. Abstracts International
A description of the US Government's first attempt at subsidizing the arts in order to provide relief for unemployed artists. An independent Federal Dance Theatre is established and despite it's problems, the group succeeds in accomplishing several notable dance programs, particulary in New York, Chicago and Los Angeles. An experiment with young choreographers is also successful as is the choreographers' use of American themes.
See also: Choreography and Performance

Lindquist, Barbara Anne, Ed.S (1989)
Central Michigan University, Michigan
The study of arts directed programs in the Kent Intermediate School District, 1987–1988
96 pp. MAI 27-03, 322   ORDER NO. 1335631
Available from: Diss. Abstracts International
This study determines the status of arts directed programs in the K-12 Kent Intermediate School District for the areas of art, vocal music, band, orchestra, dance, and drama. The results of a survey indicate that the levels of programming increased over a five year period in all areas except dance and drama.
See also: Education

Mehrhof, Joella Hendricks, Ed. D. (1986)
University of Kansas, Kansas
Utilization of funds and perceptions of corporate funding resources for university dance performance programs
185 pp. 48/02-A, 334   ORDER NO. 871,1192
Available from: Diss. Abstracts International
A description of the financial resources of university dance performance programs. It includes the extent of funding for these programs, the utilization of funds by these programs, the funding restrictions, and the comparisons of perceptions of funding between university dance professionals and corporate representatives.

Parker, Ellen, Ph.D. (1988)
New York University, New York
An investigation of the practices of selected Manhattan-based corporations and private foundations in assessing the eligibility of performing arts groups for funding
211 pp. 49/08A, 2004   ORDER NO. 882,5259
Available from: Diss. Abstracts International
The decision-making practices of four corporations and six private foundations are investigated for their methods of assessing the eligibility of performing arts groups for funding. Results of a survey show contradictions and a need for the arts to develop written communcations skills in order to compete effectively in the overcrowded subsidy market.

Paulson, Pamela, Nan, Ph. D. (1982)
University of Minnesota, Minnesota
The placement of the dance program within the college and university in relation to the congruence of goals across three administrative structures
190 pp. 43/11-A, 3536   ORDER NO. 830,8107
Available from: Diss. Abstracts International
This study determines if adminstrative structure, or location, affects the function of the dance program as perceived by dance faculty located in departments of dance, physical education, and fine arts. Function, reflected in goals, is studied by having dance faculty located across the three adminstrative structures rate the importance of selected goals on an actual scale and an ideal scale. Conclusions address congruence and actualization of goals.
See also: Education

Schuman, Barbara Jean, Ph. D. (1984)
University of Iowa, Iowa
A profile of women leaders in physical education, sport, athletics and dance organizations and a study of role models and mentors of the leaders
176 pp. 45/09-A, 2799   ORDER NO. 842,8295
Available from: Diss. Abstracts International
This study develops a profile of women who have been leaders in national physical education, sport, athletic, and dance organizations. It investigates personal and educational backgrounds and the influence of role models and mentors on their professional careers. Data for the study were taken from women national presidents from AAHPERD, AIAW, NAGWS, NAPEHE, NASPE, and NDA.

Whiteman, Erlyne F., Ph. D. (1989)
University of Southern California, California
An analysis of management competencies as viewed by selected dance administrators in dance programs in higher education in the United States
50/07-A, 1979   ORDER NO. 056,6540
Available from: Diss. Abstracts International
A determination of the management competencies as viewed by expert dance administrators in higher education in the United States using the Delphi technique. Ten dimensions are found to be important—artist, communicator, educator, facilitator, motivator, planner, resource developer, scholar, and visionary leader.

Biography

Abrahams, Ruth Karen, Ph. D. (1985)
New York University, New York
The life and art of Uday Shankar
282 pp. 48/01-A, 235   ORDER NO. 870,6299
Available from: Diss. Abstracts International
This historical investigation traces Uday Shakar's artistic development through his choreographic, performance, educational, and innovative achievements. It presents a comprehensive portrait of Shankar the artist affirming his historical significance to the field of dance. Six progressions are investigated—the Early years, the European years, the Performing years, the Teaching years, the Multimedia years, and the Declining years.
See also: Ethnology and Anthropology, History

Adler, Reba Ann, Ph. D. (1987)
New York University, New York
The dance direction of Seymour Felix on Broadway and in Hollywood from 1918 through 1953
410 pp. 49/02-A, 167   ORDER NO. 880,1510
Available from: Diss. Abstracts International
This study charts the professional career of Seymour Felix, dance director for stage and film. It traces his stage career from a child performer to Broadway dance director and then focuses on his Hollywood career from the late 1920's to the mid-1950's. An analysis of Felix's film routines is also included.
See also: Choreography and Performance.

Andreasen, Lois E., Ph. D. (1972)
Texas Woman's University, Texas
A biography of Walter Terry with emphasis upon his professional career and his contributions to the field of dance
Available from: Microform
Abstract not available.

**Barber, Beverly Anne Hillsman,
Ph. D. (1984)**
Florida State University, Florida
Pearl Primus—in search of her roots:
1943–1970
342 pp. 45/09-A, 2678   ORDER NO. 842,7288
Available from: Diss. Abstracts International
A biographical account of the professional
career of Pearl Primus from 1943 to 1970. This
study provides an examination of her various
roles as dancer, choreographer, anthropologist,
educator, scholar, lecturer, and administrator.
The nature and scope of her work with African
and Caribbean dance forms is described in relation to the socio-political conditions of the
1940's.
See also: Choreograpy and Performance, Ethnology and Anthropology

**Barker, Barbara Mackin, Ph. D.
(1981)**
New York University, New York.
The American careers of Rita Sangalli,
Giuseppina Morlacchi and Maria
Bonfanti: Nineteenth century ballerinas
308 pp. 42/07-A, 2935   ORDER NO. 812,7890
Available from: Diss. Abstracts International
Biographical studies of three ballerinas who
were instrumental in laying a foundation for
the Americanization of ballet. The three prin-
cipal Europen ballerinas are Rita Sangalli,
Guiseppina Morlacchi, and Maria Bonfanti, all
of whom were trained in Milan and performed
at La Scala before coming to America. Their
careers span the full spectrum of popular entertainment as well as opera and ballet and they
strived to set high artistic standards and
improve the lot of the dancer within society
and the theatre.
See also: Styles: Ballet, Choreography and Performance, Related Arts: Opera

Bonali, Gloria Ann, Ph.D. (1971)
Texas Woman's University, Texas.
Harriette Ann Gray: Her life and her
career as a dancer, choreographer, and
teacher 1913–1968
322 + pp. x   ORDER NO.
Available from: Mircoform
A biographical study of the personal life of
Harriette Gray, her professional career, and her
contributions to the field of modern dance as
an art form and as an academic discipline in
the United States from 1913 to 1968. Included
are descriptions of her dance education background, her association with the Humphrey-
Weidman Dance Company, her own dance
company, and her philosophy and methods of
teaching.

Brooks Schmitz, Nancy, Ed. D. (1986)
Temple University, Pennsylvania
A profile of Catherine Littlefield, a
pioneer of American ballet
315 pp. 47/08-A, 2773   ORDER NO. 862,7509
Available from: Diss. Abstracts International
The biographical description of Catherine Littlefield, director, teacher, dancer, and choreographer who is attributed with helping to
develop modern American ballet. Littlefield's
beginning repertory is based on her involvement with the Philadelphia Civic and Grand
Opera companies and later focuses on the ath-
leticism of American dancers. She successfully
blends classical ballet, modern, social, folk,
ethnic, clogging, and tap dance in her efforts
to pioneer modern American ballet.
See also: Choreography and Performance

Brunoski, Elizabeth J, Ph. D. (1983)
Adelphi University, New York
A psychobiographical study of Vaslav
Nijinsky
295 pp. 44/11-B, 3519   ORDER NO. 8404462
Available from: Diss. Abstracts International
A description of the central events of the life of
Vaslav Nijinsky in the light of psycho-analytic
theory. Biographical data indicate that deficiencies in his earliest relationships results in
a poorly modified grandiose self. Partial repara-
tion becomes available through the creatvie
function of the dance and the teachers at the
Imperial Ballet School of St Petersburg. Nijinsky's relationship with Diaghliev helps consoli-
date his gains in the narcissistic sector of his
personality. Eventually, he undergoes self-frag-
mentation and is only able to achieve a delu-
sional identity.
See also: Psychology and Therapy, Styles:
Ballet

Buckley, Suzanne Shelton, Ph. D. (1980)
University of Texas at Austin, Texas
Divine dancer: The life and work of Ruth St. Denis
581 pp. 42/07-A, 3209   ORDER NO. 812,8590
Available from: Diss. Abstracts International
A critical biography of Ruth St. Denis which focuses on her spiritual aspirations, her investigations of Buddhism, Vedanta, Christian Science, the Oxford Group and other religious groups, and on her artistic style, its roots in Art Nouveau, American variety spectacle, and the Delsarte system of expression. This study also examines St Denis' inner life as reflected in her diaries, love letters, and poems. Extended critical analysis of several of her dances is also included.

Cocuzza, Ginnine, Ph. D (1987)
New York University, New York.
The theater of Angna Enters: American dance-mime
512 pp. 48/03-A, 515   ORDER NO. 871,2740
Available from: Diss. Abstracts International
This is a study of Angna Enters, concert dancer and mime, a solo performer for more than forty years and creator of more than 150 dance-mime compositions. It is demonstrated that Enters was a significant contributor to the shape and content of American contemporary dance of the 1920's and perpertrated the influence of Dalcroze Eurhythmics in America. Included is a close examination of the significant works in her repertoire, which came to be known as the Theatre of Angna Enters.
See also: Related Arts: Theatre

Deny, Sharron Louise Kerr, Ph. D. (1974)
University of Southern California, California
Bella Lewitzky: A description of her methods and views on performance and choreography
544 pp. 34/10-A, 6430   ORDER NO. 74-9064
Available from: Diss. Abstracts International
An account of personal interviews about Bella Lewitzky and a description of her methods and views of teaching modern dance performance and choreography. Also included is a description of Bella Lewitzky as a performer and choreographer.
See also: Styles: Modern, Education

Dixon-Stowell, Brenda M, Ph. D. (1981)
New York University, New York
Dancing in the dark: The life and times of Margot Webb in Aframerican vaudeville of the swing era
822 pp. 42/07-A, 2936   ORDER NO. 812,7902
Available from: Diss. Abstracts International
Margot Webb and Harold Norton represent one of the few Aframerican ballroom teams in history. This study describes and documents their career against a background of discrimination maintaining that it was emblematic of the double standards which existed for Aframerican artists in white America. With their unique contribution largely forgotten, Norton and Webb are considered prototypes of the invisible Aframerica performer and of the touring vaudeville entertainer whose horizons were limited by lack of mainstream exposure.
See also: Styles: Social, History

Gray, Judith A, Ph. D. (1978)
University of Arizona, Arizona
To want to dance: A biography of Margaret H'Doubler
235 pp. 39/02-A, 749   ORDER NO. 781,3903
Available from: Diss. Abstracts International
A historical correlation of the life and work of dance educator Margaret H'Doubler with the development of higher education in America during the first half of the twentieth century. At the University of Wisconsin-Madison she establishes the first Orchesis group in 1919, the first dance major in 1926, and writes books and articles on kinaesthetic awareness, rhythmic structure of movement, and dance as creative art experience. Throughout her career she exemplifies the integration of art, science, and the promise of humankind.
See also: History, Education

Gutierrez, Ireneo (Neo) Jr, Ph. D. (1987)

Texas Woman's University, Texas
Luisa Triana: Biography of a Spanish dancer
285 pp. 49/04-A, 644   ORDER NO. 872,9662
Available from: Diss. Abstracts International
A study of the major influences in the life and contributions of Luisa Triana, one of the most important Spanish dancers in the United States in the second half of the 20th century. Information from Spanish history, art, dance history, periodicals, interviews, and reviews is used to assess the significance of Triana's work.
See also: History

Hansen, Martha Alice, Ed. D. (1988)

Temple University, Pennsylvania
Isadora Duncan: A literary inquiry into the somatic foundations of her art, life, and ideology during the early years 1900–1914
230 pp. 49/09-A, 2429   ORDER NO. 881,8795
Available from: Diss. Abstracts International
This study of Isadora Duncan identifies her as an individual who tapped the germinal ideas of her era and carried them into a new art expression. The somatic information presented includes five topical areas—the aesthetic, the spiritual or philosophical, the educational, the quotidien, and the moral. The study concludes that Duncan's dance reflected her internal somatic integrity, but that her personal life was governed by internal ambiguity.

Keefer, Julia L, Ph. D. (1979)

New York University, New York
Erick Hawkins, modern dancer: History, theory, technique, and performance
362 pp. 40/06-A, 2992   ORDER NO. 792,5478
Available from: Diss. Abstracts International
This study is an historical—descriptive analysis of the contributions of Eric Hawkins to modern dance. It is divided into 6 areas—history, theory, kinesiological analysis, performance, and production—and is based on observations, interviews and personal statements.
See also: Choreography and Performance

Latham, Jacqueline Quinn Moore, Ph. D. (1973)

Texas Woman's University, Texas
A biographical study of the lives and contributions of two selected contempory black male dance artists-Arther Mitchell and Alvin Ailey—in the idioms of ballet and modern dance, respectively
1,014 pp. 35/4-A, 2143   ORDER NO. 74-22,241
Available from: Diss. Abstracts International
A biographical study of the lives of Arthur Mitchell and Alvin Ailey including a critical examination of the contributions of each of the artists as dancer, choreographer, teacher, and director of professional dance companies in his respective idiom of dance. Special emphasis is placed on each artist's unique contribution to the dance field as a black male dance artist in contemporary society.
See also: Choreography and Performance

Mitchell, Lillian Leonora, Ph. D. (1982)

Texas Woman's University, Texas
Boris Volkoff: Dancer, teacher, choreographer
407 pp. 44/01-A, 257   ORDER NO. 831,2285
Available from: Diss. Abstracts International
A biographical study of Boris Volkoff, former Bolshoi Ballet dancer and the founding father of ballet in Canada. During his career in Canada he is influenced by the social, economic, and political environment. He forms the national Ballet of Canada while attempting to develop and evolve a Canadian style of expression.
See also: Styles: Ballet

Payne-Carter, David, Ph. D. (1987)

New York University, New York
Gower Champion and the American musical theatre
542 pp. 48/02-A, 180   ORDER NO. 8801561
Available from: Diss. Abstracts International
This biography first treats Gower Champion as he prepares himself for a career as a director in the 1930's. It is then organized around the Broadway musicals which he directed and choreographed. Champion's contribution to each production is described and includes his brief motion picture career. He and his wife Marge

were regarded as the definitive American dance team of the 1950's and in the 1960's he began directing and choreographing several successful Broadway shows.
See also: Choreography and Performance

Ray, Ollie Mae, Ph. D. (1976)
University of Utah, Utah
Biographies of selected leaders in tap dance
422 pp. 38/01-A, 156   ORDER NO. 776,551
Available from: Diss. Abstracts International
This study covers the biographical histories of selected dancers who made distinct contributions to tap dance from 1750 to 1970. Valid and reliable information is presented plus photos where possible.
See also: Styles: Tap

Richards, Sylvia Pelt, Ph. D. (1972)
Texas Woman's University, Texas
A biography of Charles Weidman with emphasis upon his professional career and his contributions to the field of dance
                                ORDER NO. 841,1180
Available from: Diss. Abstracts International
Abstract not Available.

Schlundt, Christena Lindborg, Ph.D. (1959)
Claremont Graduate School, California
The role of Ruth St. Denis in the history of American dance: 1906–1922
218 pp. 20/07-A, 2778   ORDER NO. 59-4428
Available from: Diss. Abstracts International
An account of the professional life of Ruth St Denis and its impact on American history. Using Dixon Ryan Fox's theory of 'civilization transfer' the author finds that the institutionalization of dance as an art form in America occurred during the dancing career of Ruth St Denis. Furthermore, it is maintained that St Denis was the greatest single element in this domestication. It chronicles the vulgarization of dance as it was forced to adjust to its only outlet, vaudeville and attributes St Denis with raising the level of taste and laying the basis of dance audience for the dancers who came after her.
See also: Styles: Modern, History, Choreography and Performance

Sloan, Ronna Elaine, Ph.D. (1983)
City University of New York, New York
Bob Fosse: An analytic-critical study
288 pp. 44/05-A, 1247   ORDER NO. 831,9801
Available from: Diss. Abstracts International
An analysis of the contributions and innovations of Robert Lewis Fosse to the American musical and a study of his growth as a creative artist. Emphasizing jazz dance, Fosse proves himself in several media and works successfully in nightclubs, theatre, television, and film. His choreography and directing are stamped with his personal style and win him entertainment awards and distinctions, including three Emmys. It is concluded that as a director-choreographer Fosse achieves total artistic control and is critically and popularly successful in musical plays and films.
See also: Styles: Jazz

Soares, Janet Mansfield, Ed. D. (1987)
Columbia University Teachers College, New York
Louis Horst: Musician in a dancer's world
219 pp. 49/06-A, 1310   ORDER NO. 881,6012
Available from: Diss. Abstracts International
This study provides a chronology of the first fifty years of Louis Horst's life, from 1884–1934, and chronicles his participation in the development of American modern dance. It focuses on the philosophical notions and practical solutions that he drew from his work with dancers and that he synthesized into his teaching of dance compostion. He is described as a musician in a dancer's world.
See also: Choreography and Performance, Styles: Modern

Turner, Eula Douglas, Ph. D. (1974)
University of Southern California, California
Eleanor Metheny: Teacher scholar
166 pp. 31/11-A, 7031   ORDER NO. 74-11,715
Available from: Diss. Abstracts International
A descriptive study of educator, Eleanor Metheny which finds that she was one of the most articulate spokespersons in the history of physical education, that she was dynamic and creative and that she was an intellectual of exceptional range. The study is based on responses from groups and persons who had studied or worked with her from 1948 to 1971.

Vallillo, Stephen M, Ph.D. (1987)
New York University, New York
George M. Cohan, Director (American
Musical Comedy)
387 pp. 48/08-A, 1933   ORDER NO. 8712787
Available from: Diss. Abstracts International
A description of George M. Cohan's career,
playwriting stye and methods, production style,
rehearsal techniques, staging, casting, use of
chorus and dances, and the scenery, lighting,
and costuming in his productions. As an actor,
singer, and dancer he entertained America for
almost forty years and his characteristic tempo
has become the standard for American musical
comedies.
See also: Choreography and Performance

**Weeks, Sandra Rivers,
Ph. D. (1980)**
*Texas Woman's
University, Texas*
Anne Schley Duggan:
Portrait of a dance
educator

331 pp. 41/05-A, 2010   ORDER NO. 802,5590
Available from: Diss. Abstracts International
A biographical study of Anne Schley Duggan,
a prominent personality in dance in American
higher education. After a brief review of her
early life and career beginnings, the study concentrates on her role in relation to the development of dance at Texas Woman's University.
The study of Duggan focuses on the years from
1936 until her retirement in 1973.
See also: Education, Administration

Children

**Arnold, Nellie Doreen Webb, Re. D.
(1972)**
Indiana University, Indiana
An interrelated arts approach to
awareness of selected composition
components in art, music, and dance
272 pp. 33/08-B, 3754   ORDER NO. 730,4320
Available from: Diss. Abstracts International
This study develops and presents an approach
to awareness of composition components com-

mon to art, music, and dance through study of
visual abstract images aesthetically perceived
in nature and artistically produced from materials indigenous to nature. Fourth through
sixth grade children receive instruction in ases-
thetic principles and their application and
then build three-dimensional art forms incorporating design, music, and dance. A tri-arts
committee evaluates their use of composition
components.
See also: Theory and Philosophy

Beveridge, Sandra Kay, Ph. D. (1973)
Ohio State University, Ohio
The relationship among motor
creativity, movement satisfaction, and
the utilization of certain movement
factors of second grade children
129 pp. 34/11-A, 7022   ORDER NO. 741,0914
Available from: Diss. Abstracts International
A study concerned with the relationships
among motor creativity, movement satisfaction, and the qualitative use of certain movement factors of second grade children. It is
found that children high in movement satisfaction do not differ from those who score low as
to their qualitative use of the movement factors. Highly creative students however, tend to
use more variety in their response to movement
problems.
See also: Psychology and Therapy.

Boorman, Joyce Lilian, Ph. D. (1980)
*University of Alberta—Canada, Alberta,
Canada*
Imagination and children: Implications
for a theory of imagination in children's
learnings
180 pp.
Available from: Microform
Abstract not available.
See also: Psychology and Therapy, Education

Brown, Ollie Mae Thomas, Ph. D. (1980)
Texas Woman's University, Texas
A comparison of the attention span of hyperactive and nonhyperactive children while performing to live and recorded dance instructions
123 pp. 41/05-A, 2003   ORDER NO. 802,5570
Available from: Diss. Abstracts International
An investigation of the effect of live and recorded music on the attention spans of hyperactive and non-hyperative children. Findings reveal a significant difference between the groups of children , but no difference between the effects of the live and recorded instructions, suggesting that accompaniment may complement live instruction in dance and positively influence attention span in children.
See also: Psychology and Therapy, Music and Rhythm

Hinitz, Blythe Simone Farb, Ed. D. (1977)
Temple University, Pennsylvania.
The development of creative movement within early childhood education, 1920 to 1970
266 pp. 38/04-A, 1982   ORDER NO. 77-21,767
Available from: Diss. Abstracts International
An account of the historical developments in the fields of early childhood education, creative movement as applied within early childhood education from 1920 to 1970. The study reveals these points of confidence—the effects of the growth of the progressive Education Movement, the impact of education as exemplified by Teachers College, Columbia University, and the embracing of the whole chiild approach by leaders in both fields.
See also: Education

Kasson, Cheryl G, Ph. D. (1986)
Colorado University at Boulder, Colorado
Children expressing emotions in dance: A phenomenological study
490 pp. 47/09-A, 3307   ORDER NO. 870,0360
Available from: Diss. Abstracts International

A description of the experience and behavior of children expressing emotions in dance, as perceived by the children and the researcher. In this investigation dance activities are described in terms of specific movements, qualities of movement, body shapes, sounds, facial expressions, and interactions. It is revealed that while children express emotions in dance, their thoughts and feelings are about the immediate experience and past or hypothetical events.
See also: Psychology and Therapy

Mandelbaum, Jean, Ph. D. (1978)
New York University, New York
A study of the relationship of an in-service program in music and movement to opportunities for creativity in selected Kindergartens
188 pp. 39/08-A, 4883   ORDER NO. 782,4095
Available from: Diss. Abstracts International
This study analyzes the opportunities for creativity which surround kindergarten music and movement experiences and relates the findings to an in-service program in music and movement provided for teachers. Results suggest that the in-service program generates more open and exploratory approaches to music and movement instruction.
See also: Education, Music and Rhythm

Sande, David Joseph, Ph. D. (1975)
University of Oregon, Oregon
The movement effort quality profiles of children in a nursery school
110 pp. 36/09-A, 5925   ORDER NO. 765,203
Available from: Diss. Abstracts International
This study investigates how the movement effort quality profiles of nursery school children vary according to gender, movement (postural or gestural), age, environment(outdoor or indoor), and activity(free or structured). Effort qualities are characterized for weight, space, time, and flow. A secondary discussion of the profiles for teachers' classroom observations.
See also: Education, Notation and Movement Analysis

**Sutlive, Josephine Laffiteau, Ed. D.
(1982)**
*University of North Carolina at
Greensboro, North Carolina*
A description of children's verbal
responses to a modern dance work in
grades kindergarten through six
168 pp. 43/03-A, 721   ORDER NO. 821,8678
Available from: Diss. Abstracts International
A description of the verbal responses children
make to modern dance work on film before
those children receive formal instruction in
dance. Subjects are asked questions to be
answered during and after viewing the film and
their responses are categorized in two dimensions—affective and objective (body, effort,
space, and relationship). Frequences and per-
centages are analyzed according to gender and
grade level.
See also: Psychology and Therapy

**Vallance, Janette Margaret, Ph. D.
(1989)**
*University of Alberta—Canada, Alberta,
Canada*
Collegial conversation: A search for
meaning in children's creative dance.
50/11-A, 3558   ORDER NO. Not Available
Available from: Diss. Abstracts International
This study explores a system of beliefs to seek
out the ground and facets of the foundations
for creative dance programs for children. The
descriptive—interpretive mode of inquiry
questions the mysterious, pre-linguistic nature
of the dance experience through reconstructed
narrative within three dance centers. Analytic
reflection by the children, parents, and colleagues uncovers hidden meanings and divines
a common universal credo.
See also: Theory and Philosopohy

Choreography and Performance

Arnold, Stepanie Kevin, Ph. D. (1977)
*University of Wisconsin at Madison,
Wisconsin*
A theatre of spatial poetry: A study of
the Modern Dance drama as it
concretizes twentieth-century visions of
gesture
273 pp. 38/12-A, 7025   ORDER NO. 780,4845
Available from: Diss. Abstracts International
A study of the development of choreographed
drama in modern western theatre, focusing on
works by Martha Graham, Kurt Joos, Jose
Limon, and Murray Louis. It examines the variety of compositional styles with a view to con-
cretizing theoretical descriptions of spatial
drama. A survey of more recent work by choreogrpahers Phoebe Neville, Bill Evans, and
Meredith Monk, reveals that modern dance
continues to vitalize a new idea of theatre.
See also: Related Arts: Theatre

Banes, Sally R, Ph. D. (1980)
New York University, New York
Judson Dance Theatre: Democracy's
body 1962–1964
497 pp. 41/12-A, 4886   ORDER NO. 811,0716
Available from: Diss. Abstracts International
This is a study of the Judson Dance Theatre,
a loosely organized collective of avantgarde
choreogrpahy in Greenwich Village, from
1962 to 1964. The twenty concerts produced
cooperatively during this time are documented. It is shown that an effort was made by
the artists to preserve diversity and freedom
using democratic methods, such as improvisation, chance, and spontaneous determination.
Several important choreographers began their
careers at the Judson Dance Theatre.
See also: History

Beck, Jill, Ph. D. (1985)
City University of New York, New York
Principles and techniques of
choreography: A study of five
choreographers from 1983
355 pp. 46/05-A, 1128   ORDER NO. 851,5607
Available from: Diss. Abstracts International

This study proposes and implements a methodology for research in choreography. Five choreographies created in 1983 are presented and analyzed. Labanotation and video documention are used to demonstrate the new research into choreography. The five analyses illustrate ways and the extent to which Labanotation score reading can reveal techniques of choreography, and in particular the nature of insights into principles of choreography afforded by videotaped records of the creative process of the dance work.

See also: Notation and Movement Analysis, Technology and Film

Berg, Shelly Celia, Ph. D. (1985)

New York University, New York
"Le sacre du printemps": a comparative study of seven versions of the ballet
428 pp. 46/03-A, 555   ORDER NO. 85-10490
Available from: Diss. Abstacts International
This study examinies in chronological order, seven significant productions of "Le Sacre du Printemps" and the ballet's importance as a seminal work in the development of twentieth century ballet. The selected ballets demonstrate a broad range of choreographic styles and varied approaches to Stravinsky's score. Choreographers include Léonide Massine, Maurice Béjart, Paul Taylor, Richard Alston, and Martha Graham, each of whom brok tradition with their choroegraphic style and innovation.

See also: Styles: Ballet

Blumenthal, Paul Steven, D. Mu. (1978)

University of Maryland, Maryland
P. T. Barnum: a work for dancers, musicians and electronic tape
(Original Composition)
55 pp. 39/09, 5196-A   ORDER NO. 790,5455
Available from: Diss. Abstracts International
A modern ballet based on some of Barnum's original circus acts. This chamber work consists of six movements which reflect elements from the lives of the personalities who helped make the famous entrepreneur a huge success.

See also: Music and Rhythm, Styles: Ballet

Byrum, Mary Carolyn, Ed. D. (1976)

University of North Carolina at Greensboro, North Carolina
An analysis of three non-objective choreographic techniques
193 pp. 37/05-A, 2716   ORDER NO. 76-24,939
Available from: Diss. Abstract International
This study consists of scripts which identify, analyse, and clarify the non-objective choreographic approaches of Alwin Nikolais, Merce Cunningham, and Jeanne Beaman. The scripts are organized to provide a guide to viewing selected films of dances by the choreographers. These teaching aids illustrate the actual characteristics of the dance and the choreographer.

See also: Education

Carriere, Diane Louise, Ph. D. (1980)

University of Wisconsin at Madison, Wisconsin
A clarification of the concept of focus in the performing art of dance
261 pp. 41/10-A, 4210   ORDER NO. 80-28,174
Available from: Diss. Abstracts International
This study demonstrates that focus is a powerful means of projection, emphasis, and expression in dance. It clarifies the concept of focus in terms of its meanings, usages, overt bodily manifestations and value as a means of communication in dance. Operational definitions of inner focus and outer focus are developed and illustrated in the context of a dance performance. Points of concentration, center of interest, eye focus, line focus, and movement focus often referred to as "focus" in dance literature are redefined.

See also: Theory and Philosophy

Challender, James Winston, Ph. D. (1986)

Florida State University, Florida
The function of the choreographer in the development of the conceptual musical: An examination of the work of Jerome Robbins, Bob Fosse, and Michael Bennett on Broadway between 1944 and 1981
427 pp. 47/08-A, 2003   ORDER NO. 8626788
Available from: Diss. Abstracts International
This study focuses on the conceptual musical and the all-powerful director/choreographer. It includes an examination of the musicals of

Robbins, Fosse, and Bennett and discusses their backgrounds and other artistic efforts. The integration of dance in musical theatre is described and other directors and choreographers are recognized to illustrate their influence on the careers of the three men.

Cohen, Barbara Naomi, Ph. D. (1980)
New York University, New York
The dance direction of Ned Wayburn: Selected topics in musical staging, 1901–1923
230 pp. 41/06-A, 2356   ORDER NO. 802,7876
Available from: Diss. Abstracts International
An illustrated study of dance direction by Ned Wayburn, 1901–1923. It covers his background in physical culture and social dance, his training and technique, and his three important genres—vaudeville, musical numbers, and chorus specialities. In addition, the study explicates Wayburn's ability to maintain his concepts of the Routine and performance heirarchy in his work.

Corey, Frederick Charles, Ph. D. (1987)
University of Arizona, Arizona
Principles for the use of stylized movement during the interpretation and performance of literature based on Martha Graham's use of classical tragedy in modern dance
169 pp. 48/09-A, 2193   ORDER NO. 872,6813
Available from: Diss. Abstracts International
An investigation of Martha Graham's choreographic use of classical tragedy using a methodology based on Aristotle's elements of tragedy. Four of Graham's ballets are analysed and as a result, five principles emerge related to rhetoric, movement vocabularies, synecdochical movement, stage properties, and costumes. By using these principles as guidelines it is argued that interpretive performers may understand, create, and utilize stylized movement that communicates the ideas, images, and actions inherent in the text being staged.
See also: Styles: Modern, Theory and Philosophy

Daugherty, Diane, Ph. D. (1985)
New York University, New York
Facial decoration in Kathakali dance-drama
214 pp. 46/03-A, 556   ORDER NO. 851,0495
Available from: Diss. Abstracts International
This study follows Kathakali actors as they transform themselves into mythological figures. It documents the preparation of the make-up materials, the painting techniques, and the craft of chutti or paste application. The discussion centers on the facial decoration worn by seven Kathakali characters. Descriptions of the techniques and designs are supported by drawings and photographs.

Dennhardt, Gregory Chris, Ph. D. (1978)
University of Illinois at Urbana-Champaign, Illinois
The director-choreographer in the American musical theatre
396 pp. 39/01-A, 26   ORDER NO. 781,1228
Available from: Diss. Abstracts International
An examination of the events that lead to the emergence of the director—choreographer artist. It also studies the careers, theories, and approaches to the staging of musical comedy and revue of seventeen artists who have served as director—choreographer specifically Agnes de Mille, Jerome Robbins, Gower Champion, Bob Fosse, and Michael Bennett, on Broadway. Sources for this study include newspaper reviews and magazine articles.

Driscoll, Kathleen, Ph. D. (1983)
University of Connecticut, Connecticut
The emergence of social structure in a modern dance company: A case study
409 pp. 44/10-A, 3167   ORDER NO. 840,1982
Available from: Diss. Abstracts International
This is a participant observation study of a semi-professional modern dance company of twelve members working in a small Canadian city. The company's work process is examined with attention on the company's hierarchy, activities involved in making the dances, division of labor, rehearsal and class processes, creative input, and individual dance roles. The analysis is based on observation notes, rehearsals and performances, supplemented by interviews and documents.
See also: Administration

Evans, Jeffrey Ernest, Ph.D. (1980)
University of Michigan, Michigan
The dancer from the dance: Meaning and creating in modern dance
296 pp. 41/02-B, 686   ORDER NO. 801,7253
Available from: Diss. Abstracts International
An illustration of how the meaning of creating is constituted from both the personal concerns of the choreographer's life and from the culture of dance, including the situation in which the creating is done. Creative Style is the central concept and it is dialectically related to the domains of Life Concerns and Choreographic Dimensions. This study presents general statements about the meaning of creating as an activity of life and about the meaning of the audience, the dancers, the medium of dance, and the body.
See also: Theory and Philosophy

Fischer, Barry, Ed. D. (1986)
New York University, New York
Graham's dance "Steps in the Street" and selected early technique: Principles for reconstructing choreography from videotape
149 pp. 47/10-A, 3595   ORDER NO. 862,5670
Available from: Diss. Abstracts International
This study identifies, reconstructs, and documents a 1930's choreography and technique of Martha Graham which has been unavailable to the public since its inception. The selected dance exerpt is entitled "Steps in the Street" from the dance suite "Chronicle". An outline of the evolving principles which emerge through the process of reconstructing the dance from videotape is presented and a summary of Graham's early professional dance explorations in the 20's and 30's is included to provide insight into her dance philosophy.
See also: Technology and Film

Fusillo, Lisa Jean, Ph. D. (1982)
Texas Woman's University, Texas
Leonide Massine: Choreographic genius with a collaborative spirit
237 pp. 43/04-A, 957   ORDER NO. 821,9612
Available from: Diss. Abstracts International
This study provides an understanding of the artist choreographer Massine and investigates the importance of artistic collaboration in his life and work. Major influences on his choreography are identified, particulary Diaghilev, selected artists, musicians with whom Massine collaborated, and other pertient events of his life. A discussion of four Massine ballets is included.
See also: Biography, Styles: Ballet

Gustafson, Sandra Elizabeth, Ed. D. (1973)
University of North Carolina at Greensboro, North Carolina
A choreographic experiment with mixed means for the purpose of communicating through the act of theatre
54 pp. 33/09-A, 4918   ORDER NO. 736,160
Available from: Diss. Abstracts International
This study describes a choreographic experiment which combines the arts to create a total effect. The work is entitled "Rural Route" and is a dance drama about the life and dreams of an old farmer. This experiment suggests a more eclectic approach to the teaching of dance composition and to the designing of courses in dance choreography.
See also: Related Arts: Theatre

Gwynn, Eleanor W. Faucette, Ph. D. (1978)
University of Wisconsin at Madison, Wisconsin
A key determinant of dance style: The structural use of the dance instrument as illustrated by the choreography of Katherine Dunham's "Rites de Passage"
254 pp. 39/06-A, 3190   ORDER NO. 781,5412
Available from: Diss. Abstracts International
This study identifies the key to choreographic style in the structured movements and in the use of the dance instrument. It also finds that the performance style of a dancer significantly affects the choreographic style, especially the dynamic line and expressive quality, but finds the design of the movements remains constant and true to the choreographic intent. Two sections of "Rites de Passage" illustrate the specific formal elements which determine its style.
See also: Theory and Philosophy

Hanstein, Penelope, Ph. D. (1986)
Ohio State University, Ohio
On the nature of art making in dance:
An artistic process skills model for the
teaching of choreography
215 pp. 47/10-A, 3640   ORDER NO. 870,3554
Available from: Diss. Abstracts International
A study of the nature of art-making in dance
and the development of a multidimensional
model for the teaching of artistic process skills.
The model, Artistic Process Skills Model, provides an alternative to craft-oriented
approaches to teaching choreography and consists of a scheme for organizing arts learning
which fosters life-time creative problem find-
ing and solving skills.

Hargrave, Susan Lee, Ph. D. (1980)
Cornell University, New York
The choreographic innovations of
Vaslav Nijinsky: Towards a dance-
theatre
182 pp. 41/01-A, 25   ORDER NO. 801,5677
Available from: Diss. Abstracts International
An exploration of both the comments from
Nijinsky and his colleagues and the ballets
themselves to compile Nijinski's approach to
the creaton of dance-theatre. This approach
and the record of his works are then placed in
theoretical—historical context through comparison with other major works in dance-theatre from his era. He is given credit fo revitalis-
ing theatrical dance and paving the way for
Massine, Nijinska, and Rambert.
See also: Styles: Ballet, History

Helpern, Alice J, Ph. D. (1981)
New York University, New York
The evolution of Martha Graham's
dance technique
265 pp. 42/07-A, 2937   ORDER NO. 812,8214
Available from: Diss. Abstracts International
This study traces the development of Graham's
technique, relates it to her choreography, and
describes its transmission at the Graham
School. It explains how Graham contributed
to dance through her technical vocabulary and
system of training and how she came to establish a modern dance tradition, creating a viable
method of training. Background information
includes biographical data on Graham's early
life, her Denishawn training, association with

Louis Horst, scope of dance training in
America, and rise of modernism in related arts.
See also: Styles: Modern, Biography

**Hodson, Millicent Kaye, Ph. D.
(1986)**
*University of California at Berkeley,
California*
Nijinsky's "New Dance": Rediscovery of
ritual design in "Sacre du Printemps"
     ORDER NO. 0375358
Available from: Diss Abstracts International
Abstract not available.

Hood, Robley, Munger, Ph. D. (1986)
University of Denver, Colorado
The Ballets Suedois: Modernism and
the painterly stage
208 pp. 47/04-A, 1118   ORDER NO. 861,2843
Available from: Diss. Abstracts International
This study explores the Ballets Suedois, an
experimental ballet troupe based in Paris
between 1920 and 1925. Four ballet productions are described with particular attention to
historical precedents, painterly characteristics,
alignment with contemporary atristic interests,
and effectiveness as dance spectacle. The study
considers the stage as a performance gallery of
modern art and painting and as the source of
balletic creation.
See also: Styles: Ballet

Lee, Sun-ock, DA (1984)
New York University, New York
The evolvement of "Yimoko III": Zen
dance choreography
190 pp. 45/08-A, 2306   ORDER NO. 842,1485
Available from: Diss. Abstracts International
This study concerns the development of a Zen
dance as it was performed in 1983. It consists
of three parts—a lecture demonstration on the
principles and philosophy of Zen dance, an
exercise for Zen dance preparation, and a
actual performance. Included is an overview of
the influence of Zen and Buddhism on the
performing arts in Japan, Korea, and the
United States.

Madden, Dorothy Gifford, Ph.D. (1962)
New York University, New York
"Always at Sea": Selected traditions of Martha's Vineyard presented in dance
211 pp. 32/04-A, 2084   ORDER NO. 62-5340
Available from: Diss. Abstracts International
This study records and abstracts those tales and traditions of Martha's Vineyard during the nineteenth century which are appropriate for choreography. Movements are invented for seven original dances in the modern dance tradition. The dances support the proposition that dance is a means by which regional lore is communicated and that it is possible to enter a community and search for traditions which are a source of rich material for choreography.
See also: Styles: Modern

Mandin, Lucille Marie, Ph. D. (1989)
University of Alberta—Canada, Alberta, Canada
An invitation to dance: The gentle art of teaching
50/11-A, 3478
Available from: Diss. Abstracts International
This is a documentation of a dance about teaching and learning. It is choreographed around a course and encapsulates emancipatory education and literature under the rubic of teaching. The dance emerges from Harris' model of teaching which stresses the importance of imagination, of creating and recreating. It features five steps: contemplation, engagement, form-giving, emergence, and release.
See also: Education

Manning, Susan Allene, Ph. D. (1987)
Columbia University, New York
Body politic: The dances of Mary Wigman
399 pp. 49/07-A, 1623   ORDER NO. 880,9388
Available from: Diss. Abstracts International
This study reconstructs the dances of Mary Wigman by synthesizing the surviving archival evidence of film clips, photographs, programs, and choreographic notes. The resulting accounts of choreographic structure and imagery become texts accessible to interpretation in broadly political terms. The study is organized by periods of Wigman's work from her early solos (1914 to 1931) to her late group dances (1943 to 1961). It is shown that her dances represent the individual body—the self- and the collective body—the community-in ways that exemplify the historical experience of her generation.
See also: Biography, History

Martin, Randy, Ph. D. (1984)
City University of New York, New York
Seeds of desire: The common ground of performance and politics
360 pp. 45/11-A, 3453   ORDER NO. 8501155
Available from: Diss. Abstracts International
This work is concerned with investigating the empirical and theoretical grounds for political performance. It includes an ethnographic study of a modern dance company tracing the making of a dance from first rehearsal to performance. Using theories of communication and culture, it exhibits the dance company in transition from symbolic, lingual forms of communication to non-lingual abstract forms and demonstrates how abstract communication is produced in the moment of performance.
See also: Theory and Philosophy

Martin, Vicki Lee, Ph. D. (1978)
Texas Woman's University, Texas
A cine-dance work: "Progression"
92 pp. 40/01-A, 7   ORDER NO. 791,5880
Available from: Diss. Abstracts International
The production of a cine-dance called "Progression" which contributes aspects of science resulting in an art work which also communicates specific elements of that science. The specific feelings expressed in this work on the social phenomena of overcrowding are alienation, tension, exhaustion, and frustration.
See also: Technology and Film

Merrill, Stina Margareta, Ph. D. (1974)
Texas Woman's University, Texas
Lighting design for modern dance: Preferences of men and women
121 pp. 36/09-A, 5923   ORDER NO. 765,061
Available from: Diss. Abstracts International
This study investigates the lighting design preferences across educational levels, genders, and dance experience. Educational level, presumably based on age and maturity, is the single most important factor governing preferences

among the designs. Gender has little effect and dance experience is a strong factor.

Miller, Raphael Francis, Ph. D. (1984)
University of Oregon, Oregon
The contributions of selected Broadway musical theatre choreographers: Connolly, Rasch, Balanchine, Holm, and Alton
383 pp. 45/07-A, 1922   ORDER NO. 842,2855
Available from: Diss. Abstracts International
This study examines the contributions of choreographers Connolly, Rasch, Balanchine, Holm, and Alton to the development of musical theatre dance. It identifys and describes several major trends and influences and focuses on the changing relationship of dance to the development of the book musical, beginning in the early 1920's and extending through the 1950's.
See also: History

Nelson, Susan Adele Lee, Ph. D. (1980)
Northwestern University, Illinois
The dance factory: A collegiate dance company as a artistic enterprise
192 pp. 41/06-A, 2334   ORDER NO. 802,6883
Available from: Diss. Abstracts International
This study examines and describes the functioning of a student performing dance company in an institution of higher education. It chronicles the experiences of the members as they struggle to establish a rationale for maintaining the group in an academic setting against institutional constraints and artistic norms of the dance world.

Neser, Gwendolyn, Ph. D. (1973)
New York University, New York
Choreographic models using a group process: Analysis and production
175 pp. 34/02-A, 899   ORDER NO. 73-19,440
Available from: Diss. Abstracts International
An investigation of the use of group process as a choreographic model. The hypothesis is tested by preparing a theatre piece entitled "Dances About Us" which is comprised of both choreographed and spontaneous movement segments. The group process is analysed by effort-shape observations.
See also: Notation and Movement Analysis

Nickolich, Barbara Estelle, Ph. D. (1979)
New York University, New York
Nikolais dance theater: A total art work
232 pp. 40/11-A, 5650   ORDER NO. 801,0385
Available from: Diss. Abstracts International
An examination of the elements of performance in Nickolais' total art work and a study of his artistic lineage. It summarizes Nickolais' evolution from realism to abstraction and points out his major contributions in terms of dance theory, a new kind of dance theatre, and the development of theatrical technology
See also: Theory and Philosophy

Overby, Lynnette Young, Ph. D. (1986)
University of Maryland College Park, Maryland
A comparison of the novice and experienced dancers' imaginary ability with respect to their performance on two body awareness tasks
137 pp. 47/10-A, 3697   ORDER NO. 862,5712
Available from: Diss. Abstracts International
This study investigates the relationships between dance experience, imagery ability, and body awareness. The subjects are expereinced and novice dancers who perform body awareness tasks and complete imagery questionnaires. The correlational analyses reveal significant differences between the groups while all subjects report using imaginal strategies to enahnce their ability to reproduce the criterion movements.

Popkin, Sheryl S, Ed. D. (1978)
Temple University, Pennsylvania
The influence of Eastern thought in the dance of Erick Hawkins
183 pp. 39/04-A, 1896   ORDER NO. 7817401
Available from: Diss. Abstracts International
An investigation of Erick Hawkins' exposure to Eastern ideas and an identification of the Eastern characteristics present in his dance. This analysis of Hawkins' interest in Eastern thought reveals it's power as a primary source of his artistry and philosophic conclusions.

Prevots-Wallen, Naima, Ph. D. (1983)
University of Southern California at Los Angeles, California
The Hollywood Bowl and Los Angeles dance, 1926–1941: Performance theory and practice
44/02-A, 324   ORDER NO. 0551678
Available from: Diss. Abstracts International
This study analyses when and why the Hollywood Bowl became a microcosm of major choreographic activity in Los Angeles from 1926 to 1940. It analyses the dance works presented and the performance theories of the artiists who created them. The documentation provides an assessment of the diverse theories that affected dance as an art form during the 1930's and 1940's.
See also: Theory and Philosophy, History

Propper, Herbert, Ph. D. (1977)
University of Michigan, Michigan
Space/symbol: The spatial concepts in selected dances of Martha Graham
298 pp. 38/06-A, 3147   ORDER NO. 77-26,338
Available from: Diss. Abstracts International
This study analyzes the use of space in Martha Graham's major dance works and the manner in which material objects are used together with the dancers to produce spatial effects. The analysis focuses on the ways in which movement, attitude, and physical relationships of dancers are related to the various set pieces, properties, costume elements, decor, and lighting of the dances. The background for the study includes an historically-oriented survey of developments in physics, mathematics, painting, and sculpture and a discusssion on the concepts of virtual space and spatial consciousness.
See also: Theory and Philosophy

Rae, Caral Yvonne, Ph. D. (1973)
Texas Woman's University, Texas
Dance commentary: An original suite of fourteen dances based upon the evolution of dance through the ages of man
328 pp.
Available from: Texas Woman's University
Abstract not Available.

Ravarour, Adrian Hill, Ph. D. (1985)
Union for Experimenting Colleges and Universities, New York
Energy flow choreography: Principles of energy transformation and transcendental dance
109 pp. 47/04-A, 1097   ORDER NO. 861,3907
Available from: Diss. Abstracts International
This study examines the philosophical and theoretical principles behind energy flow choreography, a movement technique in which the transformation of biopsychic energy enables the dancer and the viewer to experience the Transcendental Dance. Materials are drawn from Taoist and Buddhist philosophy, physics, and dance aesthetics. A series of experimental tasks are presented to assist the dancer enter the Transcendental Dance state.
See also: Theory and Philosophy

Rubin, Martin Lewis, Ph. D. (1987)
Columbia University, New York
A tradition of spectacle: Busby Berkeley on stage and screen
406 pp. 49/03-A, 362   ORDER NO. 880,9414
Available from: Diss. Abstracts International
An interpretation of Busby Berkeley's significance in the history of musical film in terms of a substantial break with theatrical practice. Precedents of the Berkeleyesque are described historically and his films are grouped into six phases, each of which is conceptualized in terms of its receptiveness to Berkeletesque spectacle.
See also: History, Technology and film

Sagolla, Lisa Jo, Ed.D. (1992)
Columbia University Teachers College, New York
Choreography in the American musical, 1960–1969: The dramatic functions of dance
186 pp.
Available from: Diss. Abstracts International
This study traces the role of dance in the American musical theatre from its origins through the 1960's. Four dramatic functions emerge and are used to describe and analyze selected musical theatre dances of the 1960's illuminat-

ing how the choreography contributes to the drama. In addition, four expressive characteristics unique to dance are explored. Recommendations are provided for a college curriculum focusing on the education of musical theatre choreographers and teachers.

Scarborough, Cindy, Ph.D. (1990)
New York University, New York
Creation and performance of six original works by six choreographers: Danced by one soloist enahanced by video introductions for analysis of audience perceptions
Available from: New York University
This study discusses a model which presents informative, artistic video introductions as enhancements to live dance performanc in an effort to alleviate confusion and foster audience appreciation and understanding of modern dance performance. Original choreographies are created for the project and audiences preview them before the live performance. An experiment is designed to examine audience responses to the model. It is recommended that dance artists become video and computer literate.

Schaefer, George E, Ph.D. (1954)
University of Rochester, New York
Ballet: 'The Lottery'
185 pp.
Available from:
Not available.
See also: Styles: Ballet

Seidel, Andrea Mantell, D.A. (1985)
New York University, New York
"Medicine Wheel:" A ritual dance drama inspired by plains Indian myths and symbols
175 pp. 48/08-A, 2112   ORDER NO. 852,2009
Available from: Diss. Abstracts International
This study focuses on the creative process of choreographing an original dance-drama, "Medicine Wheel", inspired by the sun dance ritual of the Dakota tribes. The framework is based on a system devised by Native American anthropologist Alfonso Ortiz and a performance model which analyses the ideology, mythology, and training of the participants. This contemporary dance-drama integrates

ancient symbols and metaphysical myths into a personalized artistic vision.
See also: Ethnology and Anthropology

Shafranski, Paulette Evelyn, Ph. D. (1975)
University of Southern California, California
The choreographic intent as analysed by three audiences
93 pp. 35/09-A, 5910   ORDER NO. 75-6444
Available from: Diss. Abstracts International
This study examines to what extent a choreographer's intent is translated to various audiences. A dance is created by the choreographer and is analysed to determine if the intent is communicated. A questionaire is administered to observers of a dance and also to the performers of the dance. The study finds that the choreographer's intent in form and feeling can be translated to audiences, but that content may be more difficult to convey.
See also: Theory and Philosophy

Snyder, Diana Marie, Ph. D. (1980)
University of Illinois at Urbana at Champaign, Illinois
Theatre as a verb: The theatre art of Martha Graham, 1923–1958
253 pp. 41/11-A, 4545   ORDER NO. 810,8668
Available from: Diss. Abstracts International
This study places Martha Graham's art within the context of the theatre as a whole, an essential reciprocal act involving both performer and percipient. There is a discussion on the origins of her convictions in childhood experience and the evolution of her work, its themes and techniques, from 1923 when she left the Denishawn Company until 1958 when she presented "Clytemnestra". "Clytemnestra" and the major works which preceded it are revealed as the cynosure of Graham's theatre and the "verb" which for her, is theatre.
See also: History

Sparrow, Patricia, Ph.D. (1963)
New York University, New York
The choreographic devices: Their nature and function as related to the principle of opposition
178 pp.   ORDER NO. 6406569
Available from: Diss. Abstracts International

A description of the devices which can be utilized in choreography and a demonstration of how they relate to the principle of opposition. A survey of selected professional dance teachers reveals devices they use in choreography. These findings serve as a basis for a choreographic work titled "Forms and Versions" which explores opposition factors.

Sperber, Martin, Ed. D. (1974)
Columbia University, New York
Improvisation in the performing arts: Music, dance and theatre
145 pp. 35/06-A, 3799　　ORDER NO. 74-26,621
Available from: Diss. Abstracts International
This study presents a comparative and comprehensive view of improvisation in the performing arts of music, dance, and theatre. It is found that although improvisation can be basic to performance, its greatest potential is as a means whereby students can discover themselves in relation to their respective art forms. The study defines improvisation, discuss its historical use, reports on interviews with practitioners, describes its teaching, and analyses the findings.

Steinke, Gary Lee, Ph. D. (1979)
University of Michigan, Michigan
Analysis of the dance sequences in Busby Berkeley's films; "Forty Second Street": "Footlight's Parade"; and "Gold Diggers" of 1935
175 pp. 40/02-A, 506　　ORDER NO. 791,6819
Available from: Diss. Abstracts International
An examination of the dance sequences in selected Busby Berkeley's films reveals that Berkeley created dance production which are specifically designed for the film medium. As one of the first film choreogrpahers to realize the value of cinematic technique, he approaches dance from a new perspective and establishes a standard which influences other film studios of the thirties.
See also: Technology and film

Summers, Louis Jeriel, Ph. D. (1976)
University of Missouri of Columbia, Missouri
The rise of the director/choreographer in the American musical theatre
192 pp. 37/09-A, 5448　　ORDER NO. 775,661
Available from: Diss. Abstracts International

This study traces the development of the director/choreographer. It covers the period from 1936 to 1975 and considers the careers and contributions of Balanchine, Agnes de Mille, Jerome Robbins, Michael Kidd, Herbert Ross, Joe Layton, Gower Champion, Bob Fosse, and Michael Bennett.

Trexler, Alice Elizabeth, Ph. D. (1976)
New York University, New York
"Femina Ludens" compared to exemplary games: A structural analysis of an avant-garde-derived process dance
157 pp. 38/02-A, 527　　ORDER NO. 77-16,448
Available from: Diss. Abstracts International
This study includes the problem of comparing the structural elements of the choreography "Femina Lundens" to those of exemplary games. Game-structured choreographic sections are placed into a game taxonomy for comparison purposes and a high degree of similarity is found. This non-traditional dance is identified with a pre-cursory body of avant-garde choreography, one genre of which is found to include tendencies, such as non-theatricality, process as content, and an unfinished nature of the art product.

Turner, Louise Kreher, Ph.D. (1970)
New York University, New York
The television direction of a video-tape of original choreovideo dance: An analysis of selected spatial and design elements for choreographing television dance for presentation via video-tape
236 pp. 31/05-A, 2163　　ORDER NO. 70-21,157
Available from: Diss. Abstracts International
This research studies the technical and artistic aspects of an original choreography expecially designed for television. It includes an examination of related literature and the summation of pertinent technical considerations for use as the choreovideo basis for a creative project titled "Paragram use of cameras/dancers." Through an amalgamation of television and dance, it explores the related art forms of dance, electronic music, and television as the foundation of a single creation. (A copy of the videotape is available from the Library of Performing Arts at the Lincoln Center in New York for purposes of research only.)
See also: Technology and Film.

Walther, Suzanne, Ph.D. (1990)
New York University, New York
The form of content: The dance-drama
of Kurt Jooss
336 pp.
Available from: Diss. Abstracts International
An examination of the development of ideas
in Jooss's ballets and a demonstration of how
the dramatic concept, the content behind the
movement, generates the choreographic form.
This aesthetic investigation is supplemented
by historical methods. Basic components of
dance drama, the dramatic elements, and the
aesthetic basis of his choreography are explored
and an assessment is made of Jooss' contribution to the art of theatrical dance. There is a
description and analysis of four ballets based
on direct observation.

Zupp, Nancy Thornhill, Ed. D. (1978)
*University of North Carolina at
Greensboro, North Carolina*
An analysis and comparison of the
choreographic process of Alwin
Nikolais, Murray Lois, and Phyllis
Lamhut
181 pp. 39/06-A, 3196   ORDER NO. 7824313
Available from: Diss. Abstracts International
An investigation of the perceptions of three
professional choreographers—Alwin Nikolais,
Murray Louis, and Phyllis Lamhut—concern-
ing their respective choreographic processes.
Areas studied are motivation, creative pro-
cesses, function of dancers, and evaluation of
choreography. Similarities and differences in
aesthetic philosophies as well as perceptions of
aesthetic purpose are discussed.
See also: Theory and Philosophy

Education

Acer, Charlotte Chase, Ed. D. (1987)
State University of New York, New York
Crime, curriculum and the performing
arts: A challenge for inner city schools
to consider integrated language, music,
drama and dance experiments as
compensatory curriculum for at-risk
urban minorities in Elementary school
(Volumes I and II)
843 pp. 48/12-A, 3047   ORDER NO. 880,2590
Available from: Diss. Absracts International
An investigation of the possibility that an integrated humanities program of language, music,
drama, and dance might reduce academic fail-
ure and juvenile delinquency. The priorities
of curriculum planning and early childhood
education are addressed.
See also: Children

**Adinku, William Ofotsu, Ph. D
(1988)**
University of Surrey, United Kingdom
Towards the national theatre concept:
A model for the development of dance
education within the Ghanaian
University system
268 pp. 49/08-A, 2001   ORDER NO. AACDX83028
Available from: Diss. Abstracts International
A discussion of the introduction of traditional
dance into the Ghanaian University system in
response to the concept of National Consciousness. It includes a survey of traditional
dance models and their significance for new
developments and an examination of the models as applied activities in dance education and
theatre work incorporating an African orientation.
See also: Ethnology and Anthropology

Akenson, James Edward, Ph.D. (1975)
*University of Wisconsin at Madison,
Wisconsin*
Inquiry and art in elementary social
study: Modern dance and social study in
conjunction
375 pp. 36/09-A, 5798   ORDER NO. 752,6488
Available from: Diss. Abstracts International

This study investigates the relationship between social scientific inquiry and artistic rationality and the meaning of the relationship for linking elementary social study with the art form of modern dance. It identifies a program to link both topics and finds that modern dance helps children make visible the tacit knowledge derived from social study. The study reveals that these two different forms of rationality have commonalities of method and purpose.
See also: Children, Styles: Modern

Allen, Helen M, Ed.D (1967)
New York University, New York
A study of the effectiveness of teaching folk dancing by television to third and fourth grade children
154 pp. 28/04-A, 1275   ORDER NO. 67-11,135
Available from: Diss. Abstracts International
This study compares the achievement and attitudes of third and fourth grade children taught folk dancing in two different situations, one group via closed-circuit television and the second group in a conventional gymnasium situation. On the basis of the type of experiment, the kind of analysis, and the evidence found, it is inferred that television teaching of folk dancing is as effective as the conventional method.
See also: Styles: Folk, Technology and Film

Andrews, Gladys, Ed.D. (1952)
New York University, New York
A study to describe and relate experiences for the use of teachers interested in guiding children in creative rhythmic movement
351 pp. 12-A, 3183   ORDER NO. 4540
Available from: Diss. Abstracts International
This study relates and describes experiences in creative rhythmic movement as a medium of expression. It further deals with the nature of creative expression. It consists of two parts; the first is concerned with the needs and characteristics of children in early and middle childhood and the second part is a manual about the contributions of creative rhythmic movement to the development of children in the elementary school. In this study, creative rhythmic movement is not considered as an activity in

itself, but as one means of contributing to the total development of the child.
See also: Children, Music and Rhythm

Ayob, Salmah, Ph. D. (1986)
University of Wisconsin at Madison, Wisconsin
An examination of purpose concepts in creative dance for children
330 pp. 47/04-A, 1233   ORDER NO. 861,3375
Available from: Diss. Abstracts International
This study identifies fourteen 'purpose concepts' in the creative dance literature and in four selected children's dance programs. Teachers of the programs are interviewed to discern those concepts that they perceive to be meaningful for their students. Findings indicate that children exhibit a high degree of involvement and responses relevant to the identified purpose concepts of creative dance for children.

Baker, Mary Susan, Ed. D. (1983)
Colorado University at Boulder, Colorado
Status survey of the mediated instructional materials used for dance in the area of higher education
305 pp. 44/04-A, 963   ORDER NO. 831,7639
Available from: Diss. Abstracts International
This study ascertains how higher education uses and applies mediated instructional materials found in dance theory, dance education, and dance instruction. These materials include television, video recorders, films, and audio recorders. The report of a survey finds that these materials are used in all areas of dance and that their use is increasing.
See also: Technology and Film

Ball, Wesley Allen, Ph.D. (1982)
Case Western Reserve University
A philosophical study of qualitative movement: Implications for early childhood music programs
135 pp. 43/06A, 1870   ORDER NO. 8224679
Available from: Diss. Abstracts International
This philosophical synthesis draws upon aspects of four domains of knowledge: music, movement, learning theories, and the nature of human feeling. Music is characterized as an expressive art form embodying qualities related to movement. The aesthetic properties of time-space-force in dance are applied to sound-

movement. Teaching strategies reflecting this approach are presented incorporating sensory modes of perceiving.
See also: Music and Rhythm, Children

Barry, Thais Grace, Ed. D. (1977)
Columbia University, New York
Improvisations for modern dance: Implications for dance education
109 pp. 38/01-A, 209   ORDER NO. 771,4707
Available from: Diss. Abstracts International
A demonstration of the ways in which improvisation can be used as a creative teaching device. Improvisation in dance education is explained and as well as its contribution to generating creativity and resolving the details of an idea and implementing it. Sample improvisations are given and also suggestions for students.

Benison, Betty Bryant, Ph.D. (1968)
University of New Mexico, New Mexico
A plan for programming sequential integrated dance and rhythmic activities for the elementary school level utilizing the medium of television
368 pp. 29/12-A, 4305   ORDER NO. 69-09278
Available from: Diss. Abstracts International
This study describes a teleclass (with related materials) that provides a team teaching collaboration by the television teacher and the classroom teacher to make practicable the inclusion of dance and rhythmic concepts at the fourth grade level. Surveys are used to determine the extent of dance promotion to the public via television. A teleclass is then devised using a creative design approach with dance and rhythmic concepts pertinent to the growth and development of 9 to 12 year olds.
See also: Children, Technology and Film

Bowman, Betty Ann, Ph. D. (1971)
University of Michigan, Michigan
Learning experiences in selected aspects of a dance movement sequence
107 pp. 32/03-A, 1318   ORDER NO. 712,3705
Available from: Diss. Abstracts International
A study of the learning approach of naive subjects to a basic dance movement sequence presented only by demonstration. Subjects tend to give priority to spatial aspects and basic shape, rather than temporal aspects and directional orientation. Subjects also use concepts

from their own performance and not from the performance of the demonstration.
See also: Psychology and Therapy

Brauer, Lena, Ed. D. (1975)
Rutgers University, New Jersey
Teaching approaches in modern dance
128 pp. 36/07-A, 4120   ORDER NO. 761,103
Available from: Diss. Abstracts International
An exploratory study of teaching methods employed in dance instruction and their application to non-professional modern dance instruction. Five schools of dance are studied to assess the basic elements in their teaching methods—ballet, Laban, Dalcroze, Graham, and Nicolais. The resulting elements fall within four basic components—body training, technique acquisition, body movement control, and creative activities.

Breazeale, Helene, Ph. D. (1976)
Union Graduate School
An ideal model and flexible undergraduate dance major curriculum for two-year and four-year state-supported colleges and universities
124 pp. 37/08-A, 4718   ORDER NO. 77-2710
Available from: Diss. Abstracts International
An examination of the past and present trends in dance education and a determination of the elements necessary to develop an ideal model and flexible undergraduate dance curriculum for state-supported institutions. Recommendations include methods for implementation as well as suggestions for further studies. The study supports the trend to move dance out of physical education and into the arts.

Brehm, Mary Ann, Ph. D. (1988)
University of Wisconsin at Madison, Wisconsin
Margaret H'Doubler's approach to dance education and her influence on two dance educators
261 pp. 46/06-A, 1296   ORDER NO.
Available from: Diss. Abstracts International
This study identifies and describes the characteristics of H'Doubler's classroom procedures. Organization of material is viewed in terms of lesson structure, guided exploration and classroom environment. Techniques of her approach which promote individual growth, are found to be consistent with H'Douber's

theoretical viewpoint . A working topology of her thinking, approach to dance education, and subject matter is complied and included.
See also: Theory and Philosophy

Brockmeyer, Grethchen A, Ed. D. (1976)
University of Georgia, Georgia
Development and evaluation of a teacher behavior instructional unit for eliciting creative movement performance
237 pp. 37/12-A, 7610   ORDER NO. 771,2369
Available from: Diss. Abstracts International, Microform
A description of an instructional unit composed of teacher verbal feedback behaviors directed toward the elicitation of student creative movement performance. These behaviors can be altered through participation in a microteaching program disigned to foster the change.

Browne, Thomas J, Ed. D. (1986)
Brigham Young University, Utah
Hemisphericity and its relationship to athletics, art, dance and achievement: A study among grade twelve students
140 pp. 48/01-A, 97   ORDER NO. 870,3343
Available from: Diss. Abstracts International
A study in which student participation in school programs of athletics, art, and dance is correlated with their cumulative grade point averages. No statistically significant relationships are found and it is determined that the hemispherity scores obtained using the Hermann and Brog questionnaires lacked reliability and validity.

Burdick, Dolores M. Plunk, Ph. D. (1974)
Texas Woman's University, Texas
Recommendations for professional preparation in dance for the public schools of Missouri
343 pp.
Available from: Microform
A description of the results of a survey to determine the status of movement education, rhythmical activities, and dance in Missouri public schools. Findings show that structured forms of movement are taught more than creative forms

and that there is a lack of professional preparation in the three areas. It is concluded that the deficiencies are due to lack of interest and inadequate professional education of PE teachers.
See also: Administration

Cabezas, Richard Edward, Ed. D. (1981)
New York University, New York
The education of professional dancers: In inquiry into their secondary school experiences
124 pp. 42/12-A, 5080   ORDER NO. 821,0949
Available from: Diss. Abstracts International
An investigation of the high school experiences of professional dancers in order to discover the problems encountered by career-bound dance students as they attempt to complete high school and pursue a dance career simultaneosly. A survey of 10% of the professional dancers in New York is conducted and analyzed. Twelve case studies are presented to illustrate the data gathered in the survey.

Calhoun, Miriam Eudora, Ed.D. (1963)
New York University, New York
Principles for the establishment and conduct of programs in dance for senior high school girls
152 pp.   ORDER NO. AAC6906524
Available from: New York University
A determination of the physical, mental, social, and emotional characteristics of senior high school girls and the contributions of dance to the development of these characteristics. It also summarizes the factors influencing the dance program in the senior high school and principles are formuated to serve as guides in the establishment and conduct of programs of dance for girls in these institutions. The study reveals that a dance program is enhanced if the characteristics are known and are used as the basis of developing the dance program. It also shows that students are interested in all kinds of dance, but staff are inadequately trained to teach modern dance.
See also: Administration

Chin, Donna Lisa, Ed. D. (1984)
University of Northern Colorado, Colorado
The effects of dance movement instruction on spatial awareness in elementary visually impaired students, and self-concept in secondary visually impaired students
161 pp. 45/10-A, 3111   ORDER NO. 8429824
Available from: Diss. Abstracts International
An investigation of the effects of dance movement instruction on the spatial awareness of elementary visually impaired students and on the self-concept of secondary visually impaired students. The results indicate that a physical education program, supplemented with dance movement instruction, may enhance spatial awareness and self-concept.
See also: Psychology and Therapy

Clifford, Jacqueline Anne, P.E.D. (1967)
Indiana University, Indiana
The interrelatedness of dance with music and art through a study of form as a unifying concept
181 pp. 28/04-A, 1277   ORDER NO. 67-12,909
Available from: Diss. Abstracts International
This study develops form as a unifying concept of the arts of art, music,and dance and also develops theoretical material on the interrelatedness of these three arts that can be used in the professional preparation of dance teachers. It finds that form as structure lends itself readily to an analysis of commonalities among the three arts and that the elements of line, rhythm, unity, and variety derived from dance are inherent in art and music and are essential to the attainment of form in each of the art areas.

Conroy, Mary, Ed. D. (1972)
Columbia University, New York
Curricular activities of the secondary school modern dance teacher
185 pp. 33/11-A, 6158   ORDER NO. 73-10,913
Available from: Diss. Abstracts International
This study results in a source of information for those responsible for planning high school modern dance curricula, for modern dance teacher preparation, and for the actual classroom teaching of modern dance. It is based on the curricular activities of 25 high school modern dance teachers in Los Angeles County and includes their teaching methods and the percentage of time spent on the major curricular categories. Private dance training and college dance credits are found to correlate significantly with teaching variety and levels of instruction.
See also: Styles: Modern

Cowan, Karen Lautenbach, Ph.D. (1990)
University of Wisconsin at Madison, Wisconsin
The current status of dance education in Wisconsin and developmental influences
110 pp. 51/4-A, 1028   ORDER NO. 9024759
Available from: Diss. Abstracts International
A descriptive study of the current status of dance education in Wisconsin from 1987 to 1989. Three major areas of consideration are included in this comprehensive review : dance in education, dance organizations, and dance companies. Significant events in the development of dance in education, dance organizations, and dance companies in the state which might have characterized or influenced the current status are highlighted.

Crawford, John Richardson, Ed. D. (1989)
Temple University, Pennsylvania
A comparison of organizational principles used by the choreographer, composer and painter which incorporates dance as an educational focus
247 pp. 50/10-A, 3135   ORDER NO. 900,7344
Available from: Diss. Abstracts International
This study compares the principles of formal organization in dance, music, and painting and suggests a means to interrelate these aspects among the three arts for augmenting aesthetic education and for multi-arts approaches to

composition. The study centers on dance as the educational focus based on the dynamics present during the creation and apprehension of dance, music, and painting.
See also: Theory and Philosophy

Disanto-Rose, Mary, Ed. D. (1986)
Temple University, Pennsylvania
Effect of creative dance classes on the learning of spatial concepts and the ability to analyze spatial pathways in dance video by third and fourth grade students
251 pp. 47/10-A, 3657   ORDER NO. 862,7443
Available from: Diss. Abstracts International
This study determines the effect of creative dance classes on the learning of spatial concepts and also assesses the ability of children to analyse spatial pathways in a dance video. The spatial concepts are measured by standardized and customized tests. The results suggest the value of the tests to measure spatial abilities of children, particularly the identification of visual movement patterns.
See also: Psychology and Therapy, Children, Technology and Film

Dorward, E. Marion, Ed.D. (1940)
New York University, New York
Musical education through rhythmical activity for elementary and junior high school teachers: A handbook for professional schools for teachers
373 pp.   ORDER NO. 7303106
Available from: Diss. Abstracts International
Abstract not available.

Duvall, Richard Paul, Ph.D. (1986)
Saint Louis University, Missouri
Educational criticism: Perceptions of values, criticism, and appreciation as aesthetic education across arts disciplines
263 pp. 48/04-A, 892   ORDER NO. 8715060
Available from: Diss. Abstracts International
This study focuses on teaching activities for attaining the component goals of aesthetics across the disciplines of visual arts, music, theatre, and dance in four high school programs. The goals are seen as dealing with values, criticism, and apreciation. The study is structured

out of activities perceived by teachers and supervisors to lead to the aesthetic goals.
See also: Theory and Philosophy

Franke, Johannah Schwarz, Ed. D (1970)
Columbia University, New York
Career patterns of 1961–1965 graduates of performing dance curricula in selected colleges and universities
200 pp. 31/02-A, 695   ORDER NO. 70-13,769
Available from: Diss. Abstracts International
An investigation of the effectiveness of college performing dance curricula for individual graduates of these programs in terms of their professional preparation, vocational goals, and their activities since graduating from college. Profiles of individuals are presented from their first dance classes to their post-college employment. Guidelines and responsibilites are offered to college dance departments to enhance performing and employment opportunities for graduates.
See also: Administration

Gallemore, Sandra L., Ed.D (1979)
University of North Carolina at Greensboro, North Carolina
The student teaching experience: Perceptions of student teachers, cooperating teachers, and university supervisors
278 pp.
Available from: Diss. Abstracts International
This investigation examines perceptions about the objectives of the student teaching practice. The survey instrument ranks objectives according to importance, designates the degree to which the objectives are met, and records activities and experiences which contribute to the achievement of the objectives. Comments about the reasons for achievement are analyzed and it is found that the objective most completely achieved is the demonstration of positive personal characteristics.

Goldfield, Emily Dawson, Ph. D. (1977)
University of Southern California, California
Development of creative dance for children in the United States: 1903–1973
38/10-A, 5989
Available from: Diss. Abstracts International
A presentation of the historical development and orderly growth of creative dance education for children in the United States, 1903-1973. Isadora Duncan is identified as a pioneer and inventer of a new mode of dancing while the National Dance Association is credited with consolidating the efforts and objectives of leaders in the field.
See also: Children

Googooian, Martha G, Ph. D. (1945)
University of Southern California, California
A study of creative expression courses in music and dance in selected liberal arts colleges
399 pp.
Available from: Microform
Abstract not available.
See also: Music and Rhythm

Heausler, Nancy Lea, Ph. D. (1987)
University of New Orleans, Louisiana
The effects of dance /movement as a learning medium on the acquisition of selected word analysis concepts and the development of creativity of kindergaten and second grade children
138 pp. 48/09-A, 2233   ORDER NO. 872,6761
Available from: Diss. Abstracts International
This study investigates the effectiveness of dance/movement as a method for facilitating learning of word analysis concepts and stimulating creativity. Children in the study use problem-solving and self-expression to explore the concepts and their responses are measured with standardised tests.
See also: Children

Hinckley, Priscilla Baird, Ed. D. (1985)
Boston University, Massachusetts
"Let me Dance before You": The education role of performance in a West African children's masquerade
286 pp. 46/12-A, 3575   ORDER NO. 860,1351
Available from: Diss. Abstracts International
The construction of the history of the Dodo, a masquerade dance ritual developed from a play activity. It is followed by an ethnographic description of the little boys' Dodo and the older boys' public competition Dodo. Performers, spectators, and supporters are interviewed and drawings illustrate the findings. The masquerade is presented as a social communication between the generations and as a means to take in information in new ways.
See also: Ethnology and Anthropology, Children

Hirsch, Agnes A, Ed. D. (1980)
Rutgers University of New Jersey—New Brunswick, New Jersey
An analysis of professional conceptions of modern dance education as reflected in "Journal of Physical Education and Recreation" and in "Dance Magazine". Articles from January 1965 to December 1979
142 pp. 41/09-A, 3943   ORDER NO. 810,5226
Available from: Diss. Abstracts International
The analysis of data concerning professional conceptions in modern dance education reveals that primary attention is given to the notion that creativity is imperative in a dance education program. This study also reveals that dance as an expressive art form is advocated by a significant percentage of the articles in the curriculum at every age level.
See also: Styles: Modern

Hoover, Carolyn Faye, Ph. D. (1980)
University of Oregon, Oregon
The effectiveness of a narrated dance/pantomime program in communicating selected basic health concepts of third graders
194 pp. 41/05-A, 1962   ORDER NO. 802,4861
Available from: Diss. Abstracts International
This study describes the development, performance and evaluation of dance/pantomime

programs for use in teaching concepts in safety, mental health, nutrition, and anatomy to third grade students. An objective is to examine the potential for utilizing the arts as viable educational tools. It concludes that dance/pantomime is an effective teaching method as evidenced by both cognitive and behavioral changes.
See also: Children

Ingram, Anne Gayle, Ed.D (1962)
Teachers' College, Columbia University, New York
Teaching dance as a career

226 pp.   ORDER NO. 212-678-3494
Available from: Teachers' College Reference Library
This study describes and analyzes four main dance teaching careers—college dance teacher, high school teacher, commercial studio teacher, and folk and square dance teacher. It reveals the major differences among the four areas and provides information on the preparation needed, the employment possibilities, the nature of the work, and the financial remuneration characteristic of each. The study serves to provide a basis for choosing a dance career wisely.

Jay, Danielle Mary, Ph. D. (1987)
Texas Woman's University, Texas
Effects of a dance program on the creativity and movement behavior of pre-school handicapped children
202 pp. 48/04-A, 826   ORDER NO. 871,5028
Available from: Diss. Abstracts International
An experimental study wherein pre-school handicapped speech and language delayed children participate in either a dance program or an adapted physical education program to determine whether their movement and creative behaviors are significantly affected.
See also: Psychology and Therapy, Children

Jeffries, Catherine Wilson, Ph. D. (1979)
University of North Carolina at Chapel Hill, North Carolina
Differential effects of a comparative advance organizer on performance, attitudes and practice in learning a dance skill
161 pp. 41/01-A, 155   ORDER NO. 801,3956
Available from: Diss. Abstracts International
This investigation tests the efficacy of a preinstructional strategy designed as a comparative organizer in the format of a videotape and used prior to the instructional experience of students learning to perform social dance patterns. Descriptive data indicates a more favorable attitude toward learning a new motor skill using the organizer while the amount of time spent practising is greater.
See also: Technology and Film

Kearns, Kathryn Fisher, Ed.D. (1989)
Temple University, Pennsylvania
Visual information processing: Eye movements and success in replication of beginner and advance modern dancers
205 pp. 50/10-A, 3187   ORDER NO. 900,7356
Available from: Diss. Abstracts International
In this study of visual information processing in dancers, beginning and advanced dancers are compared in their ability to replicate a stimulus videotaped dance phrase. Replication attempts are scored by a certified movement analyst and subjects are characterized as high, moderate and low successful replicators of the dance phase. A profile of the high-successful replicator emerges and generates the discussion of the implications for teachers and learners of dance.
See also: Notation and Movement Analysis

Lee, Marie Smith, Ph.D. (1959)
Columbia University, New York
Commentary on creative dance in
elementary schools with filmed
anecdotes
Available from: Microform
Abstract not available.
See also: Children, Technology and Film

**Lloyd, Marcia Lou, Ed.
D. (1986)**
University of Utah, Utah
Dance education in
American schools: 1925
to 1935

415 pp. 47/12-A, 4279   ORDER NO. 870,6384
Available from: Diss. Abstracts International
An historical documentation of the development of dance in American schools and colleges during the 1925–1935 decade. The phi-
losphies, purposes, and forms of dance are presented as well as teacher profiles and methods
of integration into the curriculum. Dance education leaders and their contributions are discussed and it is surmised that dance could not
have developed as fully had it not been for
the philosophies of progressive education and
natural activity.
See also: History

**Lord, Madeleine Charlotte, Ed. D.
(1979)**
*University of North Carolina at
Greensboro, North Carolina*
The teaching of dance: A
characterization of dance teacher
behaviors in techniques and
choreography classes at the University
level
256, 40/11-A, 5778   ORDER NO. 801,1204
Available from: Diss. Abstracts International
This study characterizes dance teacher behaviors as observed in choreogrpahy and techniques classes at the university level. Teachers'
behaviors are analyzed in terms of verbal and
non-verbal behaviors, directness and indirect-
ness of approach, the strategy flexibility, and
the dominant teaching patterns.
See also: Choreography and Performance

Lunt, Joanne Margaret, Ed. D. (1974)
*University of North Carolina at
Greenboro, North Carolina*
A procedure for systematically
describing teacher-student verbal and
nonverbal interaction in the teaching of
choreography
286 pp. 35/04-A, 2123   ORDER NO. 74-22,022
Available from: Diss. Abstracts International
A description of a procedure to systematically
describe teacher-student verbal and non-verbal interaction in the teaching of choreography. A multi-dimensional category system is
used encompassing cognitive, affective,
kinetic—kinaesthetic, and technical divisions
with behavioral categories. Four means of identification are common to all divisions, teacher,
student, verbal, and non-verbal. Both construct and content reliability are considered
acceptable for the study.
See also: Choreography and Performance

**McCutchen, Mary Gene, Ed. D.
(1978)**
*University of North Carolina at
Greensboro, North Carolina*
Expert determination of knowledge and
skills essential to the elementary
classroom teacher for the instruction of
creative dance
278 pp. 39/12-A, 7224   ORDER NO. 791,3056
Available from: Diss. Abstracts International
This study proposes the minimum knowledge
and skills which are needed by the elementary
classroom teacher for the teaching of dance to
children. The knowledge and skills are compi-
lied through semantic analysis and are verified.
The findings indicate that the greatest need of
the classroom teacher is methodology. Other
needs and priorities are described and creative
dance for children is seen as an integral part of
their education.
See also: Children

Melcer, Fannie Helen, Ed.D. (1953)
New York University, New York
Staging dance in higher education: A
study to help teachers with theater
experience in the presentation of dance
programs in higher education
265 pp.   ORDER NO. 0008026
Available from: New York University

This study determines and compiles information which is of help to teachers with limited theatre experience in the staging of modern dance presentations in institutions of higher education. The first part consists of the organization of information related to the staging of dance consistent with educational aims and the second part is a manual for teachers and students encompassing educational principles, administrative problems, program arrangement, costumes, stage sets, lighting, accompaniment, adaptng dances, and make-up.
See also: Choreography and Performance

Minton, Sandra Cerny, Ph. D. (1981)
Texas Woman's University, Texas
The effects of several types of teaching cues on postural alignment of beginning modern dancers: A cinematographic analysis
196 pp. 43/04-A, 1080 ORDER NO. 821,9619
Available from: Diss. Abstracts International
Three different approaches to verbal—visual cueing are used in beginning modern dance classes to determine their effects on postural alignment in standing and walking positions. The approaches are based on criteria for effective imagery devised by Lulu Sweigard. One conclusion is that certain types of clues may be more effecive than others in improving postural alignment.
See also: Styles: Modern, Technology and Film

Muxworthy Feige, Dian Margaret, Ed. D. (1988)
Columbia University Teachers College, New York
Gregory Bateson and Waldorf education: Gestures in the dance variations on an aesthetic epistemological theme
265 pp. 50/03-A, 575 ORDER NO. 890,6486
Available from: Diss. Abstracts International
Abstract not available.
See also: Theory and Philosophy

Nadon-Gabrion, Catherine Anne, Ed. D. (1979)
University of Massachusetts, Massachusetts
Aesthetic education: Interdisciplinary and the interrelated arts approach based on the ANISA model (Activities in movement, music, and language arts)
193 pp. 40/03-A, 1337 ORDER NO. 792,0877
Available from: Diss. Abstracts International
This study develops a set of proto-typical models based on the ANISA Curriculum Model. Learning experiences are developed through the media of movement, music, and laguage arts and are relevant to interdisciplinary approahes to teaching and learning. The model contains theories of development, curriculum, teaching, adminstration, and evaluation. It involves the arts as a symbol system and views them as an integral component of the total educational process.

Neal, Nelson Douglas, Ed. D. (1985)
University of Virginia, Virginia
Assessment of attitude change and position shift in fourth graders after participation in modern dance
131 pp. 46/10-A, 2962 ORDER NO. 852,6915
Available from: Diss. Abstracts International
An investigation of the change in children's attitudes toward dance after three dance sessions and also an assessment of the difference in dance attitude among five groups over time, genders over time, and treatments, genders, and time. The groups particpate in jazz, modern, and sport style dance. It is found that children's attitudes shift by merely participating in the program without respect to being a participant in either treatment or control conditions.
See also: Children, Styles: Modern

Nixon, Jessica Eliza, Ph.D. (1959)
Columbia University, New York
Guides for creative experiences in dance
for the teacher in the self-contained
classroom in the elementary school
Available from: Microform
Abstract not available.
See also: Children

**O'Donnell, Mary Patricia, Ed.D.
(1945)**
New York University, New York
Creative dance for lchildren: Materials
and methods for the first three grades
Available from: New York University
Abstract not available.
See also: Children

Olander, Kathleen Rae, Ed. D. (1985)
University of the Pacific, California
A survey of arts education in programs
in California public elementary schools
135 pp. 46/07-A, 1834   ORDER NO. 851,8624
Available from: Diss. Abstracts International
A description of California arts education programs with a view to asssisting administrators,
teachers, and legislators plan appropriate and
meaningful programs for elementary school
students. A questionaire survey is used to
gather relevant data as perceived by teachers
in 150 schools.
See also: Administration

**Ramirez, Emma Hocking, Ed. D.
(1980)**
Brigham Young University, Utah
Creative movement: A analysis of
methods used by experts
183 pp. 41/06-A, 2500   ORDER NO. 802,724
Available from: Diss. Abstracts International
This study consists of 1) an analysis of expert
opinions on the techniques and methods used
to develop successful creative movement programs and 2) the development of a unit of
instruction based on these findings. It is concluded that philosophies and basic foundations
are similar, but each individual has unique
ways to plan a creative movement program.
See also: Theory and Philosophy

Riley, Alan, Ed. D. (1984)
University of Toronto—Canada
The interrelationships and effects of
creative dance on the physical self-
esteem, body image and problem solving
of grade four children
45/09-A, 2734
Available from: Diss. Abstracts International
This is a case study describing the factors of
physical self-esteem, body image, and problem-
solving as relating to children's response to
creative dance. A responsive method of
research is used to explore as many dimensions
as possible. Gender differences in attitudes
towards creative dance emerge with boys experiencing more dissonance than girls. Implications for school dance programming and professional development for teachers are drawn
from the study results.
See also: Psychology and Therapy, Children

**Roman, Adylia Rose,
Ed. D. (1990)**
*Temple University,
Pennsylvania*
Dance for the hearing-
impaired in the United
States

483 pp. 51/08-A, 2550   ORDER NO. 910,0334
Available from: Diss. Abstracts International
This study explores the development of dance
for the hearing impaired in the United States.
It focuses on three applications—education,
performance, and dance therapy, and gives an
overview of dance programs for deaf children
in the school systems. It confirms the value
of dance, presents teaching methods, shares
various viewpoints, provides documentation of
dance videotapes, and identifies relevant issues
in the field.
See also: Psychology and Therapy

**Roos, Gertruida Woutrina, D.Ed.
(1989)**
University of Pretoria (South Africa)
Educative dance: Fundamentals and
practice
50/05-A, 1280
Available from: Diss. Abstracts International
An investigation of dance as an educative
medium and as a comprehensive educational

activity within the South African educational context. Dance is studied phenomenogically, emphasizing the existential implications of the child's physical, perceptual-motor involvement in dance. It confirms that dance makes a unique contribution and can be justified as a basic educational activity.

Rose, Albirda Jean Landry Charles, Ed. D (1982)
University of San Francisco, California
The effects of creative dance movement on development of a specific cognitive skill (spelling) in primary students
173 pp. 44/03-A, 669   ORDER NO. 831,6460
Available from: Diss. Abstracts International
An investigation of the relationship between learning and recall of spelling words and exposure to creative dance of children in grades two and four. The theory of this study is based on Laban's movement concepts and Piaget's origin of intelligence work.
See also: Children

Roswell, Peggy McGuire, Ph. D. (1987)
Texas Woman's University, Texas
The effects of a data based dance skills program on the motor skill performance and self-concept of moderately handicapped students
155 pp. 48/04-A, 823   ORDER NO. 871,5010
Available from: Diss. Asbstracts International
This study describes an intervention program for moderately handicapped students, aged 11 to 16 years. Teachers are trained to implement either data based dance skills instruction or the Roswell adapted dance instrument based on self-motivated, creative activities. Data is maintained on each student's progress and statistical analysis is used to reveal differences between the groups.
See also: Psychology and Therapy, Children

Sanders, Gary Elvin, Ed. D. (1988)
University of North Carolina, North Carolina
The assessment of dance movement satisfaction of elementary age children participating in a creative dance instructional program
114 pp. 50/06-A, 1594   ORDER NO. 892,1289

Available from: Diss. Abstracts International
This study describes the development of a dance movement satisfaction scale for measuring children's dance satisfaction. The instrument's reliability and validity are assessed and yield acceptable consistency scores. The treatment effects of a creative dance program are determined and it is found that the treatment groups have significantly higher satsifaction scores than the control group.
See also: Children, Psychology and Therapy

Schnoenhof, Madeleine, Ed.D. (1937)
New York University, New York
The Ann Hutchinson School at work
278 pp.
Available from: New York University
Abstract not available.

Schubert, Deborah David, Ed. D. (1985)
University of North Carolina at Greensboro, North Carolina
A survey of student evaluations of teacher/course effectiveness within dance technique courses and the development of new instrumentation
284 pp. 46/08-A, 2229   ORDER NO. 852,0612
Available from: Diss. Abstracts International
An investigation of the use of student evaluations of teacher and course effectiveness in dance technique classes for the purpose of developing a new evaluation instrument. A faculty self-evaluation form is used to measure convergent validity and this is compared with student ratings. It is concluded that the new instrument is valid and reliable.

Sgroi, Angela, Ed. D. (1989)
Rutgers—State University of New Jersey—New Brunswick, New Jersey
Adult amateur dancers: A field study of their learning
229 pp. 50/10-A, 3133   ORDER NO. 900,8016
Available from: Diss. Abstracts International
This study ascertains the nature of the teaching-learning transaction for adults who study modern dance and the impact of this learning on their lives. The findings are organized into four domains: the context, the phenomenon of learning modern dance, the teaching-learning

transaction, and the outcomes and impacts of the learning.
See also: Styles: Modern

Silva, Maristela De Moura, Ed .D. (1983)
Temple University, Philadelphia
Rudolf Laban's theory of modern educational dance: Implications for program development in elementary school
267 pp. 44/05-A, 1378   ORDER NO. 832,1277
Available from: Diss. Abstracts International
This study presents a practical basis for program development strictly based on Laban's theory of education. The components of movement are examined and translated into content for devising dance experiences for elmentary school children. It also includes a historical framework and a description of Laban's life and pertinent theoretical work.
See also: History, Children

Smith, Dorman Jesse, Ed. D. (1987)
University of Utah, Utah
Country Western dance: Analysis, description, and illustrated instructional materials
395 pp. 48/03-A, 597   ORDER NO. 871,4249
Available from: Diss. Abstracts International
This study develops, organizes, and illustrates written instructional materials for use in teaching Country Western dance. Seven dances are included with information on the type of music, dance positions, formations, direction, rhythm, footwork, body movements, leading, following, styling, and detailed step directions. The materials are sufficiently comprehensive to give dancers and instructors an adequate introduction and exposure to the many variations of Country Western dance.
See also: Styles: Social

Smith, Sylvia Alexis, Ph. D. (1984)
Southern Illinois University at Carbondale, Illinois
The effects of a cognitive-affective structured arts curriculum upon the visual perceptual skills of pre-school disadvantaged children using a visual training approach
125 pp. 46/03-A, 679   ORDER NO. 851,0066

Available from: Diss. Abstracts International
This study focuses on a cognitive-affective structured arts curriculum developed to measure its effect upon visual perceptual skills of preschool disadvantaged children. Visual art and creative movement activities are planned around preselected themes from "The Wizard of Oz". A visual training approach results in significant differences in favor of the arts curriculum.
See also: Psychology and Therapy, Related Arts: Visual

Stinson, Susan W, Ed. D. (1984)
University of North Carolina at Greensboro, North Carolina
Reflections and visions: A hermeneutic study of dangers and possibilities in dance education
170 pp. 45/05-A, 1374   ORDER NO. 841,7906
Available from: Diss. Abstracts International
An investigation of the validity of dance as an educative process with particular concern for ways which dance may limit human personhood in terms of liberation and communion. A hermeneutic methodology is used to allow the author to connect personal, professional, and social worlds of the dance educator. The process is significant as a means for curriculum planning in dance.
See also: Psychology and Therapy

Straits, Sue Ann, Ph. D. (1980)
University of Wisconsin at Madison, Wisconsin
The Alwin Nikolais artist-in-residence program at the University of Wisconsin-Madison: An ethnography of dance curriculum-in-use
434 pp. 41/09-A, 6868   ORDER NO. 802,0583
Available from: Diss. Abstracts International
This case study examines curriculum intentions, actions, and outcomes of the meeting between two distinct dance cultures. Daily dance activities are documented to capture the impact of the Alwin Nickolais artist-in-residence program at the University of Wisconsin—Madison in 1978. The focus is on 1) curriculum decisions and their impact and 2) the quality of the interchange between residency

participants. Environmental influences and social meetings are also considered.

Thomas, William Radford, III, Ph.D. (1970)

University of Texas at Austin, Texas
A status study of dance and dance curricula in selected American colleges and universities with bases for establishing a department of dance
140 pp. 31/11-A, 5807   ORDER NO. 71-11,613
Available from: Diss. Abstracts International
This study is concerned with the assessment of the growth and development of dance in American colleges and universities since it was introduced as a major area of study in 1926. It includes a discussion of the arts in our culture, an examiniation of dance as an art form, and a study of dance curriculum in higher education. The study provides information which leads to conclusions and recommendations of significance and value to dance teachers and administrators.
See also: Administration

Twillie, Gwendolyn Brown, Ph. D. (1980)

Texas' Woman's University, Texas
The effects of creative dance on the school readiness of five year old children
133 pp. 41/12-A, 5025   ORDER NO. 81-10528
Available from: Diss. Abstracts International
A study that assesses the relationship between creativity and intelligence in children. Dance lessons are developed and presented to five year olds over a six week period. Readiness and drawing tests are employed to measure the variables.
See also: Children

Valverde, Carmen Edna, Ed. D. (1987)

Rutgers—The State University of New Jersey, New Jersey
Dance as recreation: A comparison of college students' perceived values in dancing
240 pp. 49/04-A, 705   ORDER NO. 880,8238
Available from: Diss. Abstracts International

This study examines how recreational participant choices vary due to contrasting perceptions of the benefits to be realized from dancing. Surveys are used to differentiate between subjects who prefer communal forms, such as folk, square, or ballroom and those who prefer performance forms, such as ballet, tap, or jazz. Areas of similarity are found as well as variables which discriminate between the forms preferred.
See also: Psychology and Therapy

Van Hoy, Karen Lee Anderson, Ph. D. (1979)

University of Texas at Austin, Texas
A program of proposed study of five integrated arts including visual art, music, drama literature, and creative dance designed specifically for both future elementary teachers and elementary students
235 pp. 39/11-A, 6537   ORDER NO. 791,1043
Available from: Diss. Abstracts International
This study describes a humanities program integrating visual art, music, drama, literature, and dance which is proposed as a course of study for elementary teachers. This proposal emphasizes the necessity and value of individual creativity, it's stimulation provided by the arts, and it's transference into the well-being of society.

White-Dixon, Melanye P, Ed. D. (1987)

Temple University, Pennsylvania
Marion Cuyjet: Visionary of dance education in black Philadelphia
244 pp. 49/01-A, 05   ORDER NO. 880,3854
Available from: Diss. Absracts International
This study documents Marion Cuyjet's teaching approach, the structure and function of her dance school, and the role she played in the evolution of dance education in Black Philadelphia. It examines Cuyjet's roots, the phases of her professional preparation, her teaching career, and the historical development of her school. Her teaching career is described in it's socio-cultural perspective and she is attributed with producing proficient dancers and future dance educators.
See also: Biography, History

Wiesner, Theodora, Ed.D. (1958)
New York University, New York
The preparation of a manual for the teaching of dance composition through the use of folk dance materials
535 pp. 19/10-A, 3207   ORDER NO. 58-5664
Available from: Diss.Abstracts International
This study comprises of a manual presenting an approach to teaching modern dance composition through the use of elements of form found in folk dances. It is designed for the beginning teacher to help bridge the gap between technique and composition. Each chapter includes suggestions for teaching procedure, folk dances illustrative of the problem, and suggested problems for original dance studies. A list of music suitable for compositional problems is provided in the appendix.
See also: Styles: Folk, Styles: Modern

Ethnology and Anthropology

Alcide, Marie-Jose, Ph.D. (1988)
City University of New York, New York
Theatrical and dramatic elements of Haitian Voodoo
272 pp. 49/08-A   ORDER NO. 8821061
Available from: Diss. Abstracts International
This study focuses on the relationship between Voodoo and secular theatre. Theatrical and dramatic elements are analyzed according to Aristotlian criteria and it is revealed that Voodoo contains eight major theatrical elements: impersonation, mise-en-scene, audience, chorus, music, dance, scenery, and costume, and four dramatic elements: plot, character, thought, and diction.
See also: Related Arts: Theatre

Amenta, Rosalyn Marie, Ph. D. (1987)
Fordham University, New York
The earth mysticism of the Native American tribal peoples with special reference to the circle symbol and the Sioux Sun Dance rite
249 pp. 48/04-A, 950   ORDER NO. 871,4570
Available from: Diss. Abstracts International

This study analyzes historical data collected by missionaries, ethnographers, anthropologists and others to bring to light the mystical experience of Native Americans. The data is systematically examined for its mystical and philosophical content. An additional analysis is made of the metaphysical and moral philosophy of the Great Plains tribal people, the Teton Sioux, and is then applied to the reinterpretation of the mystical rite of the Sun Dance Ceremony.

Asai, Susan Miyo, Ph.D. (1988)
University of California at Los Angeles, California
Music and drama in N Omai of northern Japan
376 pp. 49/08-A, 2010   ORDER NO. 892,2001
Available from: Diss. Abstracts International
This study presents N Omai, a dance drama, not only as an art form in which music, dance, and drama unite, but as a communal expression that represents the worldview of a Japanese villager. It includes the training process, the performance context, and the audience attitudes and behavior. Music and dance are analyzed separately to determine their organizing principles and stylistic features.
See also: Related Arts: Theatre

Ashton, Martha May Bush, Ph. D. (1972)
Michigan State University, Michigan
Yakshagana Badagatittu Bayalata: A South Indian dance drama
346 pp. 33/09-A, 5337   ORDER NO. 735,319
Available from: Diss. Abstracts International
A study of the Badagatittu Bayalata, a dance drama of Southern India, which plays a role in the cultural and religious development of the community. It includes the history, temple affiliations, personnel, physical environment, music, dance, make-up, costumes, and associated ritual of the dance drama.

Atakpu, Benedict Ozengbe, D.A. (1988)
Middle Tennessee State University, Tennessee
A guide to selected traditional dances of the Bendel State of Nigeria
170 pp. 49/09-A, 2610.   ORDER NO. 882,2216
Available from: Diss. Abstracts International

A guide for the study and understanding of the history of the traditional dances of the Bendel State of Nigeria. It is designed to help prepare future dance educators in teacher training institutions and includes the historical background, costumes, instruments, preparation, formations, and steps for each dance. The importance of the various ceremonial dances and their relevance in the lives of the inhabitants is emphasized.
See also: Education

Bandem, I Made, Ph.D. (1980)
Wesleyan University
Wayang Wong in contemporary Bali
293 pp. 41/05-A, 1824   ORDER NO. 8024021
Available from: Diss. Abstracts International
This study presents a short account of the evolution of Wayang Wong as an interesting example in the development of Balinese dance. Wayang Wong, a traditional dance genre, is associated with the second temple courtyard, the appropriate location for the form in precolonial Bali. A few examples of Wayang Wong from different villages illustrate the idea of moving from kaja to kelod, the transitions being from the sacred to the secualr dance in Bali. Also included is a discussion of the historical and social functions of the dance.

Bealle, John Rufus, Ph. D. (1988)
Indiana University, Indiana
American folklore revival: A study of an old-time music and dance community
393 pp. 50/07-A, 2194   ORDER NO. 892,5101
Available from: Diss. Abstracts International
This study demonstrates the extent to which revived folklore defines a community and the individuals within it. The relevance of the music and dance symbols are extended to the larger community and serve to link the cultures within a setting of cultural pluralism.
See also: Music and Rhythm, Dance Styles: Folk

Blank, Judith, Ph. D. (1974)
University of Illinois at Chicago, Illinois
The story of the Chou Dance of the former Mayurbhanj State, Orissa
Available from: Microform
Abstract not available.

Bloom, Michael Paul, Ph.D. (1989)
Mc Gill University, Canada
The bawdy politic: Strips of culture and the culture of strip
50/04A, 830   ORDER NO. 0565381
Available from: Diss. Abstracts International
A discussion of female strip dancing as cultural practice using methods of cultural history, ethnographic field work, and theoretical critique. The study reconstructs the historical setting in which strip dancing emerged, notes the sites where it continues to evolve, and gives interpretations of strip by its practitioners.
See also: History

Callahan, Alice Anne, Ph. D. (1977)
Syracuse University, New York
"The I'N-Lon-Schka" (playground-of-the-eldest son) the June ceremonial dance of the Osages: A study in American Indian arts
252 pp. 39/02-A, 515   ORDER NO. 781,1638
Available from: Diss. Abstract International
This dissertation describes, examines and interprets the I'N-Lon-Schka with an emphasis on the arts of music, dance, and costume. After a brief history of the Osages, a consideration of dance ceremonies in primitive North American Indian societies is given followed by a detailed description of the I'on-Lon-Schka; it's music, dance movements, costume, and related crafts.

Carlson, Richard George, Ph. D. (1973)
University of Virginia, Virginia
From the "Sun Dance" to the "Ghost Dance": A social and intellectual history of the Lakotas, 1868 to 1890
ORDER NO. 802,1770
Available from: Diss. Abstracts International
Abstract not available.

Cashion, Susan Valerie, Ph. D. (1983)
Stanford University, California
Dance ritual and cultural values in a Mexican village: Festival of Santo Santiago
374 pp. 44/05-A, 1313   ORDER NO. 832,0689
Available from: Diss. Abstracts International
An investigation of La Danza de los Tastoanes, one of the ritual dance expressions of Mexico.

The study describes the event and analyzes the elements of time, space, energy, and the multivocalic nature of the dance symbol. It also examines the festival system as a nonschooling cutural institution which acts as a format and informal teaching and learning device for transmitting cultural values.

Cowan, Jane Kerin, Ph. D. (1988)
Indiana University, Indiana
Embodiments: The social construction of gender in dance-events in a northern Greek town
470 pp. 49/10-A, 3069   ORDER NO. 890,2558
Available from: Diss. Abstracts International
This study examines how gender ideas and the social relations informed by them in a small town in northern Greece are embodied, empowered, and experienced in communal celebrations which include social dancing. It argues that dance events are often problematical for males and females and it concludes that power relations are expressed and negotiated and gender inequalities reproduced in these contexts of con-sensual pleasure, sensuality, and release.
See also: Styles: Social

Cravath, Paul Russel, Ph. D. (1985)
University of Hawaii, Hawaii
Earth in flower: An historical and descriptive study of the classical dance drama of Cambodia
684 pp. 47/08-A, 2803   ORDER NO. 862,9034
Available from: Diss. Abstracts International
A documentation of the history and performance style of the Royal Ballet of Cambodia and a analysis of the dancers' mysterious elegance, and their historical, political, and aesthetic power in traditional Cambodia. This study rejects the view of an historical Indianization of Southeast Asia in favor of emphasizing a continuity of indigenous cultural forms and rituals from pre-Angkorean times.

Daniel, Yvonne Laverne Payne, Ph. D. (1989)
University of California at Berkeley, California
Ethnography of rumba: Dance and social change in contemporary Cuba
461 pp. 50/10-A, 3275   ORDER NO. 900,6294
Available from: Diss. Abstracts International
This study illuminates values and attitudes which are embodied in Cuban dance. Meaning in dance is revealed at the world-view, ritual and performance, symbolic, group, individual, and movement levels and the multivocalic nature of dance is demonstrated. The cultural contexts of rumba facilitate an understanding of the complexities surrounding social change in contemporary Cuba.
See also: Syles: Social

Deangelis, Edith Gladys Theresa, Ed. D. (1976)
Boston University, Massachusetts
The American Indian culture and its relationship to dance and games
Available from: Microform
Abstract not available.

Detwiler, Frederick Emrey Jr, Ph. D. (1983)
Pennsylvania State University, Pennsylvania
The Sun Dance of the Oglala: A case study in religion, ritual, and ethnics
373 pp. 44/03-A, 778   ORDER NO. 831,2622
Available from: Diss. Abstracts International
This study applies a phenomenological approach to the study of religion as it applies to the Oglala Sun Dance ritual complex. It includes the sources of the phenomena, a description of the social context, an account of the events of the ritual, and an analysis of the Sun Dance from a theoretical perspective. The study concludes that this ritual complex brings the social community to encounter with the sacred powers.

Dittmar, Ana M, Ph. D. (1984)
Rutgers—the State University of New Jersey at New Brunswick, New Jersey
Traditional Yugoslav dance in a changing society
171 pp. 45/07-A, 2160   ORDER NO. 842,4098

Available from: Diss. Abstracts International
This study examines some of the influences that accelerate change using traditonal dance and the Smotra Folklora, Folklore Review, as a focus. At such a festival the influences of toursim, folkdance enthusiasts, visiting Yugoslav-Americans and Yugoslav worker-migration can be seen as contributing to the continuing valuation and the marketability of traditional dance. The study also shows that traditional arts remain desirable, cultural links between the past and future and help to form the present cultural expression.
See also: Styles: Folk

Dobbin, Jay D, Ph. D. (1982)
Ohio State University, Ohio
"Do'en dee dance": Description and analysis of the jombee dance of Montserrat, West Indies
239 pp. 43/10-A, 3360   ORDER NO. 830,5318
Available from: Diss. Abstracts International
A description and analysis of the rarely performed trance ritual in which the dancers are believed to be possessed by ancestor spirits, the jombees. African and European elements are integrated to form a culturally creative and adaptive product. The demise of the dance is discussed as a function of modernization. Data are analyzed using Victor Turner's model of ritual as social drama, Mary Douglas' model of the entranced dancer as a microcosm of society, and George Simpson's analysis of Black religion in the Caribbean.

Duke, Jerry Childress, Ph. D. (1982)
Texas Woman's University, Texas
Clog dance of the Appalachian mountain region of the United States of America
113 pp. 44/01-A, 104   ORDER NO. 831,2274
Available from: Diss. Abstracts International
Appalacian clog dance steps are recorded and analyzed and variations are described. Steps are compared with step patterns of American Indians and of the dances of the countries from which the settlers of the Appalacian mountain region emigrated. Differences in Appalacian clog dance styles are attributed to inter-cultural learning and sharing.
See also: Styles: Folk

Dunn, Deborah Gail, Ph. D. (1983)
Union for Experimenting Colleges and Universities, New York
Topeng Pajegan: The mask dance of Bali (Indonesia)
253 pp. 45/10-A, 3029   ORDER NO. 842,9937
Available from: Diss. Abstracts International
The solo ritual mask dance, Topeng Pajegan, is described, documented, and analyzed revealing the significance of its ritual and theatrical components. The study concentrates on the masks themselves and the dance form. The three major dancing roles are described with photos, drawings, and a glossary of the movements and the entire process of a performance is discussed.

Fenton, Wiiliam N, Ph.D. (1937)
Yale University, Connecticut
The Seneca Eagle dance: A study of personality expression in ritual
Available from: Microform
Abstract not available.

Franken, Marjorie Ann, Ph. D. (1986)
University of California at Riverside, California
Anyone can dance: A survey and analysis of Swahili Ngoma, past and present
298 pp. 47/12-A, 4429   ORDER NO. 870,6987
Available from: Diss. Abstracts International
A general survey and description of Swahili dance based on interviews and observations in Mombasa, Kenya. In adition to descriptions of upper class dances, several dances done by more humble Swahili are presented and compared. Other categories of dance are described including women's hip dancing, religious ngoma, and young men's dances. An evolutinary sequence of elite women's dance is presented and discussed in light of current anthropological theories of dance change.

Freedman, Diane C, Ph. D. (1984)
Temple University, Philadelphia
Dance as communication code in
Romanian courtship and marriage
rituals
344 pp. 45/01-A, 230   ORDER NO. 841,0194
Available from: Diss. Abstracts International
An ethnographic analysis of dance as a meaningful code within the complex courtship and
marriage rituals of a village in Transylvania,
Romania. Movement signs of the dance code
are revealed through effort/shape analysis and
serve to express and mediate the village gender
hierarchy.
See also: Notation and Movement Analysis

Gaus, Dorothy Shipley, Ph.D. (1976)
Catholic University of America
Change in social dance song style at
Allegany Reservation, 1962-1973: The
Rabbit Dance (volumes I and II)
719 pp. 37/04-A, 1864   ORDER NO. 76-21,492
Available from: Diss. Abstracts International
An examination of the changes in social dance
song style and its connection with changes
in the environment, culture, and the musical
activities at Allegany Reservation during the
period of 1962 to 1973 when a dam and new
highway were constructed on the reservation.
Changes in the music seem related to the
decrease in social dancing and in the use of
Rabbit Dance Songs for dancing.
See also: Music and Rhythm

Gentes, Mary Josephine, Ph.D. (1987)
Univeristy of Virgina, Virgina
Hinduism through village dance drama:
Narrative image and ritual process in
South India's Terukkuttu and Yaksagana
ritual theaters
381 pp. 49/11-A, 3392   ORDER NO. 890,2463
Available from: Diss. Abstracts International
This study focuses on two village dance drama
traditions as media of religious behavior by
discussing several indigenous views of the relationship of aesthetic and religious experience
and by introducing and applying the concepts
of the "narrative imagination" and the "ritual
process" as analytical frames of reference.

Gottheim, Vivien I, D.A. (1984)
New York University, New York
Eve of Sant John's Day: A work in
words and images based on an aesthetic
inquiry into the dramatic-dance
"Bumba-Meu-Boi" in San Luis of
Maranhao, Brazil
395 pp. 46/03-A, 587   ORDER NO. 8510790
Available from: Diss. Abstracts International
This research-project is the creation of a mixed
media artwork consisting of words and images
which draw upon materials collected at the
celebration of Bumba-Meu-Boi in Sao Luis,
Maranhao, Brazil. In addition to the mixed
media work, a method of aesthetic inquiry is
developed for use by those who view the artist
as protean researcher. The author's experience
is objectified and includes a meta-critical analysis of the celebration and a review of literature.
See also: Theory and Philosophy

Hanna, Judith Lynne, Ph. D. (1976)
Columbia University, New York
The anthropology of dance ritual:
Nigeria's Ubakala Nkwa Di Iche Iche
271 pp. 37/06-A, 3738   ORDER NO. 76-28,657
Available from: Diss. Abstracts International
A study of the dance-plays of Ubakala of Nigeria to show that dance reflects , influences, and
is constitutive of other sociocultural aspects of
the system of which it is part. The relations
between the pattern of dance (text) and those
of society (context) are identified and illustrated through the analysis of six dance-play
genres.

Harding, Frances, Ph.D. (1988)
University of Exeter, United Kingdom
Continuity and creativity in Tiv theatre
370 pp. 49/05A, 1000   ORDER NO. DX82354
Available from: Diss. Abstracts International
This study is an account of a selective process
of continuity and creativity in the performance
arts of the Tiv people of Nigeria. It covers the
history of the Tiv throughout colonial rule and
into Nigerian Independence in 1960 analysing
key politicised performances. Two contemporary dance forms are described and portrayed
as transformations of Tiv society. The establishment of a Performing Arts Company is
described as are some of its performances.

Hauck, Shirley A, Ph. D. (1986)
University of Pittsburgh, Pennsylvania
Extinction and reconstruction of Aleut music and dance
303 pp. 47/12-A, 4429   ORDER NO. 870,8470
Available from: Diss. Abstracts International
This study discerns the form, content, and context of aboriginal Aleut music and dance by analyzing twenty early ethnographic descriptions according to ethnomusicological and ethnochoreographical standards. The analysis is sufficiently detailed to allow reconstructions of the performances. Examination of the Aleut cultural trait complex supports the assertion that Aleut music and dance are more closely related to Eskimo expressiveness than to Alaskan Indian traits. The examination also traces the demise of Aleut music and dance.
See also: Realted Arts: Music.

Hazzard-Gordon, Katrina Yovonne, Ph. D. (1983)
Cornell University, New York
"Atiba's a Comin": The rise of social dance formations in Afro-American culture
318 pp. 44/06-A, 1938   ORDER NO. 832,1785
Available from: Diss. Abstracts International
This study traces the sociohistoric origins and forms of black working-class culture arenas. Using social dance as a focal point, the study explores the development of ten institutional contexts in which the Afro-American has danced and finds that blacks built their own secular institutions to express their identity and community and that their socio-economic status provided the conditions for new cultural forms to emerge. Finally, the study raises questions about the relationship between culture and oppression.
See also: History

Heth, Charlotte Ann Wilson, Ph. D. (1975)
University of California at Los Angeles, California
The stomp dance music of the Oklahoma Cherokee: A study of contempory practice with special reference to the Illinois District Council Ground. (volumes I & II)
589 pp. 36/05-A, 2480   ORDER NO. 75-22,628
Available from: Diss. Abstracts International
Cherokee music together with historical and ethnographical materials pertaining to music, are used as a framework for the study of contemporary ceremonies of the 'Stomp Dance'. The dance sequence is described and the musical forms are analysed in detail. The study concludes that stomp dance music is a vital part of Oklahoma Cherokee culture and that is has value and integrity.
See also: Music and Rhythm

Ito, Sachiyo, Ph. D. (1986)
New York University, New York
Origins of traditional Okinawan dance
262 pp. 49/08-A, 2003   ORDER NO. 882,5239
Available from: Diss. Abstracts International
This study provides historical, ethnographical, and descriptive data to support the view that Okinawan dance is an indigenous art native to the unique Okinawan culture. Documentations of dance gestures from field work research, photography, videography, and Labanotation movement analysis serve as references for a comparative analysis.
See also: Notation and Movement Analysis

Kaeppler, Adrienne Lois, Ph.D. (1967)
University of Hawaii, Hawaii
The structure of Tongan dance
344 pp. 28/05-B, 1772   ORDER NO. 67-13,701
Available from: Diss. Abstracts International
In this ethnoscientific analysis of Tongan dance two basic levels of dance organization, kinemic and morphokinemic, are compared to phonemic and morphemic levels in linguistic analysis. 47 movement units are isolated using kinemic analysis and are Labanotated. Two other levels, morphokinemic and motif, are discussed and a fourth level, the whole dance structure, is described in structural and chronological detail. Six genres of Tongan dance are discussed in terms of dance movement, music, poetry, and performance. It is concluded that dance seen from an ethnographer's point of view can be enriched by the views of the participants themselves.

Keali, 'Inohomoku, Joann Wheeler, Ph.D (1970)
Indiana University, Indiana
Theory and methods for the anthropological study of dance
383 pp.
Available from: Microform
Abstract not available.
See also: Theory and Philosophy

Kehoe, Alice Beck, Ph.D. (1964)
Harvard University, Massachusetts
The Ghost Dance religion in Saskatchewan: A functional analysis
Available from: Microform
Abstract not available.

Kim, Deukshin, Ph. D. (1987)
City University of New York, New York
"Hahoe pyolsin-kut": The oldest extant Korean mask-dance theatre
290 pp. 48/12-A, 3010   ORDER NO. 880,1726
Available from: Diss. Abstracts International
This study explores hahoe pyolsin-kut as a complete cultural phenomenon—historical background, village ritual, masks, performers, stage, costumes, properties, music, dance, and dramatic values. An attempt is made to cover all aspects of Hahoe pyolsin-kut in order to discover both its theatrical quality and dramatic values.

Kim, Theresa Ki-Ja, Ph. D. (1988)
New York University, New York
The relationship between Shamanic ritual and the Korean masked dance-drama: The journey motif to chaos/darkness/void
397 pp. 50/03-A, 573   ORDER NO. 891,0578
Available from: Diss. Abstracts International
An explanation of how the chaos/darkness/void of the Korean Shaman "Song of Creation" dissolves all social, historical, and cultural orientations and enables actors and dancers to transform themselves into deities and characters for rituals and dance-dramas. It is shown that only through this depersonalization do shamans and actors function in their roles as vessels for the universal order inherent in deity or character.
See also: Theory and Philosophy

Kimber, Robert James, Ph. D. (1988)
University of Colorado at Boulder, Colorado
Performance space as sacred space in Aranda Corroboree—An interpretation of the organization and use of space as a dramatic element in the performance of selected Aborignal ritual in central Australia
317 pp. 50/03-A, 573   ORDER NO. 891,2200
Available from: Diss. Abstracts International
This study gives insight into Aboriginal Australian corroboree as a group theatre practice which in form and function pre-date the sophisticated theatre of fifth century Ancient Greece. Corroboree as ritual is examined according to the theories of Mircea Eliade. Textural sources in mythology yield archetypal figures for interpretation in mime, song, and dance giving a basis for defining social responsibility. Performance space is analyzed in terms of saturation, boundary, and projection.
See also: Related Arts: Theatre

Lawson, Mary Elizabeth, Ph.D. (1989)
Brown University
Tradition, change, and meaning in Kiribati performance: An ethnography of music and dance in a Micronesian society
548 pp. 50/08-A, 2295   ORDER NO. 900,2249
Available from: Diss. Abstracts International
An examination of the music and dance performance of the Kiribati within its context and in relation to cultural change. Cultural aspects of the study include identity, spiritual knowledge and origins, competition, and affective power. The forms and places of performance are described in both traditional and contemporary society and an analysis concludes that music and dance are a dynamic force in Kiribati.
See also: Music and Rhythm

Lee, Meewon, Ph. D. (1983)
University of Pittsburgh, Pittsburgh
"Kamyonguk": The mask-dance theater of Korea (t'alch'um, sandae, okwangdae)
396 pp. 45/02-A, 346   ORDER NO. 841,1756
Available from: Diss. Abstracts International
An exploration of Kamyonguk, a theatrical and damatic mode found in Korea, in both its

dramatic form and its theatrical representation in the context of its historical background. The study also traces Kamyonguk's relation to the folk ritual and presents characteristics of folk theatre. The actors' training, the stage, the dance and movement, the music and song, the costumes, and the masks are examined. This traditional theatre form has survived the changes of time and is recognized as a celebration of Korean national identity.
See also: Related Arts: Theatre

Lekis, Lisa, Ph.D. (1956)
Florida University, Florida
The origin and development of ethnic Caribbean dance and music
294 pp. 16/06, 1126   ORDER NO. 16,360
Available from: Diss. Abstracts International
This study traces the historical development of the ethnic dance and music of the Caribbean islands and examines their importance and significance from a sociological and anthropological point of view. The function of dance as an integral part of the life of the people is used to demonstrate how a culture may be studied through the artistic manifestations of dance and music. The influences of the original Indians, the Africans, and the colonizing Europeans are discussed and included is a survey of dance and music in the individual islands of the Caribbean.
See also: Music and Rhythm

Lewis, Ellistine Perkins, Ph. D. (1978)
University of Michigan, Michigan
The E. Azalia Hackley memorial collection of Negro music, dance, and drama: A catalogue of selected Afro-American materials
201 pp. 39/11-A, 6618   ORDER NO. 790,7122
Available from: Diss. Abstracts International
This study provides important guidelines for the use of the Afro-American material of the E. Azalia Hackney Collections in secondary school programs of multicultural music education. It provides an annotated listing of selected resources in the areas of music, dance, and drama.
See also: Education

Mace, Carroll Edward, Ph.D. (1966)
Tulane University, Louisiana
Three Quiché dance-dramas of Rabinal, Guatemula
190 pp. 27/10-A,3431   ORDER NO. 67-3854
Available from: Diss. Abstracts International
This dissertaion studies three dance-dramas or bailes performed by the Quiché Indians of Rabinal in Guatemala. Three genres are described—the historical, the religious, and the cosmic—and are shown to represent the type of primitive theatre which is still popular in Rabinal. Both Quiché and Spanish texts are presented and are studied with reference to written historical sources as well as traditions and ethnologoical information obtained in Rabinal.

Meckel, Mary V, Ph.D. (1988)
University of Nebraska at Lincoln, Nebraska
Continuity and change within a social institution: The role of the taxi-dancer
202 pp. 49/08-A   ORDER NO. 882,4944
Available from: Diss. Abstracts International
An in-depth examination of recreational establishments commonly called taxi-dance halls and the unique role of women taxi-dancers. It also examines the specific social phenomena, educational and socio-economic, which channel women into this form of employment.
See also: Styles: Social

Mills, Antonia Curtze, Ph. D. (1982)
Harvard University, Massachusetts
The Beaver Indian prophet dance and related movements among North American Indians
232 pp. 43/05-A, 1602   ORDER NO. 822,2674
Available from: Diss. Abstracts International
An investigation of the Prophet and Ghost Dance practised by North American Indians. A review of the anthropological literature shows that the dances are one type of a nativistic revitalization movement related to drastic social change. Historical data show that Prophet dances began in the east and proceeded west following white influence. Examination of ten tribes from differenct cultural areas in North America reveals that they all believed in shamanic world view and the study

concludes that the dances are still deeply rooted in North American esoteric philosophy.

Mishler, Craig Wallace, Ph. D. (1981)
University of Texas at Austin, Texas
Gwich in Athapaskan music and dance:
An ethnography and ethnohistory
405 pp. 42/11-A, 4865   ORDER NO. 820,8218
Available from: Diss. Abstracts International
In this study Gwich in music and dance is classified into two major categories: Aborrgi-nal-style and contact-traditional. Although Aboriginal-stlye dance has vanished, it can be reconstructed. Twelve contact—traditional dances are described in detail, illustrated with diagrams, and compared with other variations and prototypes. The dances are interpreted for their social significance and a profile demonstrates their chronological interface and differentiation.

Nasaruddin, Mohamed Chouse, Ph. D. (1979)
Indiana University, Indiana
Dance and music of the Desa performing arts of Malaysia
711 pp. 40/02-A, 547   ORDER NO. 791,6921
Available from: Diss. Abstracts International
An examination of the structures and common features of dance and music in the major forms of the Desa performing arts of Malaysia. Malay dance concentrates on the movements of the upper body and uses the concept of symmetrical balance. Music augments the dance and also serves a spiritual function, especially in the ritualistic opening and closing ceremonies.
See also: Music and Rhythm

Ness, Sally Ann Allen, Ph. D. (1987)
University of Washington, Washington
The 'Sinulog' dancing of Cebu city, Philippines: A semiotic analysis
705 pp. 48/12-A, 3145   ORDER NO. 880,2312
Available from: Diss. Abstracts International
This study tests a new method of observation and analysis that combines the use of Laban Movement Analysis with Peircean semeiotic analysis. An analysis of the three forms of Cebu City Sinulog dancing summarizes observations of the performance itself, relates these to informant interpretations, and analyzes semeiotic processes operating through the performances. The results indicate that style does carry cultural meaning and merits close and accurate observation.
See also: Notation and Movement Analysis

Novack, Cynthia Jean, Ph. D. (1986)
Columbia University, New York
Sharing the dance: An ethnography of contact improvisation
342 pp. 47/07-A, 2637   ORDER NO. 862,3580
Available from: Diss. Abstracts International
This study treats contact improvisation from an anthropological perspective, examining the dance form in historical, social, and cultural contexts. Theories drawn from the fields of symbolic anthropology, the sociology of art, and the study of movement behavior are used to investigate the cultural and social structures and meaning of the dance form. Comparisons with other dance forms and other realms of American culture are made to illustrate the place of contact improvisation in American cultural history.

Pantaleoni, Hewitt, Ph. D. (1972)
Wesleyan University, Connecticut
The rhythm of Atsia dance drumming among the Anlo (Eve) of Anyako
33/03-A, 1189
Available from: Diss. Abstracts International
A study of the instrumental rhythms of one part of the traditional dance, Atsia as performed on the island town of Anyako in Ghana. It describes dance-drumming as a vehicle for social expression and also presents a detailed analysis of each instrument with sample scores.
See also: Music and Rhythm

Peters, Jonathan Alexander Samuel, Ph. D. (1975)
University of Alberta, Alberta, Canada
A dance of Senghor, Achebe, Soyinka, and African cultural history
Available from: Microform
Abstract not Available.

Primus, Pearl, Ph.D. (1963)
New York University, New York
An anthropological study of masks as teaching aids in the enculturation of Mano children
234 pp.   ORDER NO. 7818147

Available from: Diss. Abstracts International
This anthropological study discusses masks as teaching aids in the enculturation of children among the Mano people of Liberia, West Africa. The basic hypothesis is that masks, manipulated in order to bring an invisible ancestral force into visible being, structure, reinforce, and formalize the learning of culture traits and values. A curriculum utilizing masks as teaching aids would encourage better understanding, uses, and development of the creative arts and would encourage better understanding of other people and cultures of the world.

Rivers, Olivia Skipper, Ph. D. (1990)
University of Wisconsin at Madison, Wisconsin
The changes in composition, function, and aesthetic criteria as a result of acculturation found in five traditional dances of the Eastern band of Cherokee Indians in North Carolina
347 pp. 51/09-A, 3122   ORDER NO. 90-30807
Available from: Diss. Abstracts International
This study describes changes in traditional Cherokee dances resulting from interaction with and acculturation into European culture. It identifies characteristics in the choreographic structure useful in reconstruction and future comparative studies. It includes a review of Cherokee history, accounts of pre-European ceremonies, choreographic analysis, and Labannotated scores.

Saleh, Magda Ahmed Abdel Ghaffar, Ph. D. (1979)
New York University, New York
A documentation of the ethnic dance traditions of the Arab Republic of Egypt
628 pp. 40/05-A, 2318   ORDER NO. 792,5289
Available from: Diss. Abstracts International
This study begins with a brief comparative overview of dance research in traditional Arab dance in the United States and Egypt. A sampling of seventeen folk dances are recorded in a documentary film along with historical, ethnological and aesthetic information. An assessment of the film as an artistic endeavour is discussed. Finally guidelines to improve the field of dance research in Egypt are given.
See also: Styles: Folk

Sandoval, Marina Consuelo, Ph. D. (1985)
University of California at Santa Cruz, California
Movement and world view: Applying Laban movement analysis and Magoroh Maruyama's paradigms to the Comanche dance and lifestyle data in three Tewa Pueblos
278 pp. 46/07-A, 1992   ORDER NO. 852,0453
Available from: Diss. Abstracts International
An exploration of the creation of meaning from body movement and cultural data using two systems—Laban Movement Anaylsis and Magoroh Maruyama's paradigms or epistomological types. These are applied to dance film footage as well as to cultural data and are used as analytical as well as interpretive tools. The Pueblo Indian culture and its Comanche dance are historically and contemporaneously described and assessed using the methodology illustrating the potential use of non-traditional observational tools in expanding understanding of cultures.
See also: Notation and Movement Analysis

Smith, Ronald Richard, Ph. D. (1976)
Indiana University, Indiana
The society of Los Congos of Panama: An ethnological study of the music and dance-theatre of an Afro-Panamanian group
340 pp. 37/04-A, 2345   ORDER NO. 79-21,604
Available from: Diss. Abstracts International
This study covers the folklore tradition of Los Congos descriptively, touching upon objects, events, and practices. The major thesis is that Congo tradition in Panama is a modern, popular expression of the social structure, activities, oral history, and ceremonial lives of the escaped slaves who surrounded the major centers of population in the Colonial era.

Sparkis, Sylvia Traska, Ph. D. (1989)
University of Illinois at Urbana-Champaign, Illinois
Folk dance as a staged attraction in Yugoslavia: A study of an evolving tradition
157 pp. 50/11-A, 3392   ORDER NO. 901,1032
Available from: Diss. Abstracts International

This ethnographic study of staged folkloric performances in Dubrovnik, Yugoslavia during the 1988 season provides information about the people involved, the forms and contents of the folklore, and the relationship between performance and tourism in Yugoslavia. The folkloric programs observed are of folk music, song, dance, theatre, games, or combinations of these.
See also: Styles: Folk

Strobel, Katherine Brown, Ph. D. (1986)
Texas Woman's University, Texas
The traditional dances of the Cumberland Plateau

145 pp. 48/04-A, 997   ORDER NO. 871,5164
Available from: Diss. Abstracts International
This study makes available a comprehensive description of the dances and dance events of the people of the Cumberalnd Plateau and provides information about the background of these dances. Data consists of videotapes of twelve regional dance events, interviews, and relevant literature. Work-play dance events, home dances, public dances, clogging, square dancing, and solo step dancing are described in detail.
See also: Styles: Folk

Sweet, Jill Drayson, Ph. D. (1981)
University of New Mexico, New Mexico
Tewa ceremonial performances: The effects of tourism on an ancient Pueblo Indian dance and music tradition
244 pp. 42/08-A, 3656   ORDER NO. 820,1955
Available from: Diss. Abstracts International
A description and analysis of the effects of tourism of the performance practices of the Tewa Pueblo Indians of New Mexico. Tewa village ritual events are compared with Tewa dance and music presentations during theatrical, tourist-orientated ceremonials Tewa Indians adjust to tourist contact through the interrelated processes of selective cultural interlacing, persistent rejuvenation, and rationalization. Tourists however, are only the

most recent of many migrating groups that have disrupted Tewa society.
See also: Music and Rhythm

Thomson, Susan Jean, Ph. D. (1989)
Harvard University, Massachusetts
Seraikela Chhau dance and the creation of authority: From princely state to democracy
273 pp. 50/08-A, 2553   ORDER NO. 892,6225
Available from: Diss. Abstracts International
This study argues that the Chhau patrons, dancers, and connoisseurs face a crisis in authority with regard to the dance's acceptance and prestige. It examines how authority is created in dance and how cultural groups and political regimes use dance to both constitute and represent their own prestige and authenticity.

Volland, Anita, Ph. D. (1975)
University of Pennsylvania, Pennsylvania
The arts in Polynesia—A study of the function and meaning of art forms in the pre-contact Pacific
384 pp. 36/12-A, 8158   ORDER NO. 76-12,356
Available from: Diss. Abstracts International
An inquiry into the relationship between the forms, functions, and meanings of the art of the New Zealand Maori. Works of art include plastic art, verbal art, and dance. Maori art forms operate largely in polysemic symbols and have multiple and simultaneous meanings which manifest an emphasis on ancestry, the past, and the continuity of social life.

Weaver, Wilhelmina Clark, Ph. D. (1970)
University of Wisconsin at Madison, Wisconsin
Dance as a cutural trait of some cutural groups of the Inca empire at the time of the Spanish conquest
370 pp. 31/11-A, 5830   ORDER NO. 71-3494
Available from: Diss Abstracts International
This study identifies the movement and non-movement elements which make it possible to specify choreographic characteristics of a cultural group. The dances of the Inca royal family show the most divergence from the common elements found among the other cultural groups of the Inca empire. Elements are com-

pared with historical developments and the interaction of dance and other cultural traits are hypothesized.
See also: History

Wild, Stephen Aubury, Ph. D. (1975)
Indiana University, Indiana
Music and dance in their social and cultural nexus
167 pp. 36/02-A, -964   ORDER NO. 75-17,072
Available from: Diss. Abstracts International
A comprehensive description of the music and dance of the Walbiri Aborigines of central Australia. Dances are primarily to commemorate the ancestor's acts, while songs are magical—both are the central focus of all rituals. Walbiris songs and dances have important ecological, sociological, and psychological functions and these are detailed in the study.
See also: Music and Rhythm

Wong, Peter Kim-Hung, Ph. D. (1989)
University of Wisconsin at Madison, Wisconsin
Cultural influences on dance in the T'ang dynasty and the movement characteristics of a dance of the period
398 pp. 50/09-A, 2684   ORDER NO. 891,7678
Available from: Diss. Abstracts International
An investigation of the cultural background of the dance from the earliest dynasty to the T'ang dynasty and of the cultural influence on the common dance in the T'ang dynasty. A reconstructed T'ang dance drama is selected for analysis using Labanotation, Laban movement analysis, and an analysis method designed by the author. Findings provide information for choreography of Chinese dance and broaden the vocabulary in oriental dance.
See also: Notation and Movement Analysis, Choreography and Performance

Wortman, Mary Alice, Ph. D. (1972)
Ohio University, Ohio
The concept of Machismo in the poetry, music, and dance of the Gaucho of the Rio De La Plata
214 pp. 33/08-A, 4279   ORDER NO. 74-4252
Available from: Diss. Abstracts International
An exploration of the manisfestations of a Spanish-American concept of males superiority called machisma through studying the

dance, poetry and music of Argentina and Uraguay. Dance forms are studied for expression of machisma in their movements and meanings and are found to be significant by representing acts of courtship and conquest of women.

Youngerman, Suzanne, Ph. D. (1983)
Columbia University, New York
"Shaking is no Foolish Play": An anthropological perspective on the American shakers-person, time, space, and dance-ritual
276 pp. 44/12-A, 3738   ORDER NO. 840,6574
Available from: Diss. Abstracts International
This historical reconstruction of the Shaker settlement in America in the 1970's culminates in an extended study of the development of the form and function of the Shaker dance—ritual which served as a model for Shaker culture in that it both expressed and shaped beliefs and actions, helping to bridge the gap between ideology and social organization.
See also: History

Yousof, Ghulam-Sarwar, Ph. D. (1976)
University of Hawaii, Hawaii
The Kelantan Mak Yong dance theatre. A study of performance structure
405 pp. 38/01-A, 30   ORDER NO. 77-14,607
Available from: Diss. Abstracts International
A description of the Mak Yong dance theatre form which incorporates the elements of ritual, stylised dance, vocal and instrumental music, song, story, improvised and formal language, as well as stylised acting. It is found on the east coast of the Malay peninsula and today the performances are done in two styles—for entertainment and for spiritual and healing purposes. Several different types of Mak Yong performances are described and conventions and structural patterns are also discussed.
See also: Choreography and Performance

History

Albig, Pegeen Horth, Ph.D. (1979)
Florida State University, Florida
A history of the Robert Joffrey Ballet
(Vols I and II)
565 pp. 40/06-A, 2987   ORDER NO. 792,6708
Available from: Diss. Abstracts International
A historical and analytical survey of the first
twenty years of the Joffrey Ballet Company
(1956–75). The study traces the company from
its formation to its first crest of maturity as one
of America's three major classical companies.
Source materials include books, critics'
reviews, privately owned scrapbooks, and
interviews of persons connected with the company.
See also: Styles: Ballet

Barclay, Thomas Brian, Ph.D. (1958)
University of Toronto, Ontario, Canada
The role of the dance and dance lyrics
in the Spanish comedia of the early
eighteenth century
97 pp.
Available from: Mircroform
Abstract not available.

Brandman, Russella, Ph. D. (1977)
Florida State University, Florida
The evolution of jazz dance from folk
origins to concert stage
649 pp. 38/05-A, 2422   ORDER NO. 77-24,743
Available from: Diss. Abstracts International
This study traces the origins and development
of jazz dance, describes contemporary concert
jazz forms, and draws conclusions concerning
relationships between early traditional and
contemporary forms. The study includes discussions of African dance, early practices of the
slave trade, jazz music development, religious,
social, and secular dance forms and festivals,
and the West Indies influence. Summaries of
contemporary concert jazz choreography are
presented and comparisons are made between
traditional and contemporary forms.
See also: Dance Styles: Jazz

Brooks, Lynn Matluck, Ed. D. (1985)
Temple University, Pennsylvania
The dances of the processing of Seville
in Spain's golden age
499 pp. 46/03-A, 555   ORDER NO. 850,9321
Available from: Diss. Abstracts International
This study reveals new perspectives on Seville's
history, its spiritual traditions, and on the
nature of religious, popular, theatrical, and
court dance in the Golden Age. It illuminates
the processional dance works themselves, their
choreographers, and religious tradition. An
investigation into church attitudes and imperial decline determines the fate of Sevilles'
unique religious dance.

**Buckman, Susan Donna, Ph. D.
(1984)**
Texas Womans University, Texas
Dance in Denver's pioneer theatres:
1859–1871
208 pp. 45/12-A, 3466   ORDER NO. 850,2643
Available from: Diss. Abstracts International
An investigation of the role of dance on the
frontier society of Denver, Colorado from 1859
to 1871. The study identifies who danced, what
they danced, the nature of the theatres, and
the audiences who watched. Performances that
took place in legitimate and variety theatres
are described and several persons are identified
as having perfomed dance in entr'acte and
major dance productions.

Chumbley, Joyce, Ph. D. (1976)
University of Hawaii, Hawaii
The world of Moliere's comedy-ballets
405 pp. 33/09-A, 5337   ORDER NO. 73-5260
Available from: Diss. Abstract International
An overview of Moliere's comedy-ballets in
their 17th century setting. It traces the close
relationship between them and earlier French
theatre and places them in historical context
with regard to Louis XIV, his family, and his
courtiers.
See also: Styles: Ballet

Clark, Sharon Leigh, Ph. D. (1973)
New York University, New York
Rock dance in the United States,
1960–1970: Its origins, forms and
patterns
397 pp. 34/12-B, 5788   ORDER NO. 741,2833

Available from: Diss. Abstract International
A study of the origins, forms, and patterns of rock dance as one aspect of civilization in the United States, 1960-1970. Findings of the study indicate a link between the subcultures of youth, women, and blacks and the general society. It also indicates that rock dance was a non-verbal attempt of emancipation from assigned societal roles.
See also: Styles: Social

Colley, Thomas, Ph. D. (1974)

Wayne State University, Michigan
A historical study of the Society of Stage Directors and Choreographers through 1973
319 pp. 35/12-A, 8061   ORDER NO. 75-13,306
Available from: Diss. Abstracts International
A historical study of the labor union representing directors and choreographers on Broadway, off Broadway, and in resident theaters. It includes the union's objectives, its agreements and contracts, the Workshop Foundation, and its role in the future of American theatre as an industry and as an art.
See also: Choreography and Performance, Administration

Costonis, Maureen Needham, Ph. D. (1989)

New York University, New York
Ballet comes to America, 1792–1842: French contributions to the establishment of theatical dance in New Orleans and Philadelphia
466 pp. 50/09-A, 2707   ORDER NO. 900,4272
Available from: Diss. Abstracts International
This study examines contributions of French dancers who brought ballet to America and analyzes the ways in which theatrical dance productions replicated the Paris Opera's example. Max Weber's theory of organizational design is used to analyze and compare the American and Paris administrative operations. The data reveals continuity and growth in ballet presentations during the period.
See also: Styles: Ballet, Administration

Craig, Jenifer Pashkowski, Ph. D. (1982)

University of Southern California at Los Angeles, California
Contemporary accounts of dance from the American West in the nineteenth century
43/04-A, 1078   ORDER NO.
Available from: Diss. Abstracts International
Contemporary journalistic sources are selected for this study of dance in the pioneer society of the nineteenth century American West. Six cultural views of dance events are documented exposing attitudes concerning dance at this time in American history. These contexts include the traveling pioneers, rural social life, urban social life, frontier theatre, saloons and dance halls, and church dance. The summary presents a new interpretation of the development of twentieth century American dance.
See also: Ethnology and Anthropology

Croghan, Leland, Ph.D. (1968)

New York University, New York
New York burlesque: 1840–1870: A study in theatrical self-criticism
402 pp.   ORDER NO. 6811784
Available from: Diss. Abstracts International
This study examines the nature and extent of burlesque criticism and determines burlesque's place in the stream of American critical humor. It uses primary sources: memoirs of early writers, newspaper reviews, and playbills and includes a chronicle history, by theatre, of burlesque writers, performers, and managers from The Beggar's Opera in 1750 to G.L. Fox's burlesques of Edwin Booth in 1870. Nearly 300 titles are considered and the literature supports the hypothesis that burlesque served a social function beyond its entertainment value.

Culberston, Anne E., D. Mus. Ed. (1985)

Indiana University, Indiana
Music and dance at the John C. Campbell Folk School in Brasstown, North Carolina, 1925–1985
166 pp. 47/12-A, 4315   ORDER NO. 870,8595
Available from: Diss. Abstracts International

A historical study of the John C. Campbell Folk School and the work of its founders—Olive Dame Campbell and Marguerite Butler(-Bidstrup). It provides a description of the music and dance activities at the school which include country, English ritual, and Danish folk dancing. Summer youth porgrams and the community use of the school are also outlined.
See also: Dance styles: Folk

De Metz, Ouida Kaye, Ph. D. (1975)
Florida State University, Florida
The uses of dance in the English language theatres of New Orleans prior to the Civil War, 1806–1861
133 pp. 36/02-A, 604   ORDER NO. 75-17,285
Available from: Diss. Abstracts International
This study describes the diversity and popularity of dance in the New Orleans theatres during the first half of the nineteeth century. Romantic classical ballet and character dance are described as extremely popular while jigs, equestrian, and rope dancing are also highly favored.
See also: Related Arts: Theatre, Choreography and Performance

Delamater, Jerome Herbert, Ph. D. (1978)
Northwestern University, Illinios
A critical and historical analysis of dance as a code of the Hollywood musical
689 pp. 39/08-A, 4556   ORDER NO. 790,3244
Available from: Microform
This study historically surveys and critically analyzes three aspects of dance in the Hollywood musical: the dance forms used in the choreography, the approaches to filming dance and the relationships that the dances have with the total film. The study closely details the work of Busby Berkeley, Fred Astaire and Gene Kelly. Dance directors, performers, and specific films are analyzed in terms of their contributions to dance in film and to the movement toward integration.
See also: Technology and Film, Choreography and Performance

Emery, Leonore Lynne Fauley, Ph.D. (1971)
University of Southern California, California
Black dance in the United States from 1619 to 1970
502 pp. 32/02-A, 770   ORDER NO. 71-21,454
Available from: Diss. Abstracts International
A history of the Negro and dance in the United States from slave ships of 1619 to contemporary concert dancers of 1970, including black West Indian dance from 1518 to 1900. Minstrel, secular, and sacred dance are examined and findings focus on black cultural heritage, minstrel sterotyping, color distinctions, and the influence on contemporary social dance.

Esses, Maurice I, Ph. D. (1986)
University of Toronto—Canada
Dance and instrumental "differences" in Spain during the seventeenth and eighteenth centuries
48/11-A, 2756
Available from: Diss Abstracts International
This study investigates the complementary phenomena of dance and instrumental variations prominent in Spain during the 17th and early 18th centuries. It draws upon a wide range of primary material as it explores the musical ties between Spain and the rest of Western Europe. It then examines the instrumental sources which contain dance pieces. The extensive use of dancing throughout Spanish society is discussed and 75 dance-types are analyzed.
See also: Music and Rhythm

Gerbes, Angelika Renate, Ph. D. (1972)
Ohio State University, Ohio
Gottfried Taubert on social and theatrical dance of the early eighteenth-century
330 pp. 33/08-A, 4578   ORDER NO. 73-2001
Available from: Diss. Abstracts International
An examination of early 18th century social and theatrical dance as discussed by German writer Gottfried Taubert. Information is provided about the role and teaching methods of the dance master including style, etiquette, attire, reverences, protocol, and decorum. It concludes that Taubert was attempting to promulgate that which was best in the French

tradition—the "Galant" dance of the late 17th century.

Glann, Janice Graham, Ph. D. (1976)
Bowling Green State University, Ohio
An assessment of the functions of dance in the broadway musical: 1940/41–1968/69
315 pp. 37/08-A, 4711   ORDER NO. 77,2691
Available from: Diss. Abstracts International
A description of the ways in which dance contributes functionally to the total structure of the Broadway musical. An analysis of four hundred twenty two dance sequences reveals that dance contributes a broad array of dramatic functions, particularly plot and atmosphere.
See also: Related Arts: Theatre.

Griffith, Betty Rose, Ph. D. (1975)
California State University at Long Beach, California
Theoretical foundation of dance in higher education in the United States 1933–1965
377 pp. 36/09-A, 5860   ORDER NO. 76-5243
Available from: Diss. Abstracts International
This study identifies the concepts which theoretically justify dance in higher education in the Unitied States from 1933 to 1965. Being an historical study, the data are derived from the literature concerning dance, general education, physical education, and philosophy. A significant influence is exercised by concert dancers while the most influential educators are seen as Margaret H'Doubler, Gertrude Colby, John Dewey, and Susanne Langer. A case is made for keeping dance associated with physical education and concern is shown for the steady erosion of dance from physical education to fine arts.
See also: Education

Hansell, Kathleen Kuzmick, Ph. D. (1980)
University of California at Berkeley, California
Opera and ballet at the Regio Ducai Teatro of Milan, 1771–1776: A musical and social history
1161 pp. 41/07-A, 2821   ORDER NO. 802,9419
Available from: Diss. Abstracts International
A history of the growth of ballet and opera in Milan 1771–1776 heralding it's most important era. Operas and ballet produced at this time illustrate general trends in Italian musical theatre and the preferences of the Milanese who demanded the best. Novel aspects of Noverre's pantomimes and ballets are introduced . Noverre who worked at Milan 1774–1776 rejects the Italian style and the construction and music of his ballets reveal the extent of his innovations.
See also: Styles: Ballet, Choreography and Performance, Related Arts: Opera

Hindman, Anne Andrews, Ph. D. (1972)
University of Georgia, Georgia
The myth of the Western Frontier in American dance and drama: 1930–1943
362 pp. 33/07-A, 3836   ORDER NO. 73-34,089
Available from: Diss. Abstracts International
An historical discussion of the myth of the Western Frontier and its impact on the evolution of American theatre and dance with special emphasis on the 1930's and 1940's. The myth, as represented in selected dramas and dances, provides an affirmation of cultural aspirations and helps forge cultural identity.
See also: Related Arts: Theatre

Horwitz, Dawn Lille, Ph. D. (1982)
New York University, New York
Michel Fokine in America, 1919–1942
235 pp. 43/07-A, 2158   ORDER NO. 822,7193
Available from: Diss. Abstract International
This study covers the American performances of Folkine and his wife, Vera Folkine, as well as all the ballets created by him in this country, many of which were in the area of popular entertainment. It also discusses his methods of teaching and his attempts to create an American ballet. The results are presented in topical

chapters and then chronologically within each chapter.
See also: Styles: Ballet, Choreography and Performance, Biography

Jenkins, Jane R, Ph. D. (1978)
University of North Carolina at Greensboro, North Carolina
Social dance in North Carolina before the twentieth century—an overview
148 pp. 39/06-A, 3450   ORDER NO. 782,4302
Available from: Diss. Abstracts International
An examination of the historical materials concerning social dance in North Carolina in the 21st century. The study concludes that social dance of the early settlers is participated in as a recreational pursuit, despite opposition from the clergy. Further, the dances of the lower socio-economic inhabitants reflect their work and lifestyles while the social dance of the upper classes are well documented and authenticated.
See also: Styles: Social

Kassing, Gayle Irma, Ph. D. (1978)
Texas Woman's University, Texas
Dance on the St. Louis stage: 1850 1870

297 pp. 40/02-A, 546   ORDER NO. 791,5873
Available from: Diss. Abstracts International
A presentation of the history of dance on the St. Louis, Missouri stage from 1850 to 1870. Major performers and the works in which they perform are identified. The theatrical trends in St. Louis before, during, and after the War Between the States are described. The study is divided into chronological theatrical seasons.
See also: Related Arts: Theatre

Kmen, Henry Arnold, Ph.D. (1961)
Tulane University of Louisianna, New Orleans
Singing and dancing in New Orleans: A social history of the birth and growth of ball and opera, 1791–1841
582 pp. 23/11- , 4334   ORDER NO. 63-2209
Available from: Diss. Abstracts International

This study traces in detail the growth of opera in New Orleans to its maturity, analyzing quality, difficulties overcome, methods of production and promotion, and the dependence on dancing. The importance of social dancing is described with evidence of over eighty ballrooms catering to public and private dancing events. Strong connections are shown to exist between New Orleans opera and the love of dancing in that city. Included are lists of the ballrooms, concerts combined with balls, opera performances, and composers from 1796 to 1841.
See also: Styles: Social, Related Arts: Theatre, Related Arts: Opera

Marsh, Carol, Ph. D. (1985)
City University of New York, New York
French court dance in England, 1706–1740: A study of the sources
365 pp. 46/02-A, 296   ORDER NO. 8508713
Available from: Diss. Abstracts International
A systematic study of six treatises and seventy five notated choreographies published between 1706 and 1740 describing the French style of dance which flourished in England during that time. It includes information about the dancing masters Tomlinson and Isaac and investigates the English choreographies. Musical sources are identified and distinctions are made between English and French styles. The appendix includes information on over 150 dancing masters and bass lines for twenty of the dances.
See also: Music and Rhythm

Martin, Jennifer Kaye Lowe, Ph. D. (1977)
University of Michigan, Michigan
The English dancing master, 1660–1728: His role at court, in society, and on the public stage
172 pp. 38/03-A, 1127   ORDER NO. 77-18,074
Available from: Diss. Abstracts International
A description of the role of the dancing master at court, in society, and on the public stage and an examination of the part he played in English dance as these three areas evolve. Dance practices are described and also the dancing masters role. Dancing masters include Isaac, Josiah Priest, and John Weaver.

Martinez-Hunter, Sanjuanita, Ph. D. (1984)
Texas Woman's University, Texas
The development of dance in Mexico: 1325–1910
236 pp. 45/12-A, 3726   ORDER NO. 850,2659
Available from: Diss. Abstracts International
A study of the development of dance in Mexico from the Pre-Hispanic period to the Mexican Revolution of 1910. It is demonstrated that the people of Mexico express and interpret their responses to historical events via dance and that the expression of dance origins, styles, and rhythms provides the link between history, folklore, and cultural heritage.
See also: Ethnology and Anthropology

McConnell Anne, Ph. D. (1972)
University of Arizona, Arizona
The opera-ballet: Opera as literature (Portions of text in French)
433 pp. 33/08-A, 1145   ORDER NO. 72-73,377
Available from: Diss. Abstracts International
A description of the opera-ballet as a fragmented and sensual response to the moral decadence of the Regency period in France (1690's–1720). Imitating the Fetes of the Regency courts, these ballets gave the nobles a fantasy world free from the problems that accompanied their morality. Their decline coincided with the society's search for more permanent and structured forms and values.
See also: Styles: Ballet, Related Arts: Opera

Monty, Paul Eugene, Ph. D. (1986)
New York University, New York
Serena, Ruth St. Denis, and the evolution of belly dance in America (1876–1976)
466 pp. 48/01-A, 09   ORDER NO. 870,6323
Available from: Diss. Abstracts International
A descriptive historical account of the evolution of belly dance in America from its introduction at the Philadelphia Centennial Exposition in 1876 until the first convention for professional belly dancers in 1974. It attributes Ruth St Denis with inspiring an interest in orientalism and ethnic styles through her interpretive dances after the turn of the century. Her student, Serena, develops a theatrical interpretive choreography using belly dance as

its base in the 1960's and belly dance seminars become popular in the 1970's.
See also: History

Perkins, Janet Blair, Ph. D. (1988)
University of Wisconsin at Madison, Wisconsin
Images of movement and dance in ancient Greek art: A qualitative approach
346 pp. 49/12-A, 3535   ORDER NO. 89-03034
Available from: Diss. Abstracts International
A qualitative assessment of the movement suggested by ancient sculptures and drawings which provides, with the support of Plato and Aristotle, a broad definition of the ancient dances. The concepts relating to this assessment are seen in the visual recording of movement and are paralleled in Plato's description of the role of gymnastics in the execution of the dance art.
See also: Theory and Philosophy

Phillips, Partricia Ann, Ed. D. (1973)
Boston University of Education, Boston
A philosophical, historical, and cultural analysis of the American square dance (volumes I and II)
667 pp. 34/04-A, 1679   ORDER NO. 73-23,596
Available from: Diss. Abstracts International
A history of modern square dance and its role in education with evidence that the American square dance thoughout its evolution has provided a vehicle through which to study the history of the United States. The study maintains that square dance is an integral part of the culture and reflects its cultural values.
See also: Styles: Social (Square)

Ramsay, Margaret Hupp, Ph. D. (1986)
New York University, New York
Grand Union (1970–1976), an improvisational performance group
246 pp. 47/12-A, 4239   ORDER NO. 870,6775
Available from: Diss. Abstracts International
A history of the Grand Union Performance/ Dance Group, a collaborative improvisational company noted for its minimalist choreographer, Yvonne Rainer. It gives a description of the Grand Union performance style with reviews of the works and Ranier's own work is traced and examined. The company's touring

and performance history is detailed and its management, technical aspects, themes, and audience involvement are discussed. Finally, it looks at the impact of the company on the next generation of dancers.
See also: Choreography and Performance

Riis, Thomas Laurence, Ph.D. (1981)
University of Michigan, Michigan
Black musical theatre in New York, 1890–1915
401 pp. 42/09-A, 3804   ORDER NO. 8204745
Available from: Diss. Abstracts International
This study sketches the history of black involvement in American musical theatre in the nineteenth century and provides an overview of events leading up to 1898. Traveling shows are featured and also the first black shows in New York. Major show people and the songs they composed and sang are ennumerated and described. It is noted that whether in dancing, singing or acting, the energy and grace of the performers impressed the critics, dance especially.
See also: Music and Rhythm

Rock, Judith, Ph. D. (1988)
Graduate Theological Union
Terpsichore at Louis Le Grand: Baroque dance on a Jesuit stage in Paris
559 pp. 49/07-A, 1623   ORDER NO. 881,6901
Available from: Diss. Abstracts International
An examintion of the meeting of baroque style and classical aesthetic in the ballets produced by the French colleges of the Society of Jesuits from 1660 to 1761. It includes the ballets' technique and production process, their relationship to audiences and to the Jesuit's educational goals, the ballets as the feminine element of the Jesuit theatre, and the problems and possibilities of restaging the ballets.
See also: Styles: Ballet

Ruyter, Nancy Lee, Ph.D. (1970)
Claremont Graduate School, California
Reformers and visionaries: The Americanization of the art of dance
277 pp. 31/12-A, 6766   ORDER NO. 71-13,731
Available from: Diss. Abstracts International
This study is an intellectual history of the modern American theatrical dance in its first flowering. It describes how theatrical dance enters the mainstream of American culture and

achieves status as a respectable art form. It begins with the domination of nineteeth century ballet and follows with the American Delsarte movement, the modern American theatrical dancers of the twentieth century, and then includes the historical background of educational dance in America. It is demonstrated that to become a uniquely American art form, it is necessary for the dance to align iteslf with American values and aspirations.
See also: Theory and Philosophy

Schoettler, Eugenia, Ph. D. (1979)
Kent State University, Ohio
From a chorus line to "A Chorus Line": The emergence of dance in the American musical theatre
313 pp. 40/01-A, 30   ORDER NO. 791,6359
Available from: Diss. Abstracts International
This study traces the evolution of dance in the American musical theatre from the early 20th century posturing chorus lines, to the opening of the musical "A Chorus Line" in 1975. Included in the scope of the study is the relationship of the choreography to all elements of the production, the choreographer as director, dancers as actors, and the dancer as total theatre personality.
See also: Choreography and Performance

Tucker, Iantha Elizabeth Lake, Ed. D. (1984)
New York University, New York
The role of Afro-Americans in dance in the United States from slavery through 1983: A slide presentation
293 pp. 45/07-A, 2032   ORDER NO. 842,1483
Available from: Diss. Abstracts International
This study comprises of a written document to accompany a slide presentation focusing on the historical background of Afro-American dance heritage and a narrative summary explaining the events, time frame, dance areas, and selected dance artists. The information is divided into specific fields of dance in which Afro-Americans have played an influential role and the major time periods are based on the historical structure of Lynn Emery's "Black Dance in the United States from 1619 to 1970." (Slides are available for consultation at New York University, School of Education library.)

Wagner, Ann Louise, Ph. D. (1980)
University of Minnesota, Minnesota
The significance of dance in sixteenth
century courtesy literature
234 pp. 41/07-A, 2999   ORDER NO. 810,2178
Available from: Diss. Abstracts International
A presentation of the significance of dance
education as evidenced by interpretations of
meaning and valuing found in the courtesy
treatises of the sixteenth century which focus
on the kind of training necessary for the civic
responsibilities of the Renaissance aristocracy.
The study includes more specfic pedagogical
issues as well as moral, social and aesthetic
considerations.
See also: Education, Theory and Philosophy

Wagner, Charlotte A, Ph.D. (1968)
New York University, New York
Theatrical narrative dance in England:
1747–1775
202 pp. 32/02-A, 699   ORDER NO. 69-11,866
Available from: Diss. Abstracts International
An examination of the dances and pantomimes of eighteenth century London. It is
explained that London dance has its origins in
Tudor and Stuart masque and French opera-
ballet and that the antimasque genres survived
the demise of the masque proper in the Resto-
ration dances and dramatic operas. John
Weaver, Marie Salle, Garrick and Noverre are
attributed with significant influence on dance
for the London stage during this period.
See also: Related Arts: Theatre

**Warner, Mary-Jane Evans, Ph. D.
(1974)**
Ohio State University, Ohio
Gavottes and Bouquets: A comparative
study of changes in dance style between
1700 and 1850
287 pp. 35/05-A, 3162   ORDER NO. 74-24,423
Available from: Diss. Abstracts International
This study discusses dance style from
1700–1850 using the gavotte as the basic
example to illustrate changes that occurred.
The discussion begins with the gavotte's origin
as a sixteenth century group dance and as a
social courtesy where bouquets were presented.
Ensuing changes included more difficult steps,
slower tempo and altered spatial patterns. Ulti-
mately the dance changed to become a theatrical "period piece".

**Westfall, Suzanne Ruth, Ph. D.
(1984)**
University of Toronto, Canada
The entertainment of a noble patron:
Early tudor household revels
45/09-A, 2699
Available from: Diss. Abstracts International
An examination of the performers that the
aristocracy retained, the entertainments
(plays, dances, sports) thay they produced, and
the reasons the nobility found theatrical art
worthy of their attention and money.

Witherell, Anne Louise, Ph.D. (1981)
Stanford University, California
Louis Pecour's 1700 "Recueil de
Dances"
368 pp. 41/11-A, 4538   ORDER NO. 8109017
Available from: Diss. Abstracts International
A reconstruction and analysis of the earliest
published collection of eighteenth-century
French ballroom choreographies, the 1700
"Recueil de Dances" by Louis Pecour. The
"Recueil" contains nine danses á deux to music
by Lully, Colasse, and Campra. The reconstruction is facilitated by a dance notation system first published by Raoul Feuillet in 1700
and by reference to early eighteenth century
dance manuals. The dances are analyzed in
relationship to the music and floor patterns
and figures are described.
See also: Choreography and Performance

**Wynne, Shirley Spackman, Ph.D.
(1967)**
Ohio State University, Ohio
The charms of compliassance: The
dance in England in the early
eighteenth century
157 pp. 28/11-A, 4748   ORDER NO. 68-3093
Available from: Diss. Abstracts International
This study considers the problems of historical
stylistic development in dance and how characteristics of style can be applied to dance
forms in early eighteenth century England.
The growth of Classical and Expressional styles
are discussed and contrasted from their origin
in the early Renaissance to the end of the
eighteenth century. John Weaver is credited
with introducing an embryonic Expressional
style in England in the early eighteenth century and the causes for its appearance at this
time and place are explored.

Music and Rhythm

Anthony, James Raymond, Ph.D (1964)
University of Southern California, California
The opera-ballet of Andre Campra: A study of the first period French opera-ballet
839 pp. 26/03-A, 1683   ORDER NO. 641,2458
Available from: Diss Abstracts International
A study of the contribution of the opera-ballet to the evolution of new concepts of musical forms and musical dramaturgy in the French lyric theatre of the early eighteenth century. Four opera-ballets by Andre Campra (1660—1740) are analyzed for their musicodramatic innovations. The appendices inlcude the musical organization of Campra's opera-ballets, the production details of all performances through 1740, and short biographical sketches of the most important singers and dancers.
See also: History, Related Arts: Opera, Styles: Ballet

Bartee, Neale King, Ph. D. (1977)
University of Illinois at Urbana-Champaign, Illinois
The developmentof a theoretical position on conducting using principles of body movement as explicated by Rudolf Laban
218 pp. 38/14-A, 6384   ORDER NO. 780,3930
Available from: Diss. Abstracts International
The writings of Rudolf Laban are examined as a basis for improving the use of body movement in conducting. Susanne Langer's theory of musical meaning is used as a philosophical base for the analysis of tonal motion in music. Deficiencies in conducting theory and practice are noted and it is concluded that conductors can improve their ability to use expressive gestures by studying movement.

Benson, Norman Arthur, Ph.D. (1963)
University of Minnesota, Minneapolis
The itinerant dancing and music masters of eighteenth century America
488 pp. 25/04- ,2551   ORDER NO. 64-7226
Available from: Diss. Abstracts International
This study traces the activities of selected eighteenth century dancing and music masters in the culture-communities of Charleston, Williamsburg, Philadelphia, New York, and Boston. The patronage offered to these itinerant masters by the court, church, and theatre is viewed as a perogative of an aristocratic class structure whose antecedents lie in the Baroque society of continental Europe. Nevertheless, these music and dancing masters play a prominent role in the development of America's music culture.

Blatt, Arthur, Ph.D. (1964)
New York University, New York
Rhythmic responses of normal elementary school children: An investigation of the developmental differences in the rhythmic response of the normal child when rhythmic stimulii is utilized as contrasted with music stimulii
81 pp. 25/02-A, 1315   ORDER NO. AAC6408460
Available from: Diss. Abstracts International
An investigation of the developmental difference in the rhythmic responsiveness of middle to upper-middle class children whenever a pure rhythmic stimulus is used in contrast to a musical stimulus. Rhythmic responsiveness is evaluated by physical movement. Children are placed in four age groups and movies are taken of each child's reaction to the stumulii. Degree and quality of movement are rated. Results show that rhythmic responsiveness diminishes with age: the younger children liking to move to rhythm and the older children preferring planned group activities.
See also: Music and Rhythm

Canty, Dean Robert, D. Mu. (1980)
University of Texas at Austin, Texas
A study of the pasodobles of Pascual Marquina; including a brief history of the Spanish pasodoble and specific analysis of the performance practices of pasodobles from three established categories (volumes I and II)
720 pp. 41/04-A, 1270   ORDER NO. 802,1538
Available from: Diss. Abstracst International
Abstracts not available.

Cox, Rosann McLaughlin, Ph. D. (1974)
Texas Woman's University, Texas
Musical accompaniment for dance: Preference of males and females at four educational levels
121 pp. 36/09-A, 5616　　ORDER NO. 76-5054
Available from: Diss. Abstracts International
An investigation of differences in preference for musical accompaniment for dance by gender and educational level. The findings show that as students mature their preference becomes more sophisticated and attuned to more structure and formality. Females furthermore, tend to exhibit more sophisticated preference at an earlier educational level.
See also: Psychology and Therapy

Dunner, Leslie Byron, D. Mu. (1982)
University of Cincinnati, Ohio
Stravinsky and dance: A conductor's study of "Renard"
145 pp. 43/08-A, 2486　　ORDER NO. 822,3039
Available from: Diss. Abstracts International
A presentation of those events leading to the composition of "Renard", its performance history, and an in-depth analysis of its compositional traits and performance problems. "Renard" is considered an experimental masterpiece in miniature combining music, dance, and drama in a non-operatic form. The driving rhythms and dance forms provide the perfect musical construction necessary for choreography and Stravinsky's approach is seen as influencing the development of twentieth century compositional style.

Engelhard, Doris Louise, MUS. D. (1980)
University of Arizona, Arizona
Song and dance as an approach to teacher preparation in music for primary classroom teachers
200 pp. 41/04-A, 1462　　ORDER NO. 802,2834
Available from: Diss. Abstracts International
The presentation of a pattern of musical preparation for prospective elementary classroom teachers. This pattern is based on a eclectic approach which focuses on the selected pedagogical principles of Kodaly, Orff, and Dalcroze. The instruction sequence is based on a vocal approach empasizing movement and includes more than 100 songs, rhymes, and movement activities.
See also: Children, Education

Ensign, Cynthia Jane Peterson, Ph.D. (1976)
University of Wisconsin at Madison, Wisconsin
An examination of the effects of range, frequency and duration of movement on rhythmic synchronization
224 pp. 37/10-A, 6343　　ORDER NO. 7629,910
Available from: Diss. Abstracts International
This investigation examines the effects of differences in range, frequency, and duration of movement on voluntary rhythmic synchronization—the capacity to coordinate two or more rhythmic events. The coordination consists of a knee action sequence as a movement event with a series of metronome ticks as a sound event. Implications are offered with respect to the theory of rhythmic perception and these are discussed along with the effects themselves.
See also: Science

Godowns, James Stephens, D. Mus. (1983)
Indiana University, Indiana
The contribution of French court dance to performance of the Couperin organ masses
Available from: Micrographics, Doheny Library, USC
Abstract not available.

Hatton, Gaylen A, Ph.D. (1963)
University of Utah, Utah
'Toxcatl' Ballet
219 pp. 24/05-A, 20596　　ORDER NO. 63-7118
Available from: Microform
The musical score for the ballet "Toxcatl" based on an Aztec legend. The score is based on a twelve note theme which is the source of the melody, harmony, and counterpoint. The music is descriptive and reflects the moods of the legend, but is not a duplication of the musical sounds and styles familiar to the Aztec culture.

Hoehn, William Todd, Ph. D. (1981)
Ohio State University, Ohio
The ballet music of Constant Lambert:
A study of collaboration in music and
dance
277 pp. 42/07-A, 2924   ORDER NO. 812,9017
Available from: Diss. Abstracts International
An examination of Lambert's four origingal
ballet scores and the presentation of summary
conclusions regarding the character and treatment of melody and rhythm, form, harmony,
and orchestration. The composer's style of
writing for the ballet is described while much
of the study is devoted to an historical survey
of attitudes and practices of composers and
choreographers in the collaborative production of ballets from the time of Noverre to the
1980's.
See also: Styles: Ballet

Holloway, Jane Howell, Ed. D. (1974)
Columbia University, New York
The study and analysis of selected dance
forms in the keyboard music of the
Baroque period: A pedagogical guide for
elementary pianists in college
126 pp. 35/02-A, 844   ORDER NO. 74-18,719
Available from: Diss. Abstracts International
Using the Baroque dance as primary source
material, this study presents an instructional
approach to enhance the study of keyboard for
elementary pianists, by understanding the art
in terms of it's historical aesthetic, and technical aspects. Elements of Baroque musical style,
character, styles of performance, and practice,
based on treatises of the period, are discussed
and suggestions for the interpretations of
Baroque dances are provided.
See also: History

Hughes, Sarah Mahler, D.MA. (1985)
University of Kansas, Kansas
Seventeenth-century dance
characteristics in the organ masses of
Francois Couperin (1668–1733)
140 pp. 47/02-A, 341   ORDER NO. 860,8475
Available from: Diss. Abstracts International
An analysis of dance characteristics in two
masses written in 1690 by Francios Couperin,
French keyboard composer and teacher. It
explores the role of dancing and dance music
in the cultural life at court and presents brief
descriptions of the histories and characters of

seventeenth and eighteenth century dances.
Following a discussion of the organ and organ
masses, the dance-like elements—meter,
rhythm, tempo and phrasing—and the individual dance types—gavottes, menuets, sara-
bandes, gigues, entr·es graves, and correntes
are described.
See also: History

**Kaloyanides, Michael George, Ph. D.
(1975)**
Wesleyan University, Connecticut
The music of Cretan dances, a study of
the musical structures of Cretan dance
forms as performed in the Irakleion
Provinces of Crete
247 pp. 36/04-A, 1891   ORDER NO. 75-22,999
Available from: Diss. Abstracts International
An examination of the musical structures of
five major Cretan dance forms as performed in
central Crete. The study gives an overview of
present-day Cretan musical heritage, provides
detailed musical analysis of five Cretan dance
forms, including dance steps, and concludes
with a discussion of the social setting at which
dancing occurs.
See also: Styles: Folk

**Kilpatrick, David Bruce, Ph. D.
(1975)**
*University of California at Los Angeles,
California*
Function and style in Pontic dance
music
348 pp. 36/09-A, 5628   ORDER NO. 76,5120
Available from: Diss. Abstracts International
This study provides descriptive information on
the folk dance music of the Pontic (Black Sea)
Greeks and includes a brief analysis of the
dance movements and techniques of the uni-
fied folk art. The two basic modes of dance,
smooth and agitated, are analyzed in relationship to the musical accompaniment and trance
dance is examined. The appendix includes
transcriptions of dance tunes and Labanoted
dance scores.
See also: Styles: Folk

Kuo, Yu-Chun, Ph.D. (1988)
University of California at San Diego, California
"Ring": Concerto for dance and music. (Original composition)
76 pp. 50/01-A   ORDER NO. 890,8010
Available from: Diss. Abstracts International
A description of a concerto for dance and music involving a dance solo with a music ensemble of flute, cello, piano, and percussion. The full score includes a graphic dance notation which suggests the intensity and movement of the choreography and the lighting design.
See also: Notation and Movement Analysis

Larson, LeRoy Wilbur, Ph. D. (1975)
University of Minnesota, Minnesota
Scandinavian-American folk dance music of the Norwegians in Minnesota
507 pp. 36/04-A, 1892   ORDER NO. 75-21,062
Available from: Diss. Abstracts International
This study is based on the collection of 166 instrumental folk dance melodies recorded in the state of Minnesota. 13% are documented as being of Scandanavian origin. The repertory consists of waltzes. Schottisches, polkas, mazurkas, two-steps, and one square dance. Included are chapters on musical traditions, city and rural dances, home entertainment and Scandinavian-American dance types.
See also: Styles: Folk

Lastrucci, Carlo Lawrence, Ph.D. (1941)
Stanford University, California
The professional dance musician
951 pp.
Available from: Microform
Abstract not available.

Leshock, Malvina M., D. MA. (1984)
Temple Univeristy, Philadelphia
"The Ebony and Ivory Horse": Ballet for orchestra. (Musical score and essay)
186 pp. 45/06-A, 1568   ORDER NO. 822,3185
Available from: Diss. Abstracts International
"The Ebony and the Ivory Horse" is a three act ballet for orchestra based on a tale from "The Thousand and One Nights". The ballet is organized to create logical, balanced placements for the exposition of pure dance. Narra-

tive function is executed through balletic mime and naturalistic gesture accompanied by a musical structure and the dramatic function. The score inconjunction with dance, creates a sound space congenial to choreographic forms. The abject despair of this dance mirrors parallels found in contemporary society.
See also: Style: Ballet

MacPherson, William Alan, Ph. D. (1984)
Harvard University, Massachusetts
The music of the English country dance, 1651–1728: With indexes of the printed sources
788 pp. 45/12-A, 3476   ORDER NO. 850,3553
Available from: Diss. Abstracts International
A systematic study of country-dance music and it's sources (1651–1728) as a large repertoire of popular music. Country dancing as a social activity in 17th and 18th century England is discussed and the changing character for the tune-repertoire is shown to reflect the increasing popularity of the dance. The music is analysed from the view of tune relationships and illustrative musical examples are abundant throughout the text.
See also: History

McVoy, James Earl, Jr, Ph. D. (1977)
University of Rochester, New York
Analysis of "Orion, a Ballet"
119 pp. 37/11-A, 6831   ORDER NO. 778,319
Available from: Diss. Abstracts International
Music for a ballet in two acts based on a scenario synthesised from several myths surrounding the constellation of Orion. The scenes deal with his relationships with mortals, goddesses and his ultimate transformation into a constellation.
See also: Styles: Ballet

Mehraban, Ho-sein Shirazi Zadeh, Ph. D. (1978)
Northwestern University- Evanston, Illinois
Folk music of Fars Province, Iran: A section of children's games, folk songs, and dances
214 pp. 39/10-A, 6013   ORDER NO. 790,7914
Available from: Diss. Abstracts International
A compilation of Iranian folk music from Fars Province which also serves as a resource for

music educators and music lovers in the United States and Iran. Information in the study results from observing ceremonial occasions in Iran and recording the music and folk songs. The study describes the folk musical instruments, children's singing games, folk songs of Fars, and folk dances.
See also: Styles: Folk

Moe, Lawrence Henry, Ph.D. (1956)
Harvard University, Massechuetts
Dance music in printed Italian lute tablatures from 1507 to 1611
Available from: Microform
Abstract not available.

Morrow, Robert Russel, Ph.D. (1970)
University of Rochester, New York
A collection of dance music of Europe: 1200–1600 transcribed and arranged for school instrumental ensembles
Available from: Microform
See also: Education, History

Owen, Jerry Michael, Ph. D. (1974)
University of Iowa, Iowa
Three formats for the dance for winds, percussion, and six string instruments
40 pp. 35/07-A, 4597   ORDER NO. 75-1240
Available from: Diss. Abstracts International
This music composition is conceived primarily as music for dance. It contains references to many historical styles of musical composition, such as expressionism, classicism, neo-classicism, and impressionism. It's three movements and Prolog have a duration of approximately five minutes.

Pepin, M. Natalie, S.N.J.M.,
Mus. A.D. (1972)
Boston University, School of Fine and Applied Arts, Boston
Dance and jazz elements in the piano music of Maurice Ravel
299 pp. 33/04-A,1772   ORDER NO. 72-25,126
Available from: Diss. Abstracts International
An analysis of the influence of dance on the piano music of Maurice Ravel whose work is permeated with rhythms and melodies having some choreographic aspect. The results show Ravel's attraction to Spanish and neo-classical dance forms and also waltz types. The analysis

concludes with his use of Americana and jazz elements.

Pond, Marden Jensen, D. A. (1985)
University of Northern Colorado, Colorado
Music for a choreographic narrative and a supporting study: Composing for theatrical dance. (Volumes I and II). (Original score)
654 pp. 46/04-A, 836   ORDER NO. 851,2652
Available from: Diss. Abstracts International
A music composition which coincides with the story, "The Little Prince" by St Exupery. A supporting research document accompanies the composition and covers topics that are of importance to the composer or musician who is involved in the productions of ballet or other dance forms. This study includes discussions on ballet and dance history, twentieth century developments, the collaborative process in music/dance production, and the compositional technique used in the score for "The Little Prince".
See also: Styles: Ballet

Pruett, Diane Milhan, Ph. D. (1978)
University of Wisconsin at Madison, Wisconsin
A study of the relationship of Isadora Duncan to the musical composers and mentors who influenced her musical selection for choreography
309 pp. 40/05-A, 2346   ORDER NO. 791,8929
Available from: Diss. Abstracts International
This study identifies and discusses the relationship between the American modern dance choreographer Isadora Duncan (1877–1927) and the musical mentors whose compostions and theoretical writings influenced the dancer's choice of music and subsequently the evolution of her art.
See also: Biography, Choreography and Performance

Putnam, Mark Glenn, D.MA (1989)
Memphis State University, Tennessee
"B'resheet"—a ballet inspired by the commentaries of Rashi. (Original composition)
94 pp. 50/06-A, 1477   ORDER NO. 982,2001
Available from: Diss. Abstracts International

A description of a musical composition conceived as a ballet in order to reflect the story of creation as revealed by Hebrew scholar Rashi. This association with dance requires special musical consideration causing the music to be composed with emphasis on rhythmic and formal parameters. "B'resheet" is in two parts and is approximately 18 minutes long.
See also: Styles: Ballet

Rausch, Carlos, D. MA. (1985)
Columbia University, New York
"A Legend of the Andes": Ballet in one act
466 pp. 46/03-A, 551   ORDER NO. 851,1544
Available from: Diss. Abstracts International
The music orchestration of a one act ballet based on the Peruvian play "Ollanta", discovered in the nineteeth century. The essay includes the sources of the drama, a list of musical settings based on the drama, sources of the music, Renaissance and Baroque dance forms, structure of the work, and the musical language related to the drama. Considerations of timing and tempi conclude the description.
See also: Styles: Ballet

Rinzler, Paul E., D.A. (1988)
University of Northern Colorado, Colorado
"Layers", an original composition for wind ensemble based on African rhythm
198 pp. 49/08-A, 2016   ORDER NO. 8821353
Available from: Diss. Abstracts International
"Layers" is a composition for wind ensemble based on African polyrhythm. The African dance ensemble is chosen to illustrate the essentials of African polyrhythm as well as to provide a model for composition. The roles that instruments play in the African dance ensemble are divided into sections. New musical material is composed for each of these roles and the result is "Layers" incorporating polyrhythm, additive rhythm, a fixed-time background, and repetition.

Russell, Tilden A., Ph. D. (1983)
University of North Carolina at Chapel Hill, North Carolina
Minuet, scherzando, and scherzo: The dance movement in transition, 1781–1825
336 pp. 44/04-A, 906   ORDER NO. 831,6659
Available from: Diss. Abstracts International
This study describes how the dance movement during the period 1781–1825 is treated in a variety of traditional and innovative manners in the chamber and symphonic works of minor and major European composers. It is suggested that the dance movement in transition is a paradigm of the displacement of Classical values by Romantic ones and that the dance movement is a key to the sources of musical Romanticism. German and English aesthetic influences shape the radical changes in music at the turn of the nineteenth century.
See also: History

Santos, Ramon Pagayon, Ph. D. (1972)
State University of New York at Buffalo, New York
Ang putting waling- waling: A musico-dance drama in three acts: Story, libretto and music (original composition, musical (volumes I and II)
208 pp. 33/08-A, 4461   ORDER NO. 73-5172
Available from: Diss. Abstracts International
Description—two volumes of a three act stage work that combines the media of music, dance, and pantomime. Story is inspired by the history of the Philippine people and focuses on conflict between the Philipines and Western cultures. The Libretto is in the national language with an English translation. The project features native Philipine instruments.
See also: Ethnology and Anthropology

Sheehy, Daniel Edward, Ph. D. (1979)
University of California, Los Angeles, California
The *Son Jarocho:* The history, style, and repertory of a changing Mexican musical tradition
401 pp. 40/04-A,1744   ORDER NO. 792,1454
Available from: Diss. Abstracts International
This study discusses the historical development of the Son Jarocho and includes its role in

the festive *fandango*, a unique instrumentarium with an associated dance tradition based on the zapateado. It concludes with a discussion of changing style characteristcs as a result of urbanization, commercializaton, and growth of the tourist industry.

Stewart, John Dean, Ph. D. (1973)
Indiana University, Indiana
Metrical and tonal stability in the dance music of the Fitzwilliam Virginal book
188 pp. 34/04-A, 1956   ORDER NO. 73-23,035
Available from: Diss. Abstracts International
An examination of 122 dance pieces of the "Fitzwilliam Virginal Book" in relation to the criteria for metrical and tonal stability. The underlying assumption is that these two elements are not mutually exclusive, rather they reinforce each other.

Sydor, Elizabeth Ernst, Ed. D. (1985)
Columbia University Teachers College, New York
Atrox: The composition, performance and analysis of a chamber composition for abstract choreography
173 pp. 46/09-A, 2611   ORDER NO. 852,5526
Available from: Diss. Abstracts International
A description of the merger of abstract music and non-literal choreography in an organically sturctured, multi-level presentational form. The presentation is clarified by the analysis of both choreographic and musical gesture in relation to a continuum of concrete to abstract gesture. The conception of music as an art of hearing and dance as an art of sight is broadened and valued through the kinaesthetic experience and perception of both performer and audience.
See also: Theory and Philosophy

Tate, Patricia Coleman, D.A. (1985)
University of Northern Colorado, Colorado
"The Dance of the Seven Veils": A historical and descriptive analysis
261 pp. 46/08-A, 2127   ORDER NO. 852,3390
Available from: Diss. Abstracts International
This study analyses the material upon which a reconstruction of the original "Dance of the Seven Veils" can be based. It also investigates revisions and provides a basis for future choreo-graphic reconstructions or interpretations. The study summarizes Strauss' intention for the dance and explains how the dance serves the opera "Salome" as the dramatic climax. It concludes with the significance of the study to the fields of opera and dance.
See also: History, Choreography and Performance, Related Arts: Opera

Whitman, James Kerry, Ph. D. (1975)
State University of New York at Buffalo, New York
The dance of Shiva
20 pp. 37/08-A, 4691   ORDER NO.
Available from: Diss. Abstracts International
A musical compostion os Shiva's dance consisting of five parts—preservation, illusion, destruction, release, and creation. The musical form corresponds to the process of transformation and each of the five sections depicts an action of Shiva.
See also: Ethnology and Anthropology

Winchell, Richard Marvin, D.Mus. (1982)
Florida State University, Florida
Music for dance. (original composition)
48 pp. 43/10-A, 3254   ORDER NO. 830,6175
Available from: Diss. Abstracts International
A musical composition in one movement scored for woodwind, brass, and percussion instruments and written specifically to be choreographed for modern dance.

Wrazen, Louise Josepha, Ph. D. (1988)
University of Toronto, Canada
The "Goralski" of the Polish Highlanders: Old World musical tradition from a New World perspective
49/09-A, 2447   ORDER NO. 0564023
Available from: Diss. Abstracts International
This study describes the "goralski", a dance event of the Polish Highlanders (Gorale) and the effects of immigration on the musical culture of the people. It traces the path of the Highlander traditional music complex from the Old World of the past (Poland) to the New World of the present (Canada) and notes changes in structure and performance. The dance event is seen as epitomizing "Highlander-ness" in that it is a complete cultural artifact.
See also: Ethnology and Anthropology

Notation and Movement Analysis

Greenfield, Sarah Curtice, Ph. D. (1975)
University of Arizona, Arizona
Notation systems for transcribing verbal and nonverbal behavior in adult education research: Linguistics (phonetics and phonemics), paralinguistics, proxemics, the micro analysis of the organized flow of behavior, haptics, dance notations, and kinesics
500 pp. 36/04-A, 1981   ORDER NO. 75-22,544
Available from: Diss. Abstracts International
The location, examination, and description of notation systems that are used for transcribing human communicative behavior. Systems include linguistic, paralinguistic, proxemic haptic and kinesic and several dance notation systems (Labanotation, effort-shape, and Motif Writing). Steps are outlined to design a multi-disciplinary experiment to explore adult learning and teaching behaviors as they relate to communication.
See also: Education

Gregory, Robin Winifred, Ph. D. (1977)
University of Wisconsin at Madison, Wisconsin
The formulation of charted verbilizations in the study of human movement
264 pp. 38/11-A, 6601   ORDER NO. 772,8250
Available from: Diss. Abstracts International
A procedure for translating bodily movement into the language of words. Charts are used to categorize verbal meaning relative to the space, time, and force meanings abstracted from human movement. Notation systems are surveyed and a choreography is analysed to complete the charts. Hypothetical statements are subsequently derived from the charts and discussed in detail.

Lepczyk, Billie Frances, Ed.D. (1981)
Columbia University Teachers College, New York
A contrastive study of movement style in dance through the Laban perspective
171 pp. 43/05-A, 1328   ORDER NO. 822,3185
Available from: Diss. Abstracts International
This study concerns the indentification of the distinctions between movement styles in dance through the Laban perspective. The styles chosen for analysis are ballet, Martha Graham, and Twyla Tharp. Materials analyzed include dance technique, vocabulary, and dance works. Movement qualities are complied in a chart which serves as the basis of the discussion on distinctions between the styles.
See also: Theory and Philosophy

Mariani, Myriam Evelyse, Ph. D. (1986)
University of Wisconsin at Madison, Wisconsin
A portrayal of the Brazilian Samba dance with the use of Labananalysis as a tool for movement analysis
528 pp. 48/04-A, 766   ORDER NO. 870,8099
Available from: Diss. Abstracts International
The study of the Samba dance within its cultural context as an African influence on Brazil. The Samba movements are analytically described as performed by the participants of the Schools of Samba during the Carnival in Rio de Janeiro. The pattterns and variations of the rhythmic and movement characteristics are described using Laban Movement Analysis and Music Rhythmic Analysis. A comparison is also made between Africanisms and contemporary Brazilian movement characteristics to show similarities and differences between these two patterns.
See also: Styles: Social, Ethnology and Anthropology

Moses, Nancy Heise, Ed. D. (1980)
Boston University, Massachusetts
The effects of movement notation on the performance, cognitions, and attitudes of beginning ballet students at the college level
166 pp. 41/08-A, 3479   ORDER NO. 810,2244
Available from: Diss. Abstracts International

This study determines the effects of Sutton Movement Writing notation on the performance, cognitions, and attitudes of college beginning ballet students. It finds that teaching ballet with the aid of dance notation has some merit in terms of performance and knowledge gained, but has no significant effect on attitude.
See also: Styles: Ballet, Education

O'Neill, Donna Kathlyn, Vansant, D.Ed. (1982)

University of Oregon, Oregon
The development of a refined movement analysis and it's relationship to motor creativity among grade two children
141 pp. 43/02-A, 396   ORDER NO. 821,5312
Available from: Diss. Abstracts International
This study addresses the problems of indentifying and assessing creativity in children's dance. It describes the development and validation a measure to assess motor creativity and investigates the relationship between scores on different tests. The new tests are found to be a valid measure of motor creativity as exemplified in dance movement.
See also: Children

Preston-Dunlop, Valerie Morthland, Ph. D. (1981)

University of London, Goldsmiths' College, England
The nature of the embodiment of choreutic units in contemporary choreography
401 pp. 43/11-A, 3459   ORDER NO. 830,5137
Available from: Diss. Abstracts International
A reassembling of how Rudolf Laban's original choreutic concepts can be broadened and reassembled to provide a rich resource for the analysis of contemporary choreography. An analytic method devised through notation is described and used to compare choreutic styles. When viewed in context with the spatial practice of other dance artists, teachers, and theorists this resource is regarded as central to analyzing choreutic content and style of a work. Choreographies of Humphrey, Nijinska, and Grossman are compared to illustrate the method.
See also: Theory and philosophy, Choreography and Performance

Smith, A William, Ph. D. (1988)

Ohio State University, Ohio
Descriptive analysis of fifteenth-century Italian dance and related concepts found in Antonio Cornazano's dance threatise "Libro Dell 'Arte Del Danzare" (citta del vaticano, Biblioteca apostolica Vaticana, Codice Capponiano 203) and in the dance treatise of Domenico Da Piacenza, Cornazano's teacher, "De Arte Saltandi et Choreas Ducendi"
689 pp. 49/08-A, 2028   ORDER NO. 882,0352
Available from: Diss. Abstracts International
An examination of selected terminology within the fifteenth century Italian dance treatises of Antonio Cornazano and his teacher Domenico da Piacenza. Dance terms are identified, listed in context, and analyzed. The terms are used to examine Labanotated reconstructions of nineteen formal step-actions found in the treatises. An English translation of Cornazano's dance text is offered.
See also: History

Stampp, Michele Susan, Ph. D. (1980)

University of Nevada at Reno, Nevada
Expressive movement and psychopathology: An exploratory study
216 pp. 41/12-B, 4691   ORDER NO. 811,1690
Available from: Diss. Abstracts International
A comparison of body movement style between three subject groups—normal, anxious depressed, and hostile depressed to determine if the subjects could be differentiated on the basis of expressive movement behavior. Movement analysis techniques are used to assess movement behavior variables: effort-shape, postural-spatial, and gestural. The results indicate that movement variables can be reliably measured and that normal and psychiatric subjects significantly differ in expressive movement behavior.
See also: Psychology and Therapy

Psychology and Therapy

Allen, Beverly Joyce, Ph. D. (1989)
Ohio State University, Ohio
The effect of dance/ movement on the self- concept of developmentally handicapped fourth and fifth grade students
215 pp. 50/12-A, 3886   ORDER NO. 901,1115
Available from: Diss. Abstracts International
This study determines the effect of a two week intensive dance/movement education program on the self-concept of developmentally handicapped children as measured by the Piers-Harris Children's Self-Concept Scale. The results indicate strong linear correlations between the qualitative and quantitative data, but no significant difference in the self-concepts.
See also: Children.

Allison, Patrica Robinette, Ed. D. (1976)
University of Alabama, Alabama
An instrument to measure the creative dance attitudes of grade five children
165 pp. 37/12-A, 7608   ORDER NO. 771,2164
Available from: Dis. Abstract International
This study constructs an instrument to measure attitudes related to creative dance experience of 5th grade children. It attempts to determine differences in attitudes based on gender and race using the Creative Dance Attitude Inventory.
See also: Children

Alves-Masters, Judy, Ph. D. (1979)
University of Georgia, Georgia
Changing self-esteem of women through Middle Eastern dance
263 pp. 40/07-A, 4256   ORDER NO. 800,1020
Available from: Diss Abstracts International
The author uses the medium of Middle Eastern dance to show that women who perform the belly dancing role, experience an increased positive self-esteem in terms of self-perceived attractiveness, femininty, sensuality, and sexuality. Subjects enrolled in an introductory belly-dancing course, are evaluated in terms of their self-expression and self-perception at two time intervals.

Beal, Rayma Kirkpatrick, Ed. D. (1985)
University of Cincinnati, Ohio
The effect of a dance/movement activity program on the successful adjustment of aging in the active/ independent older adult
157 pp. 46/10-A, 3127   ORDER NO. 852,6548
Available from: Diss. Abstracts International
An investigation of the effectiveness of a dance/movement activities program on several indicators of mental health in active/independent older adults. Subjects are assigned to either the treatment group participating in dance sessions or to the control group participating in regular activities. Mental health is measured by the Beck Depression Inventory and the Life Satisfaction Index.

Bernstein, Penny Lewis, Ph. D. (1978)
Humanistic Psychology Institute
Toward an implicit theory of dance- movement therapy
157 pp. 39/03-B, 1082   ORDER NO. 78-16279
Available from: Diss. Abstracts International
Abstract not available.

Berrol, Cynthia Florence, Ph.D. (1978)
University of California at Berkeley with San Francisco State University, California
The effects of two movement remediation programs on selected measures of perceptual-motor ability, academic achievement, and behavior on first grade children manifesting learning and perceptual-motor problems
200 pp. p. 5443   ORDER NO. 7904667
Available from: Diss. Abstracts International
A determination of the effects of two remedial movement interventions on measures of performance and behavior using first grade children with learning and perceptual-motor problems. The interventions are dance/movement

therapy and sensory-motor activities. Experimental groups of children receive dance/movement-problem solving techniques and also increased stimulation to the tactile and vestibular systems of the CNS. Controls continue in usual physical education activities. Results are inconclusive due to inappropriate and unpredictable measures testing the variables.
See also: Children

Boarman, Alice Marie, Ed. D. (1977)
Oregon State University, Oregon
The effects of folk dancing upon reaction time and movement time of senior citizens
67 pp. 38/09-A, 5329   ORDER NO. 773,2544
Available from: Diss. Abstract International
An examination of folkdancing as a potential modality for altering the speed of reaction and speed of movement of senior citizens. Analysis of variance suggests that folkdance neither influences simple reaction time nor movement time of older individuals.
See also: Styles: Folk, Science

Boswell, Betty, Boni, Ph. D. (1982)
Texas Woman's University, Texas
Adapted dance for mentally retarded children: An experimental study
176 pp. 43/09-A, 2925   ORDER NO. 830,3103
Available from: Diss. Abstracts International
An examination of the efficacy of participation in an adpated dance program based on a model facilitating change in selected dynamic balance and rhythmic skills of mentally handicapped children. Subjects are assigned to either an adapted dance program or a movement exploration program. Although two movement models are employed, the resultant patterns of change demonstrate similarity.
See also: Children

Brennan, Mary Alice, Ph. D. (1976)
University of Wisconsin at Madison, Wisconsin
Investigation into the relationship between creative ability in dance, field independence, and creativity
308 pp. 37/07-A, 4209   ORDER NO. 76-23,306
Available from: Diss. Abstracts International
An examination of the relationships among creative ability in dance, field independence—dependence, and selected attributes of creative

persons. The study describes the development of measures used to assess creative ability in dance, and includes an expert rating instrument and movement performance tests.

Browning, Gloria Seaman, Ph. D. (1972)
Texas Woman's University, Texas
The influence of the alpha rhythm during mental practice while acquiring a specific tap skill
201 pp.   ORDER NO.
Available from:
This study investigates three types of learning situations, physical practice instruction, mental-physical practice instruction, and alpha mental practice instruction and finds that mental practice is more effective when the subjects are generating alpha rhythms.
See also: Styles: Jazz and Tap

Capy, Mara Myrtle, Ed. D. (1983)
University of Massachusetts, Massachusetts
A developmental project for advanced dance-movement therapists in Israel: An intercultural experiment
345 pp. 44/04-A, 1025   ORDER NO. 831,7427
Available from: Diss. Abstracts International
This study describes, analyzes, and evaluates a cross-cultural endeavor for advanced dance-movement therapists jointly sponsored by Antioch, New England and Haifa University, Israel. The project fills in the gaps in Israeli therapist's backgrounds and plans a Dance-Movement Therapy Program for Haifa University. It provides historical and theoretical substantiation and includes the design and function of a teacher training component.
See also: Education, Administration

Carter, Frances Helen, Ph.D. (1965)
University of Iowa, Iowa
Selected kinesthetic and psychological differences between the highly skilled in dance and in sports
80 pp. 26/10-A, 5850   ORDER NO. 66-3416
Available from: Diss. Abstracts International
In this investigation two groups of physical education majors, one highly skilled in dance and the other highly skilled in sports, are compared with respect to measures of balance, personality assessment, and tests of time estimation. Results show that the dance group scored

higher on the balance tests and had superior performances in the tempo forward and the moderate tempo with varying space patterns. Personality measures also show significant differences between the groups.

Chodorow, Joan, Ph. D. (1988)
Union for Experimenting Colleges and Universities, New York
Dance/movement as active imagination: Origins, theory, practice
150 pp. 49/10-B, 4530   ORDER NO. 8901435
Available from: Diss. Abstracts International
This study explores the value of dance/movement to psychotherapy, particularly as a form of active imagination. It also offers an understanding of the origins of movement in the psyche. A biographical narrative is followed by the uses of dance/movement in the practice of psychotherapy and a description of the levels of the psyche.

Cole, Ivy Lee, Ph. D. (1979)
Texas Woman's University, Texas
Dance therapy with a nonverbal, autistic child: A documentation of process
248 pp. 40/12-A, 6188   ORDER NO. 801,2157
Available from: Diss. Abstract International
An analysis of videotapes which record the therapeutic process occurring between the investigator and a non-verbal autistic boy. As the relationship grows the child's self-contacts reveal a growing ability to express and communicate. Results support the hypothesis that the movement patterns manifested in a client-centered approach to dance therapy are specific indicators of the therapeutic process.

Dibbell-Hope, Sandy, Ph. D. (1989)
University of California/School of Professional Psychology at Berkeley/ Alameda, California
Moving toward health: A study of the use of dance-movement therapy in the psychological adaption to breast cancer
276 pp. 54/08-B, 3689   ORDER NO. 8926360
Available from: Diss. Abstracts International
An investigation of the use of dance-movement therapy for the psychological adaptation to breast cancer. Psychological data are derived from interviews and self-report measures.

While the therapy does not show overall efficacy, there are indications that it can be effective for certain types of women.

Diller, Vivian Felice, Ph. D. (1980)
Yeshiva University, New York
The ballet dancer: In-depth psychobiographical case studies
315 pp. 41/08-B, 3175   ORDER NO. 810,3722
Available from: Diss. Abstracts International
This study investigates the character of the ballet dancer using an in-depth psychobiographical case study approach which focuses on recurring representational configurations and their origins and functional significance. It concludes that the ballet profession provides dancers with the fulfillment of their talents and aspirations and also with a fragile solution to their conflicts and needs, especially in the narcissistic realm.
See also: Styles: Ballet

Eler, Barbara Jean, Ph. D. (1986)
New York University, New York
Social interaction in a drama dance group of hospitalized schizophrenics
163 pp. 47/08-A, 2003   ORDER NO. 8625621
Available from: Diss. Abstracts International
A description of the behaviors of hospitalized schizophrenics for indications of social interaction during selected periods of six drama-dance workshops. Non-verbal and verbal behaviors are observed unobtrusively with video camera and then scored. Results show that drama-dance workshops have potential for encouraging interactive behaviors. This study demonstrates support for combining dance and drama as a treatment modality for hospitalized schizophrenics.

Fox, Jacqueline Elizabeth, Ph. D. (1987)
University of Michigan, Michigan
Dance in a sightless world: A phenomenology
265 pp. 48/06-A, 1431   ORDER NO. 872,0264
Available from: Diss. Abstracts International
This study describes the lived-world of five visually-impaired children and examines their behavior through an experience of dance. A phenomenological research approach is used to develop a case study on each child and then a thematic analysis of the cases is conducted

to produce the findings. Spatiality, loneliness, and separation are the major themes that emerge while it is found that dance classes are beneficial in decreasing "blindism" behavior and increaseing self-esteem.

Goodrick, Terry Suzanne, Ph. D. (1986)
Ohio State University, Ohio
Sensitivity to choreographic styles in dance as related to age, experience, and cognitive differences
270 pp. 48/01-B, 283   ORDER NO.
Available from: Diss. Abstracts International
In this study style sensitivity is conceptualized in terms of perceptual learning theory, individual differences in verbal and perceptual ability, and Gestalt psychology. Sensitivity to choreographic style is tested on adults, sixth graders, and first graders with results indicating that age differences are similar to those for other arts. Dance experience is regarded as the strongest predictor of style sensitivity.
See also: Theory and Philosophy

Green, Eleanor Ruth, Ph. D. (1970)
Texas Woman's University, Texas
A study of the stability of perception for two extreme perceptual types, the visual and haptic, in relation to learning dance movements
322 pp.   ORDER NO.
Available from: Microform
This study determines if two extreme perceptual types, the visual and the haptic, remain stable when learning dance movements taught with distinct methods emphasizing similar and different perceptual modalities. Following tests and evaluations, it is concluded that the types do remain stable even when exposed to disticntly different teaching methods.
See also: Education

Griffin, Vivian Joy, Ed. D. (1983)
Brigham Young University, Utah
Hemisphericity in athletes and dancers
116 pp. 44/07-A, 2083   ORDER NO. 832,1334
Available from: Diss. Abstracts International
An exploration of the relationship of college students' hemispherity and their participation in dance performance or on athletic teams. Relationships of their cumulative grade point average and gender with brain dominance are

also investigated. Significant relationships are found between all variables—GPA, gender, and hemispherity.

Halstead, Carol Elizabeth Decker, Ed. D. (1980)
Wayne State University, Michigan
An analysis of attitudes and definitions by selected teachers and pupils toward dance in general and dance in the classroom
150 pp. 41/10-A, 4330   ORDER NO. 810,7261
Available from: Diss. Abstracts International
This study provides detailed data about teachers' attitudes concerning dance in the classroom and provides statistics concerning attitudes about dance from the student population. The Creative Dance Attitude Inventory is used to elicit responses from students and an interview format is used to gather data from teachers following a classroom-based program in dance.
See also: Education

Hatch, Frank White, Ph. D. (1973)
University of Wisconsin at Madison, Wisconsin
A behavioral cybernetic interpretation of dance and dance culture
102 pp. 34/10-B, 5237   ORDER NO.
Available from: Diss. Abstracts International
This descriptive study consist of a system analysis of dance and dance culture. A feedback theory of self-governed behavior is used to describe the dancer as a dynamic control system. Highly coordinated interactions of dancers with each other and with their audience are explained in terms of mutual social tracking. A cybernetic theory of cultural behavior is applied to the symbolic movement of dance to show how dance acts as a control feeder of cultural expression and communication. A summary explains why older levels of dance behavior persist and coexist with newer developments to form a living record of culture.
See also: Ethnology and Anthropology

Holcomb, James Marion, Ph. D. (1977)

United States International University/ School of Performing Arts, California

The effects of dancing and relaxation sessions on stress levels of senior citizens

104 pp. 39/10-B, 5069   ORDER NO. 790,8422

Available from: Diss. Abstracts International

This experimental study discusses the causes and effects of stress and describes training sessions in ballroom dancing and relaxation methods of an experimental group of senior citizens. Measures for levels of stress are compared with a control group to ascertain if the ballroom dancing reduces stress levels.

See also: Styles: Social

Jette, Nadine Marie, Ed. D. (1975)

Brigham Young University, Alabama

The effects of modern dance and music on body image and self concept in college women

106 pp. 37/01-A, 178   ORDER NO. 76-15,452

Available from: Diss. Abstracts International

An investigation of the effects of modern dance with musical accompaniment and music with rhythmical activities on body image and self-concept in college women.

See also: Styles: Modern, Music and Rhythm

Johnson, Ray, Ph. D. (1980)

University of Oregon, Oregon

Analysis of selected factors related to the element of space in movement creativity

115 pp. 41/08-A, 3528   ORDER NO. 810,1842

Available from: Diss. Abstracts International

The development of a space analytic model based on the uses of space to evaluate movement creativity. This model evaluates dynamics, contour, and focus and finds these to be significant predictors of movement creativity.

Kaslow, Florence Whiteman, Ph.D. (1969)

Bryn Mawr College, Pennsylvania

Dance and movement therapies: A study in theory and applicability

519 pp. 30/12-A, 5529   ORDER NO. 70-10,012

Available from: Diss. Abstracts International

This study is concerned with the body as a target of therapeutic intervention and presents the view that the body is an instrument of expression and communication. The history of the therapeutic uses of dance is traced and the dance therapy of today is examined. A theory of movement therapy is discussed and it is concluded that research is necessary to elevate the practice of movement therapy to the level of tested knowledge.

Kavaler, Susan Ivy, Ph. D. (1974)

Adelphi University, New York

The effects of dance therapy on mentally retarded children

163 pp. 35/05-B, 2435   ORDER NO. 74-24,640

Available from: Diss. Abstracts International

This study examines the effects of a dance therapy program on a group of mentally retarded school children. The program includes isolation and coordination of body parts, exercise games, exploration of space and rhythm, and improvisaton. It concludes that dance therapy does not significantly change the motor performance, self-concept, and body awareness of mentally retarded children.

See also: Children

Klem, Yonah, Ed.D. (1985)

Northern Illinois University, Illinois

Toward a general theory of body psychotherapy based on the theories of Reichian and dance-movement therapies

219 pp. 46/07-B, 2461   ORDER NO.

Available from: Diss. Abstracts International

An examination of Reichian and dance-movement therapy theories to discover if there are enough similarities to develop a general theory of body psychotherapy. A comparison of the theories and a critical evaluation of the concepts are made and hypotheses are presented. Implications for the general field of psychotherapy are then discussed.

See also: Theory and Philosophy.

Leventhal, Marcia Binnie, Ph. D. (1982)

Florida Institute of Technology, Florida

Dance therapy for the special child: An integrative treatment model

287 pp. 43/10-B, 3367   ORDER NO.

Available from: Diss. Abstracts International

Dance as therapy is viewed from several perspectives in order to isolate it as a discrete phe-

nomenon. It is discussed in relation to pure and basic dance, the body therapies, the body-mind interaction, the mother-child relationship, and to perceptual motor development. The review includes a discussion of the pioneers in dance therapy and an analysis of the theories and methods used with children. It is suggested that dance therapy for the special child is widely variable, but that there are a few uniquely developed conceptual theories.
See also: Children

Levy, Francine Joan, Ed. D. (1981)
Rutgers the State University of New Jersey at New Brunswick, New Jersey
Dance therapy: Foundations and organization of theory and practice
786 pp. 42/04-B, 1588   ORDER NO.
Available from: Diss. Abstracts International
An analysis of the historical development of the field of dance therapy in the United States from an institutional, theoretical, and practical perspective. This study views dance therapy as a form of psychotherapy that relies largely on dance/movement as its primary medium of self-expressionn and communicaiton. It chronicles dance therapy from the 1940's to the 1970's and includes the pioneers, trends, patient populations, and profiles of leading dance therapists.
See also: History

Lindner, Erna Caplow, Ph.D. (1986)
Coumbia Pacific University, California
Therapeutic Dance/ Movement for Older Adults
256 pp.
Available from: Diss. Abstracts International
See also: Education

Marcow, Vivien Joy, Ph. D. (1986)
Union for Experimenting Collegs and Universities, New York
Passionate learning: The process of educating the creative arts therapist
85 pp. 47/05-A, 1661   ORDER NO. 861,7905
Available from: Diss. Abstracts International

In this study thinking about learning with passion is applied to the process of educating the creative arts therapist. Learning is examined within the context of human development and is followed by a description of the evolution of the creative arts therapy fields and their respective professional training periods. A performance piece, "Yellow Bird", is meant to be viewed in relationship to the study.
See also: Education

Marek, Patricia Anabel, Ph. D. (1975)
University of Tennessee, Tennessee
Dance therapy with adult day hospital patients
88 pp. 36/11-B, 5806   ORDER NO.
Available from: Diss. Abstracts International
An examination of the effects of dance therapy in an adult therapy program. An experimental group participates in daily dance therapy sessions and the control group in verbal therapy sessions. Subjects are rated several times and ratings are compared at the beginning and end of the experiment.

McConnell, Judith Ann, Ph. D. (1988)
Ohio State University, Ohio
Effects of movement training on body awareness, self-concept, and antisocial behavior in forensic psychiatric patients
110 pp. 49/09-B, 4066   ORDER NO. 882,4568
Available from: Diss. Abstracts International
This study compares a 20 dance session movement training program combining creative dance techniques with a 20 session problem solving discussion group program. Dependent variables include body awareness, self concept, and antisocial behavior.

Miles, James Baker, Ed.D. (1962)
North Texas State University, Texas
An analysis of relationships between experiences in correlated courses in art, music, and modern dance and certain behavioral changes related to aesthetic experience
70 pp. 23/09-A, 3309   ORDER NO. 63-1415
Available from: Diss. Abstracts International
A study of the relationship between a twelve week program of coordinated laboratory experiences in art, music, and modern dance and

the development of four factors related to aesthetic experience. These factors are aesthetic perception, aesthetic attitude, physiological responsiveness, and level of freedom from restraint. At the conclusion of the experiment it is found that aesthetic attitudinal changes can be effected through multi-arts programs particularly if they are correlated rather than isolated.

Montague, Mary Ella, Ed.D. (1961)
New York University, New York
The effects of dance experiences upon observable behaviors of women prisoners
320 pp. ORDER NO. 6201445
Available from: Diss. Abstracts International
This is a study of the effects of dance on observable behaviors of women prisoners. Data concerning traits which characterized the inmates is gathered and a planned series of dance experiences is conducted. The over-all conclusion drawn suggests that participation in a series of systematic dance experiences contributed to participants in a variety of ways. Desirable changes in inmate behavior tended to occur.

Murphy, Timothy Fredric, Ph. D. (1982)
Boston College, Massachusetts
Teaching the dance: Nietzsche as educator
212 pp. 43/02-A, 472 ORDER NO. 821,6112
Available from: Diss. Abstracts International
This study shows that Nietzsche considers himself a philosopher because he attempts to educate readers about living patterns. Nietzshe proposes the dance as the symbol of successful education because it integrates people back into nature. His political concerns are also considered.
See also: Education

Murray, Patricia Ann, P. Ed (1982)
Indiana University, Indiana
Extraversion—Introversion and the use of locomotor space in modern dance
113 pp. 43/04-A, 1080 ORDER NO. 82-21545
Available from: Diss. Abstracts International
This study determines the relationship between extraversion—introversion and the amount of locomotor space used in modern dance improvisation. The study also involves

the construction, validation, and reliability determination of a test to measure locomotor space. Recommendations to teachers of modern dance pertain to relationships between movement behavior and personality constructs.
See also: Styles: Modern, Education

Oglesby, Carole Ann, Ph. D. (1969)
Purdue University, Pennsylvania
Influence of perceived aspects of parental and peer expectancies, warmth, and authority, on self-identification as active and competent movement performers
179 pp. 30/6-A, 4814 ORDER NO. 70-8936
Available from: Diss. Abstracts International
An investigation of the influence of parents and peers on girls self-perception as active and competent movement performers. Aspects measured were parental warmth, parental and peer expectations, and parental authority.

Oshuns, Margaret Gwen, Ph. D. (1977)
Ohio State University, Ohio
An exploratory study of creative movement as a means of increasing positive self-concept, personal, and social adjustment of selected seventh grade students
191 pp. 38/02-A, 555 ORDER NO. 77-17,121
Available from: Diss. Abstracts International
This exploratory study determines whether creative movement increases self-concept in a select group of seventh grade students. The content is based on Barbara Mettler's movement techniques. The results reveal a reduction in anxiety and an increase in positive relations with school and others, such as peers, teachers, and adults.
See also: Children

Powell, J Robin, Ph. D. (1985)
New York University, New York
Body awareness: The kinetic awareness work of Elaine Summers
284 pp. 46/03-A, 648 ORDER NO. 851,0524
Available from: Diss. Abstracts International
A description of the theory and practice of Elaine Summer's work in kinetic awareness within the context of other body awareness

practitioners and theorists who have evolved parallel aproaches to dealing with problems of tension and stress. Summer's work is regarded as multi-directional in its movement of body parts in order to release holding patterns and to balance the body in performance and everyday life.

Puretz, Susan Luskin, Ed. D. (1973)
New York University, New York
A comparison of the effects of dance and physical education on the self-concept of selected disadvantaged girls
90 pp. 34/06-A, 3124   ORDER NO. 73-30,114
Available from: Diss. Abstracts International
A study of the development of self-concept in disadvantaged elementary school students by exposing them to modern educational dance as a substitute for physical education. The results indicate significant positive findings in self-concept of a long term nature of those students who had received modern educational dance instead of physical education.
See also: Education, Children

Robbins, Bonnie, Ph.D. (1988)
New York University, New York
The effectiveness of movement strategies in reducing physically aggressive behaviors in five to twelve year old children hospitalized for severe conduct disorders
149 pp.   ORDER NO. 8825263
Available from: Diss.Abstracts International
An assessment of the effectiveness of particular movement strategies in decreasing physically aggressive behaviors in five to twelve year old children hospitalized for severe conduct disorders. Findings support continued use of movement as a therapeutic intervention with this population.
See also: Children

Schneider, Friedrech Johann, Ed. D. (1977)
Boston University, Boston
The effect of movement exploration and mime on body-image, self-concept, and body-coordination of seventh grade children
267 pp. 38/09-A,5335   ORDER NO. 7732782
Available from: Diss. Abstracts International

An investigation of the effect of a specially designed program of movement exploration and mime on body image, self-concept, and body coordination of seventh grade children. It concludes that body image and self concept do not change significantly, but body coordination is improved.
See also: Children

Schwartz, Vera Simon, Ed. D. (1980)
Rutgers University of New Jersey, New Jersey
The relationship of dimensions of Jungian psychological type of college major, either physical education or dance, and preferred approach to teaching human movement
153 pp. 41/01-A, 159   ORDER NO. 801,4252
Available from: Diss. Abstracts International
An examination of the personality characteristics of two groups involved in teaching human movement, the physical education specialist and the dance specialist. The Myer-Briggs Type Indicator is used to measure extraversion—introversion and sensing—intuiting. Findings conclude that dance majors tend toward intuition and physical education majors tend toward sensing while both groups tend toward extroversion.

Shaw, Sylvia Jean, Ph. D. (1988)
University of Alberta—Canada, Alberta, Canada
Attitudes of Canadians of Ukrainian descent toward Ukrainian dance
49/11-A, 3302   ORDER NO. AAC0564324
Available from:
This study discusses the attitudes of Canadians of Ukranian descent regarding the desire to keep Ukranian dance exclusive, the need for background materials, the political issues, and the value of the dance. Ukranian dance is found to be highly valued and an important component of the Ukranian heritage. experience.
See also: Styles: Folk, Ethnology and Anthropology

Siegel, Elaine Vivian, Ph. D. (1981)
Union for Experimenting Colleges and Univeristies, New York
"The mirror of our selves": A psychoanalytic study in dance-movement therapy
458 pp. 42/10-B, 4212   ORDER NO. 8205659
Available from: Diss. Abstracts International
This study uses psychoanalytical egopsychology to construct a theoretical framework for the comprehensive conceptualization of dance-movement therapy. Body-mind unity is emphasized and human motility is given priority as an ego apparatus. Freud's writings corroborate the development of psychoanalytic dance-movement therapy and it is supported that dance-movement therapy is a primary, rather than an adjunctive treatment mode.

Silver, Judith A, Ph. D. (1981)
University of Toronto (Canada)
Therapeutic aspects of folk dance: Self concept, body concept, ethnic distancing and social distancing
42/10-A, 4373   ORDER NO.
Available from: Diss. Abstracts International
This study reviews literature related to the psychological and therapeutic functions of dance, especially folk dance participation. Based on this literature, a program of international folk dances is presented experimentally to determine if it would lead to improved self-concepts, more positive attitudes about classmates and reduced distancing between ethnic groups. The results are discussed in terms of the dance literature, social learning theory, and ethnic contract hypotheses.
See also: Styles: Folk

Skye, Ferial Deer, Ed. D. (1988)
South Dakota State University, South Dakota
A study of the effects of dance education on stress in college-age American Indian women
171 pp. 49/07-A, 1706   ORDER NO. 881,5830
Available from: Diss. Abstracts International
This study examines the effects of a culturally-based dance education model on the reduction of stress in American Indian women. A survey is conducted and the results are used to develop a dance education model which provides movement experiences designed to reduce stress factors and develop coping mechanisms through movement-related relaxation.
See also: Education

Sloss, Joan Nora, Ed. D. (1983)
Temple University, Philadelphia
Experiencing oneself in dance: A phenomenological study of centeredness, relatedness and projection
282 pp. 44/05-A, 1248   ORDER NO. 832,1278
Available from: Diss. Abstracts International
A phenomenological analysis of essential aspects of the dancer's experience—centeredness, relatedness, and projection. The analysis reveals several ways in which these aspects are independent structures of the dancer's art. The philosophical approach is supported by the existential philosophy of Maurice Merleau-Ponty and Jean Paul Sartre, and by Maxine Sheets-Johnstone's phenomenological studies of dance. The study concludes with an account of the essential function of imaginative consciousness (visualizations) for physical performance and theatrical projection.
See also: Theory and Philosophy

Taylor, Willie Lee, Ed. D. (1977)
University of Georgia, Georgia
The effectiveness of ballroom dance instruction on the self-concept and mobility of blind adults
144 pp. 38/11-A, 6605   ORDER NO. 780,6047
Available from: Diss. Abstracts International
This investigation tests the notion that self-concept mean scores and mobility scores of blind adults will change after they participate in a ballroom dance program. The major conclusions are that ballroom dance training will significantly improve the mobility efficiency of blind adults and that the level of skill acquisition in ballroom dance correlates positively with their levels of mobility and self concept, thus showing that an instructional program in ballroom dance based on orientation and mobility concepts is worthwhile.
See also: Styles: Social

Trigg, Marilyn Gertude, Ed. D. (1978)
University of North Carolina at Greensboro, North Carolina
The effects of varying amounts of creative modern dance activities on creative-thinking ability and self concept
201 pp. 39/12-A, 7227   ORDER NO. 791,3061
Available from: Diss. Abstracts International
An investigation of the effect that varying amounts of creative modern dance activities have on subjects' creative thinking abilities and self-concepts after 10 weeks. The findings show neither significant effects on the items being tested nor any significant relationship between them.
See also: Styles: Modern

Trujillo, Lorenzo Alan, Ed. D. (1979)
San Francisco State University, California
The effects of a Hispanic ethnic dance curriculum upon high school students' self concept and academic performance
234 pp. 40/04-A, 1851   ORDER NO. 79-23019
Available from: Diss. Abstracts International
This study examines the relationship of the participation of a group of high school students in a Hispanic ethnic dance curriculum to their various aspects of behavior, especially self-concept. It also measures their gain in knowledge of specific aspects of Hispanic culture. The study concludes that the participants showed a significant gain in their self-concept and academic performance.
See also: Ethnology and Anthropology, Education

Venson, Gloria Mathis, Ph. D. (1977)
Southern Illinois University at Carbondale, Illinois
The effects of time related modern educational dance programs on the self-concept of fourth, fifth and sixth-grade girls in a Southern urban city
96 pp. 38/05-A, 2569   ORDER NO. 77-24,043
Available from: Diss. Abstracts International
In this study girls in modern educational dance programs are compared with a like group of girls in the regular school program for the purpose of examining the effect on self-concept. Each modern educational dance class has two major goals—to develop a movement vocabulary and to provide opportunities for improvisation through creative movement. The investigation finds that modern educational dance does contribute to the variance of self-concept and presents implications for classroom and dance teachers.
See also: Education, Children

Wilson, Timothy Robert, Ed. D. (1985)
University of Houston, Texas
The effect of creative movement and contact improvisation experiences on self-awareness
315 pp. 46/06-A, 1556   ORDER NO. 851,7718
Available from: Diss. Abstracts International
An investigation of the effect of creative movement and contact improvisation on self-awareness. A journal format is used by subjects to record data consisting of qualitative cataloging and coding of self-awareness indicators. Profiles are developed from the data and these emphasize differences among the subjects and suggest implications for dance, therapy, and education.
See also: Education

Related Arts:
Literature

Davis, Floyd Herman, Jr, Ed. D. (1972)
Ball State University, Indiana
The dramaturgical functions of song, dance and music in the comedies of John Dryden
202 pp. 33/06-A, 2888   ORDER NO. 72-30,146
Available from: Diss. Abstracts International
An analysis of Dryden's dramaturgical use of song, dance, and music as they contribute to plot, character, and setting in selected comedies. It is argued that dance serves to complicate the plot, bring characters together, introduce atmosphere and transform mood. Together with songs and music, dance enhances, reinforces, and synthesizes elements of comedy in Dryden's works.
See also: Related Arts: Theatre

Gordon, Sarah Ellen, Ph. D. (1973)
Texas Christain University, Texas
The great dance: A study of Eliot's use of the dance metaphor in the Four Quartets
155 pp. 34/06-A, 3394   ORDER NO. 73-31,605
Available from: Diss. Abstracts International
As one of the central metaphors of the Quartets, the dance has it's origins in the philosophy of Plato and Plotinus and is historically associated with the nuptical apprehension of the divine and with the mystic's attempt to convey experience through language. In this study it is shown that the symbol of the cosmic dance provides Eliot with a means of explaining the mystery of being.
See also: Theory and Philosophy

Johnson, Cynthia June, Ph.D. (1983)
Rice University
The dance motif in Zola's "L'Assommoir"
303 pp. 44/02-A, 499   ORDER NO. 8314943
Available from: Diss. Abstracts International
This study examines the relationship of dance to literature using the vocabulary and plot of "L'Assommoir" by Emile Zola. The text is divided into sections like the acts of a ballet and Zola uses word choice, associatoin of gesture with characters, and stage techniques to evoke the ballet analogy. The emphasis on movement and the dance heighten symbolic values in the text and illustrate the importance of dance and the figure of the dancer in the arts as a whole in nineteenth century Paris.
See also: Styles: Ballet

Krance, Charles Andrew, Ph.D. (1970)
University of Wisconsin at Madison, Wisconsin
Tersichore in the night: Dance patterns and motifs in 'Voyage Au Bout De La Nuit'
421 pp. 31/04-A, 1804   ORDER NO. 70-13,920
Available from: Diss. Abstracts International
This study demonstrates that the composition and structure of twentieth century author Céline's novel, "Voyage au bout de la nuit" has certain dance-like patterns. The dynamic quality of the novel reflects the transposition into literature of terpsichorean time and space relations. An examination of several parallel principles between the novel and dance reveals to what extent the stylistic and thematic structures of "Voyage" are influenced by Céline's passion for dance.

McKinney, Barbara Joan, Ph. D. (1974)
University of Minnesota, Minnosota
Images of dancing in sixteenth-century English poetry
145 pp. 35/02-A, 1055   ORDER NO. 74-17,307
Available from: Diss. Abstracts International
A study of dance imagery in the poerty of 16th century Tudor England where nearly everyone danced. Dance imagery is mimetic of the Tudor passion for order and ceremony, but also reflects the less ordered aspect of society, for example in the Dance of Death and Bacchanalian Dances. Other dances blended ideas as a means of resolving contraries. These dance images are vehicles for synthesizing and commenting on the poetic process.

Mirabella, Bella Maryanne, Ph. D. (1979)
Rutgers University, New Jersey
Part I—Mute rhetoric dance in Shakespeare and Marston. Part II—The Machine in the Garden: The theme of work in 'Tess of the D'Urbervilles'. Part III—Art and imagination in Edith Wharton's 'The House of Mirth'
141 pp. 40/07-A, 4056   ORDER NO. 792,8425
Available from: Diss. Abstracts International
This essay explores the relationship of two dramatic devices, dance and disguise, and the roles they play in selected Shakespearean plays. Dance is used as both a literary convention and a dramatic device in addition to being a popular pastime which is often linked with disguise as in a masked dance.
See also: Related Arts: Theatre

Napoli, Joanne, Ph. D. (1972)
University of Massachusetts, Massachusetts
The meaning of the dancer in the poetry of William Butler Yeats
33/06-A, 2945   ORDER NO. 72-33,013
Available from: Diss. Abstracts International
A discussion of the dancer image in William Butler Yeat's poetry. This image reveals wide and fascinating implications for potenial spiri-

tual development and is a metaphor for a state of consciousness which Yeats strove to attain all his life.

Pyron, Mary Virginia, Ph. D. (1987)
Vanderbilt University, Tennessee
"Sundry measures": Dance in Renaissance comedy
221 pp. 48/09-A, 2345   ORDER NO. 872,5924
Available from: Diss. Abstracts International
This study presents a panorama of dance included in the extant English plays listed as comedies, romantic comedies, and tragicomedies from 1558 to 1625. Dance serves in characterizations, rituals of courtship, puns and wordplay, and plot structures. The study places English Renaissance dance in its social and literary context and suggests a new metaphor for dance. The appendix lists all the comedies containing dancing and includes information about the amount and kind of dancing within each play.
See also: History

Salvati, Julianne Mia, Ph. D. (1981)
University of Rhode Island, Providence of Rhode Island
W. B. Yeats and his "Sweet Dancer"
158 pp. 43/02-A, 307   ORDER NO. 821,5356
Available from: Diss. Abstracts International
Between 1976 and 1939, Yeats wrote a series of dramas in which the climatic scenes are expressed through dance. This study defines the nature and scope of the dancer's dramatic impact in his dance-plays and shows how each dance sequence suggests a unique and powerful statement concerning Yeats' understanding of the human condition.

Sheerwood, Sandra Mason, Ph. D (1977)
University of Illinois at Urbana-Champaign, Illinois
The new poetry of William Carlos Williams: Poetic uses of music and dance
177 pp. 38/10-A, 6125   ORDER NO. 780,4155
Available from: Diss. Abstracts International
A study of imaginery and structure of Williams' poetry which reveals not only his knowledge and understanding of the arts of music and dance, but of their importance in this poetic schema and of the thoroughness of their incor-

poration into the object of the poem. This study explores the rationale for Williams' choices of music and dance as dynamic models of the poetic experience.

Shelley, Paula Diane, Ph. D. (1985)
University of California at Los Angeles, California
The use of dance in Jacobean drama to develop character
211 pp. 46/12-A, 3538   ORDER NO. 860,3991
Available from: Diss. Abstracts International
This study argues that dance is used to develop character in the Jacobean plays no less effectively than peotry or music. Dance is shown to credibly motivate the actions of characters and to lend cohesion to plays often thought disjointed. Using examples from the plays of Middleton, Ford, Webster, and Shakespeare, amongst others, the modes of dance are identified and discussed in detail.

Stanton, Lilian, Ph. D. (1973)
University of Notre Dame, Indiana
Art in the dance: A study of the use of the fine arts in Anthony Powell's "A dance to the music of time"
269 pp. 34/07-A, 4288   ORDER NO. 74-73
Available from: Diss. Abstracts International
A study by Powell's awareness of the interrelatedness of all the arts with the dance art. It includes the use of dance pattern, ritual and specific references to the fine arts to effect a fusion of time within the narrator's perception of the past, present, and future. Repetitions of pattern in the dance are compared to unchanging life patterns.

Strickland, William Franklin, Ph. D. (1973)
Florida University, Florida
e.e. cummings dramatic imagination: A study of three plays and a ballet
204 pp. 35/02-A, 1123   ORDER NO. 74-19,192
Available from: Diss. Abstracts International
Not Available.
See also: Styles: Ballet

Vashi, Nataraj G, Ph.D. (1952)
University of Illinois at Chicago, Illinois
Dance in Sanskirt literature from Panini to Bharata Muni

Available from: University of Illinois at Chicago
Abstract not available.
See also: Ethnology and Anthropology

Vickers, Clinton John, Ph. D. (1974)

University of Massachusetts, Massachusetts
Image into symbol: The evolution of the dance in the poetry and drama of W. B. Yeats
205 pp. 35/01-A, 484   ORDER NO. 74-15,047
Available from: Diss. Abstracts International
An investigation of the relationship between the dance in W. B. Yeats' poems and plays of the 1890's and the occult rituals of that time. An examination of dance as a metaphor for life as well as of death, and a detailing of the evolution of the dance in the poems from image to symbol is included.

Welton, John Lee, Ph. D. (1974)

Southern Illinois University, Illinois
Interpretive movement: A training approach for performers of literature
354 pp. 35/02-A, 1276   ORDER NO. 74-18,881
Available from: Diss. Abstracts International
The description of a program of training for teachers of performers of literature in which movement is used to sensitize the interpreter to himself/herself and to the literature that is being performed. Interpretive movement based on synesthesia is used as the method for sensitizing while the 'kinevocal technique' is used as a basis of the exercises.
See also: Education

West, Jeanne M, Ph. D. (1983)

Kent State University, Ohio
Shelley and the dance: A study of "Queen Mab," "Alastor," "Prometheus Unbound," and "The Triumph of Life"
167 pp. 44/12-A, 3700   ORDER NO. 840,6154
Available from: Diss. Abstracts International
A study of Shelley's use of dance images and rhythmical movement in his exploration of the potential of the human imagination for transforming the universe. His love for the art of dance helps him fashion a new cosmic dance. Qualities of the dance can be seen enriching many of Shelley's images and imbuing them with freedom and unlimited movement.

White, Judith Simpson, Ph. D. (1979)

University of Virginia, Virginia
William Yeats and the dancer: A history of Yeat's work with dance theatre
155 pp. 40/09-A, 5051   ORDER NO. 800,4630
Available from: Diss. Abstracts International
This dissertation traces the history of Yeats' work with dance theatre placing it within the context of the total arts movement of the Symbolist era and the development of modern dance and ballet. The focus is on theatrical and poetic qualities Yeats felt dance could add to his verse drama, particulary those found in Japanese dance drama and in the ballet of Ninette de Valois.

Yun Chang Sik, Ph. D. (1972)

Princeton University, New Jersey
The tragic theatre: The "No" and Yeat's dance plays
324 pp. 33/07-A, 3608   ORDER NO. 72-29,841
Available from: Diss. Abstracts International
A critical study of tragic theater as manifested in the No' theater of Japan and the dance plays of W. B. Yeats. In the final chapter the aesthetics of music and dance as elements of the tragic theater are briefly essayed and dance is viewed as a reconciling image.
See also: Related Arts: Theatre

Related Arts:
Opera

Allanbrook, Wye Jamison, Ph.D. (1974)

Stanford University, California
Dance as expression in Mozart opera
361 pp. 35/03-A, 1684   ORDER NO. 742,0168
Available from: Diss. Abstract International
In opera the expressive nuances of dance are revealing and useful. This study analyses the dances frequently used in Mozart's operas and includes a survey of examples and comments of theorists on the characteristics of rhythmic patterns and affects. The dances fall into both a social and affective hierarchy which in turn reflects a basic condition of eighteenth century

life in which dance, demeanor and character are closely connected.
See also: History

Peterson, Daniel, Ph.D. (1986)
New York University, New York
Reading bodily action from the operatic score: A new approach to the operatic criticism domain with reference to Gaim Carlo Menotti's "The Telephone"
282 pp. 47/04-A, 1110   ORDER NO. 8614343
Available from: Diss. Abstracts International
A discussion and description of the three elements of operatic criticism—music, text, and bodily action. The approach is demonstrated with references to the score of Gian-Carlo's "The Telephone" and to a movement score written with Labanotation, a conventional system for writing movement. Eight passages from the two scores are examined for the way the three elements interact in affecting dramatic tension.

Related Arts:
Painting

Majzels, Claudine, Ph. D. (1977)
University of Pennsylvania, Pennsylvania
The dance in the art of Pieter Bruegel the elder
288 pp. 38/03-A, 1075   ORDER NO. 77-19,889
Available from: Diss. Absracts International
An analysis of the dance imagery in Bruegel's paintings, prints, and drawings showing that folk lore and folk dance can provide the artist with a wealth of humor and wit wherein movement is a metaphor for meaning. Bruegel reinvents the dances of his time as a choreographer in two dimensions and stimulates the beholder to join in the liveliness of his vision.
See also: Styles: Folk

McQuillan, Melissa Ann, Ph. D. (1979)
New York University, New York
Painters and the ballet, 1917–1926: An aspect of the relationship between art and theatre
826 pp. 40/11-A, 5635   ORDER NO. 801,0379

Available from: Diss. Abstracts International
This dissertation investigates the broad art historical questions presented by the artists who painted the ballet from 1917 to 1926. Although the painters separate responses are different, their collective developments centered on the theatrical-ballet companies bring significant attention to the costume, decor, theatre design, and ballet style of that period.
See also: Styles: Ballet

Shackelford, George Thomas Madison, Ph. D. (1986)
Yale University, Connecticut
The dance compositions of Edgar Degas
308 pp. 47/11-A, 3897   ORDER NO. 870,1083
Available from: Diss. Abstracts International
Studying Degas' painting and sculpture in light of his drawings, this dissertation argues that the drawings are not preparatory works, but random explorations from which Degas derives inspiration for more complicated artistic efforts. His interest in the ballet as urban entertainment and the ballet's place in Parisian society of the late nineteeth century provides the focus of the first chapter which is followed by analyses of the dance works themselves and the ways in which their formal qualities effect their respective interpretations.
See also: Styles: Ballet

Related Arts:
Theatre

Bethune, Robert William, Ph. D. (1985)
University of Hawaii, Hawaii
The effect of Kabuki training on the western performances of Western acting students
357 pp. 48/07-A, 1586   ORDER NO. 87-23866
Available from: Diss. Abstracts International
This study develops a methodology for analysing live performance based on Kabuki acting, Laban movement analysis, speech science, dance ethnology, and ethnomusicology. The methodology is applied to performances by Nakamura Matagoro of the National Theatre of Japan and is also applied to a group of Western acting students in a program conducted by

Matagoro. The analyses show how the student performances change over time.
See also: Notation and Movement Analysis

Campbell, C. Jean Bailey, Ph. D. (1976)
Bowling Green State University, Ohio
An approach to human movement for the stage
235 pp. 37/08-A, 4610   ORDER NO. 772,690
Available from: Diss. Abstracts International
This study develops an approach to human movement based on selected facts and principles from several related disciplines—anatomy, physiology, and mechanical physics. The writings of Rudolf Laban provide movement analysis and the study concludes that an understanding of expressive movement is valuable to actors and directors.
See also: Notation and Movement Analysis, Science

Davis, Marion Lorene, Ph. D. (1961)
University of Wisconsin at Madison, Wisconsin
The modern dance as dramatic theatre (A comparison of selected elements)
437 pp. 22/01-A, 358   ORDER NO. 61-1524
Available from: Diss. Abstracts International
This study suggests objective lines based on theatre elements along which to pursue the analysis of the formal elements of dance. It provides a method of critical investigation which gives concrete shape to the elusive aspects of dance. Dance language is discussed as a further dimension common to the analytical study of the performing arts in general.
See also: Theory and Philosophy

Johnson, Norman W., Jr, Ph. D. (1989)
University of Oregon, Oregon
Period movement style and the waltz: A choreo-kinetic model for actor training
302 pp. 50/05-A, 1139   ORDER NO. 891,8946
Available from: Diss. Abstracts International
This study describes the waltz's evolution through three major sylistic phases and reveals a body of information capable of providing the actor, director, or acting teacher with approaches to the study and formation of a nineteenth century movement style. Through choreo-kinesic evaluation it examines specific postures and gestures, spatial relationships, movement qualities, rhythms, and contextural influences of the waltz.
See also: History, Styles: Social

Maschio, Geraldine Ann, Ph. D. (1981)
University of Wisconsin at Madison, Wisconsin
The Ziegfeld Follies: Form, content, and significance of an American revue
211 pp. 42/08-A, 3348   ORDER NO. 812,5734
Available from: Diss. Abstracts International
A study of the revue as produced by Florenz Ziegfield from 1907 to 1931. The Ziegfeld Follies exemplifies achievements made in the theatrical arts and offers insight into the nature of society during these years. Although derivative in substance, the revue is described as innovative in form presenting beautiful women, topical comedy, music, dance, lavish costumes, and scenery in a tightly constructed, cogent production.
See also: History

Wilson, John Michael, Ph. D. (1973)
University of Wisconsin at Madison, Wisconsin
A natural philosophy of movement style for theatre performers
417 pp. 34/07-A, 4474   ORDER NO. 73-21,187
Available from: Diss. Abstracts International
A study of the significance of articulateness in the theatre performing arts, where the medium of expression is the human body, the mode is visible movement and the objects of expression are the evolving self-images of mankind. An anthrometric model is developed, the four universal qualities of movement are presented and psychological theories of perceptual-motor principles are discussed related to the training of actors and dancers.
See also: Theory and Philosophy, Psychology and Therapy

Related Arts: Visual

Edwards, Charles Malcolm, Ph.D. (1985)
New York University, New York
Greek votive reliefs to Pan and the nymphs
924 pp. 46/08-A, 2109   ORDER NO. 8522032
Available from: Diss. Abstracts International
A collection and study of the votive reliefs dedicated to Pan and the nymphs during the Classical and Hellenistic periods in Greece. The work is divided into text and catalogue. The text explores aspects of the cults of the nymphs and Pan in mythology and in the remains of cave santuaries. The reliefs consist of prototypes such as the Round Dance and mantle dancers. The catalogue lists 113 preserved reliefs. Each piece is described and discussed in terms of date and iconography.

Science

Becker, Theodore Jay, Ph. D. (1984)
Indiana University, Indiana
Kinetic and kinematic parameters of landing impact forces in the dance jump and leap
281 pp. 45/09-B, 2866   ORDER NO. 842,6637
Available from: Diss. Abstracts International
An investigation of the kinetic and kinematic factors of the landing technique characteristically performed by dancers at the terminal portion of the jump and leap. The parameters of the landing which reveal the most information about the impact forces are determined and described. These are jump distance, knee flexion, leap distance,and full heel compression contact.

Burris, Maureen Smith, Ed. D. (1979)
University of Southern Mississsippi, Mississippi
The effects of a six-week aerobic dance and folk dance program vs. the effects of a six-week aerobic jogging program on the cardiovascular efficiency and percent of body fat in postpubescent girls
95 pp. 40/03-A, 1344   ORDER NO. 791,9684
Available from: Diss. Abstracts International
This study compares the effects of a six-week aerobic dance and folk-dance program on cardiovascular efficiency and percent of body fat. Results indicate that both programs increase cardiovascular efficiency and reduce percent of body fat and that there is no significant difference between them.
See also: Styles: Folk

Chambers, Vinton Blaine, Ed. D. (1980)
Brigham Young University, Utah
The effects of dance on selected physiological variables
112 pp. 41/07, 2994   ORDER NO. 810,2741
Available from: Diss. Abstract International
This experimental study determines the contribution of beginning level dance classes toward specific fitness parameters. A second goal compares fitness components of advanced women dancers with varsity women athletes.

Chatfield, Steven John, Ph. D. (1989)
Colorado University at Boulder, Colorado
A physiologic and aesthetic cross-sectional analysis of modern dancers

144 pp. 50/07-A, 1830   ORDER NO. 892,3488
Available from: Diss. Abstracts International
This study determines differences in select aesthetic and physiologic capabilities between several ability levels of modern dancers and non-dancers. Predictors include resequencing errors and time, thigh skinfold, outward femoral rotation, hyperextension, endurance, and per cent fat. Correlations reveal trends of

improving physiologic parameters with increasing dance competence.
See also: Styles: Modern

De Guzman, Joseph Acosta, Ed. D. (1979)
Columbia University, New York
The effects of a semester of modern dance on the cardiovascular fitness and body composition of college women
249 pp. 40/09-A, 4955 ORDER NO. 800,6799
Available from: Diss. Abstracts International
This study investigates the effects of a semester of elementary modern dance instruction on the aerobic fitness and body composition of sedentary college—aged women. It finds that cardiovascular fitness may be improved and that body energy expended can be classified as light to moderate.
See also: Styles: Modern

Fitt, Sally Sevey, Ed. D. (1975)
University of California at Los Angeles, California
The assessment of the inter-rater agreement and validity of observation techniques for the identification of neuromuscular excitation patterns
91 pp. 36/10-A, 6537 ORDER NO. 768,988
Available from: Diss. Abstracts International
A description of the selection and evaluation of observers trained to identify the neuromuscular excitation patterns of isolated and complex tasks which are simultaneously recorded electromyographically. The observations are deemed objective and valid and immediate and long-range research implications are discussed.

Fuller, Pamela Elizabeth, Ph. D. (1976)
Texas Woman's University, Texas
Dance injuries: An audio-slide presentation
135 pp. 37/07-B, 3340
Available from: Diss. Abstracts International
A presentation of audio-slides on common dance injuries which are created to be used by teachers of undergraduate dance majors. A pre-test, post-test experiment is used to evalutate the presentation and concludes that those who view the presentation have significantly greater knowledge about dance injuries that those who do not.
See also: Education

Hays, Joan Camille Francis, Ph. D. (1971)
University of Texas at Austin, Texas
The contribution of beginning modern dance to cardiovascular fitness in college women
170 pp. 33/01-A, 181 ORDER NO. 72-19,601
Available from: Diss. Abstracts International
Heart rates of individuals in beginning modern dance and beginning gymnastics are monitored via radio telemetry to determine cardiovascular change. Findings conclude that these beginning skill classes do not create or provide enough strenuous activity to cause improvement in cardiovascular fitness.
See also: Styles: Modern

Lessard, Elizabeth C, Ph. D. (1980)
Texas Woman's University, Texas
Biomechanical analysis of the classical grand plié and two stylistic variations
99 pp. 41/08-A, 3478 ORDER NO. 810,4345
Available from: Diss. Abstracts International
A biomechanical analysis of the effect of torso movements on the grand plié. Computer technology is used to obtain moments of force at the joints and the excursion of the center of gravity. Dominant muscle group action and patterns of contractions are also examined. The investigation recommends that since the addition of torso movements increases the level of difficulty, stylistic variations of the grand plié should not be included in the training of the beginning dancer.
See also: Styles: Ballet

Nichols, Lucille Marie, Ed. D. (1975)
Columbia University, New York
Structure in motion: The influence of
morphology, experience, and the ballet
bar on verticality of alignment in the
performance of the plié
151 pp. 36/06-A, 3490   ORDER NO. 75-27,066
Available from: Diss. Abstracts International
This study objectively views factors which
influence the postural alignment of the dancer.
The primary concern is whether the degrees
of difficulty experienced by individuals in the
execution of the same skill (plié) can be determined by examination of morphological characteristics. The findings show that neither spi-
nal ratio nor verticality have any effect on
deviation. However, the lack of flexibility of
the body is a limitation in the development of
a consistency of movement.
See also: Styles: Ballet

Olson, Kevin, Ph. D. (1984)
Ohio State University, Ohio
An isotonic universal gym weight
training program for dancers to increase
strength, dispel myths, and increase
subjective and objective dance
technique
92 pp. 45/01-A, 118   ORDER NO. 841,0415
Available from: Diss. Abstracts International
An investigation of the effects of weight training on the strength and technique of dancers.
Body composition, maximum strength, body
distortion, and both subjective and objective
ballet technique are measured and compared.
The main conclusion of the study is that weight
training is not detrimental to dancers.

**Pappalardo, Margaret Doyle, Ed. D.
(1980)**
Boston University, Massachusetts
The effects of discotheque dancing on
selected physiological and psychological
parameters of college students
190 pp. 40/12-A, 6192   ORDER NO. 801,3336
Available from: Diss. Abstracts International
This study determines the effects of disco dancing on body weight, maximum oxygen uptake,
blood pressure, heart rate and also the psychological parameters of body image, self-concept
and anxiety in relation to body cathexis.
See also: Styles: Social

**Plastino, Janice Gudde,
Ph. D. (1977)**
*University of Southern
California, California*
Biomechanical
quantification of specific
ballet movements using
tri-axial cinematography
38/10-A, 5994   ORDER NO. Not Available
Available from: Diss. Abstracts International
An investigation of the mechanical properties
identified in certain ballet techniques. A comparison of the performces of intermediate and
professional dancers reveals several differences,
particulary based on age and flexibility. The
study concludes that technical ability is not
the only criterion for judgement of a dancer's
quality.
See also: Styles: Ballet

**Richardson, James Alexander, Jr,
Ed. D. (1978)**
University of Arkansas, Arkansas
Anxiety and energy expenditure in
modern dance
79 pp. 39/06-A, 3454   ORDER NO. 782,3293
Available from: Diss. Abstracts International
A study of the energy expenditure of females
while performing modern dance and the
changes in heart rate and oxygen uptake from
rehearsal to performance, with implications for
anxiety levels and work definitions.
See also: Styles: Modern

Sweigard, Lulu E, Ph.D. (1939)
New York University, New York
Bilateral asymmetry in the alignment of
the skeletal framework of the human
body
196 pp.   ORDER NO. AAC 7303449
Available from: New York University
This study in posture produces reliable data
on the alignment of the skeletal structure and
points to other research needed to substantiate
or to redirect procedure in the alleviation of
postural difficulties. The study discovers some
of the bilateral asymmetries in the alignment
of the skeletal framework and the extent to
which these asymmetries tend to occur
together.

Styles: Ballet

Allen, William T., Ph.D (1954)
University of Rochester, New York
"Ballet: 'La Belle Dame Sans Merci' "
185 pp.
Available from: University of Rochester
Abstract not available.

Bacon, Camille Howard, Ph. D. (1982)
University of California at Berkeley, California.
Shakespeare into dance: The ballet of "Romeo and Juliet"
185 pp. 43/08-A, 2498   ORDER NO. 830,0421
Available from: Diss. Abstracts International
This study focuses on three stagings of the ballet "Romeo and Juliet" (Galeotti's, Lavrovsky's, and Tudor's) and compares them with performances of "Romeo and Juliet" as a drama on the English stage in the eighteenth, nineteenth, and twentieth centuries. The ballets chosen define dance tradition at a given period and reflect the aesthetic theories and tastes of their choreographers. The study uses contemporary reports, muscial scores, stage plans, production pictures, journal entries, and the recorded memories of the performing and producing artists.
See also: Choreography and Performance, Related Arts: Theatre

Brown, Glenda Jean, Ph. D. (1977)
University of Illinois at Urbana-Champaign, Illinois
Modes of aesthetic experience in the ballet de cour, 1581–1650
243 pp. 34/12-A, 7738   ORDER NO. 74-11,956
Available from: Diss. Abstracts International
An exposition of the different elements which make up the ballet de cour and an analysis of the structural patterns and modes which permit combinations of these elements within any given ballet. Cohesiveness in these ballets is communicated by the languages of poetry, movement, and music and thus an aesthetic ritual is created

Chazin-Bennohum, Judith, Ph. D. (1981)
University of New Mexico, New Mexico
Livrets of ballet and pantomimes during the French Revolution
375 pp.
Available from: University of New Mexico
Abstract not available.
See also: History

Christopher, Luella Sue, Ph. D. (1979)
The American University, Washington D.C
Pirouettes with bayonets: Classical ballet metamorphosed as dance-drama and its usage in the People's Republic of China as a tool of political . . .
431 pp. 40/02-A, 1063   ORDER NO. 791,8507
Available from: Diss. Abstracts International
This study describes the abandonment of romantic ballet and the development of a revolutionary dance drama in the period of the Chinese Cultural Revolution in the mid-1960's and 70's. It is argued that this development is geared to inculcatiing Maosit percepts of egalitarianism and to encouraging cooperative efforts to build a self-reliant Communist system.
See also: History

Debold, Conrad II, Ph. D. (1982)
Emory University, Georgia
"Parade" and "Le Spectacle Interieur": The role of Jean Cocteau in an avant-garde ballet
253 pp. 43/07-A, 2139   ORDER NO. 822,1522
Available from: Diss. Abstracts International
This study's analysis of "Parade" focuses on Cocteau demonstrating how he infuses his personality and his poetic imagination into the characters he invents for the ballet—the Prestidigitateur Chinois, the Petite Fille Americaine, and the acrobats. Through an exploration of the meanings of these characters, this study shows how Cocteau invites the audience into his personalized world and backstage to discover the truth and mystery of "Parade's" spectacle interier.

Federico, Ronald Charles, Ph.D. (1968)
Northwestern University, Illinois
Ballet as an occupation
228 pp. 29/07-A, 2354   ORDER NO. 69-1828
Available from: Diss. Abstracts International
A sociological study of ballet as an artistic occupation based on a sample of 146 dancers employed in American ballet companies. It is found that most dancers are young, female, and unmarried. They come from upper middleclass families, urban environments, and typically have a 12th grade education. Occupational factors are discussed relative to economic resources, audience support, and competition with the other arts. It is concluded that ballet is unusual in that it is both physical and intellectual, an uncommon combination in American society.

Garafola, Lynn, Ph. D. (1985)
City University of New York, New York
Art and enterprise in Diahilev's Ballets Russes. (Volums I and II)
762 pp. 46/02-A, 301   ORDER NO. 850,8698
Available from: Diss. Abstracts International
A multidisciplinary study of a ballet troupe that between 1909 and 1929 moved the art of ballet from the periphery to the center of European cultural consciousness. It analyses this phenomenon in three ways—the alliance of ballet with major contemporary trends in music, painting and drama, the develoment of a self-sustaining financial base, and the creation of a new audience of socialites, intellectuals, and artistic taste makers.
See also: History

Garwood, Ronald Edward, Ph. D. (1985)
Stanford University, California
Moliere's 'comedies-ballets'
303 pp. 46/12-A, 3536   ORDER NO. 860,2474
Available from: Diss. Abstracts International
A scholarly analysis of Moliere's comedies-ballets using elements of dance and music as well as of literature. The study shows how Moliere creates new types of plays where 'total' entertainment and the interplay of the elements exists alongside the interplay of thematic elements to provide a communication genre on

several levels in which the inclusion of ballet is essential.
See also: Related Arts: Literature

Gintautiene, Kristina, Ph. D. (1984)
New York University, New York
"The Black Crook": Ballet in the gilded age (1866–1876)
233 pp. 45/08-A, 2284   ORDER NO. 842,1441
Available from: Diss. Abstracts International
This study describes and analyzes the extravaganza ballet "The Black Crook," which was produced in New York in 1866 signaling ballet's return to prominence in the post-Romantic period of dance history. To discern the production's uniqueness, five antecedent years of theatrical dance are analyzed and to determine it's influence, dance in the decade following "The Black Crook" is also investigated.
See also: History

Glasow, E. Thomas, Ph. D. (1985)
State University of New York, New York
Moliere, Lully, and the comedy-ballet
153 pp. 46/10-A, 2858   ORDER NO. 852,8258
Available from: Diss. Abstracts International
An historical and textual study of the artistic collaboration of Moliere, the dramatist, and Lully, the composer, between 1661 and 1971 when both men produced several comedy—ballets together. As a team they worked to combine music, comedy, and dance in original ways and their colloboration proved an important step in the evolution of French opera, despite their later conflict of interest and the eventual dissolution of the partnership.
See also: History, Related Arts: Opera

Hansen, Robert Craig, Ph. D. (1977)
University of Minnesota, Minnesota
Scenic and costume design for the Ballet Russes between 1909 and 1929
537 pp. 38/10-A, 5801   ORDER NO. 780,2673
Available from: Diss. Abstracts International
An examination of the stylistic revolution of scenic and costume design in the Ballets Russes reflecting the first two decades of artistic development of Western Europe. The study discusses the origins of the Ballets Russes, the introduction of Russian scenic and costume design, the era's avant-garde and new classicism, and the last years of the company. It

includes a chronological list of productions and designers.
See also: Choreography and Performance, History

Hoffer, Diane Lynn, Psy.D. (1981)
Nova University
The classical ballet dancer: A psyco-social analysis of the dance personality profile
212 pp. 43/10-B, 3364
Available from: Diss. Abstracts International
This study investigates and describes the personality profiles of professional classical ballet dancers in order to determine if there is a profile unique to this group of individuals. The specific psychological manifestations and personality characteristics as measured by tests and interviews, are seen to be the result of the dancers' unique socialization process, experiences, and personality dynamics.
See also: Psychology and Therapy

Johnston, Elizabeth Carrington, Ph.D. (1964)
Harvard University, Massachuetts
The English masque and the French court ballet, 1581–1640
Available from: Harvard University
Abstract not available.
See also: History

La Pointe, Janice McCaleb, Ph. D. (1980)
Texas Woman's University, Texas
Birth of a ballet: August Bournoville's "A Folk Tale," 1854
414 pp. 41/12-A, 4888   ORDER NO. 811,0522
Available from: Diss. Abstracts International
A discussion of "A Folk Tale," a ballet choreographed by Bournonville, from its inception in 1853 to the restaging by the choreographer in 1874. The process Bournonville used to write his libretto is discussed based upon folkloric and archival sources, previously published stories, and theatrical performances. Also

included are biographies of Bournonville and his two composers.
See also: Biography, Choreography and Performance

Lehman, Rhea H, Ph. D. (1986)
University of Wisconsin at Madison, Wisconsin
Virtue and virtuosity: America's vision of the romantic ballet, 1827–1840
320 pp. 47/08-A, 3245   ORDER NO. 861,4380
Available from: Diss. Abstracts International
This study examines thirteen years of intense ballet activity and growth during the age of Jackson. It describes the rapid succession of dance artists from abroad and the accompanying rapid audience development. Despite its success, ballet in America was subject to moral indignation and censure. This study interprets extant documents of the Romantic ballet as significant indices of American culture and includes an exploration of a gender ideology implicit in the Romantic mythology surrounding the ballet performances.
See also: History

Lindsey, Mort, Ed D. (1974)
Columbia University, New York
The composition, performance and analysis of an original musical work, "The Seven Ages of Man": A chamber ballet based on text by William Shakespeare
122 pp. 35/06-A, 3795   ORDER NO. 74-26,598
Available from: Diss. Abstracts International
This is an analysis and detailed discussion of the process of composing a chamber ballet. The composition is in seven movements and utilizes the departments of music, theater arts, and dance in an integrated performance. The work combines with poetry and dance and expresses through musical styles and moods the seven stages of life in Shakespeare's "As You Like it." The ballet is choreographed in contemporary style and the complete work is performed by a narrator, one dancer, and a chamber orchestra consisting of seven players and a conductor.
See also: Choreography and Performance, Related Arts: Theatre

Nosse, Carl Eugene, D. Mus. (1973)
Florida State University, Florida
"Richard Cory" (original ballet)
124 pp. 35/02-A, 1146   ORDER NO. 74-18,018
Available from: Diss. Abstracts International
A description of "Richard Cory," an orginal
ballet portraying a man who has separate personalities. It is based on a poem of the same
name written by Edward Arlington Robinson.
Instrumentation, narrative, and harmonies are
integrated with the development of the poem's
motives.
See also: Choreography and Performance

**Palmiotto, Carol Elaine; Wilson,
Kristine Lee, Ed.D (1984)**
*United States International University/
School of Performing Arts, California*
An historical account of the United
States tours of the Royal Ballet of Great
Britain from 1949–1970
373 pp. 45/05-A, 1241   ORDER NO. 841,7510
Available from: Diss. Abstracts International
A study of the nature and characteristics of
the Royal Ballet of Great Britain during the
1949–1970 tours of the United States. The
areas of investigation include the conditions
in Great Britain before the company was
formed and during the initiation of tours, the
conditions during the American tours, and the
nature of operating decisions pertaining to
artistic performances, logistical support, and
financial control. Key thematic data is supported by direct quotations and a summary of
information from interviewees is included. It
is found that success is due to personalities such
as Ninette de Valois and Sol Hurok while the
decline of the tours is ascribed to union inter-
ference.
See also: Administration

Raskind, Lisa Bonoff, Ph. D. (1983)
*University of California at Los Angeles,
California*
A magical flight: A study of religious
symbolism in the romantic ballet
337 pp. 45/01-A, 211   ORDER NO. 840,9231
Available from: Diss. Abstracts International
An investigation of the response elicited by
the romantic ballet through a symbolic analysis
of the major ballets presented at the Paris
Opera Theatre from 1820-1845. A compar-
ision of romantic symbolism with similar

expressions is religious settings reveals the religious nature of romantic expression, and the
relation of symbolic and social change to the
religious dimension of human life.
See also: Theory and Philosophy

Ries, Frank W. D, Ph. D. (1980)
Indiana University, Indiana
Jean Cocteau and the ballet
371 pp. 41/03-A, 852   ORDER NO. 802,0037
Available from: Diss. Abstracts International
A discussion and analysis of Cocteau's involvement with balletic compositions between 1912
and 1959. It includes an investigation of his
own writings, the writings of his contempories,
and the observations of the dancers, musicians,
and artists involved in each ballet. The creation and performance of the ballets is dealt
with in chronological order and the organization includes discussion of the influence of
each ballet on later dance compositions.
See also: Biography, Choreography and Performance

**Shell, Caroline Goodrich, Ph. D.
(1980)**
Texas Woman's University, Texas
The concepts and practices of
elementary pointe technique level
students
41/08-A, 3481   ORDER NO. 810,4351
Available from: Diss. Abstracts International
A description of a handbook on elementary
pointe technique at the college level. The
instructional materials are based on the physical and technical needs of student and teacher
and are offered as a alternative to the content
of tradtional ballet manuals.

Swift, Mary Grace, Ph.D. (1967)
University of Notre Dame, Indiana
The art of dance in the USSR: A study
of politics, ideology, and culture
509 pp. 28/10-A, 4069   ORDER NO. 68-4086
Available from: Diss. Abstracts International
A history of the art of ballet in Russia during
the Soviet period; from the Russian Revolution
until the 1960's. The influence of communist
doctrine on all the arts is discussed with particular attention given to the ballet. Despite Party
propaganda and controls, vast facilities for
amateur ballet and folk dance exist in the

USSR while Soviet ballet has achieved world fame through cultural-exchange tours.
See also: History

Styles: Jazz

Walsh, John J, Ph.D. (1954)
Yale University, Connecticut
Ballet of the Jesuit in Italy, Germany, and France
185 pp.
Available from: Yale University
Abstract not available.

Wiles, Patricia Joyce Wade, Ph.D. (1988)
Texas Tech University, Texas
A study of "Job, a Masque for Dancing" by Ralph Vaughan Williams
352 pp. 50/02-A, 300   ORDER NO. 8908533
Available from: Diss. Abstracts International
This study describes the unusual synthesis of music, dance, and stage design in the production of "Job, a Masque for Dancing," a ballet based on William Blake's engravings in the "Book of Job." An overview of the English masque and the dance world of the 1920's provides historical and contemporary background. Gestural and visual elements of Blake's illustrations are explored as sources of inspiration for Williams' score and de Valois' choreography. Both the music and choreography are extensively analyzed and illustrated with a focus on the interrelatedness of the syncretic texts.
See also: Music and Rhythm

Woodbury, Virginia Garton, Ed. D. (1985)
Temple University, Pennsylvania
Ballet as a special case of dance: Implications for program development
159 pp. 46/08-A, 2186   ORDER NO. 852,1166
Available from: Diss. Abstracts International
This study proposes that dance is a discrete field of physical activity constrained by form and rules. Classical ballet is examined as a special case of dance and five theoretical propositons are presented which account for a means of identifying steps and poses as being balletic. Training and performance in ballet monitor the propositions in a practical sense.
See also: Theory and Philosophy.

Begho, Felix O, Ph. D. (1985)
New York University, New York
Black dance continuum: Reflections on the heritage connection between African dance and Afro-American jazz dance
731 pp. 46/03-A, 540   ORDER NO. 851,0749
Available from: Diss. Abstract International
This study examines Afro-American jazz dance and its relation of jazz music. It identifies the African heritage of jazz dance and associative developments in changing socio-political conditions from slavery to the present. The alliance of dance and music is examined against the background conditions of Afro-Americans and Nigerians as Africans.
See also: History, Ethnology and Anthropology, Music and Rhythm

Fortunato, Joanne Alba, Ph. D. (1974)
University of Southern California, California
Major influences affecting the development of jazz dance, 1950–1971
212 pp. 34/11-A, 7024   ORDER NO. 74-11,687
Available from: Diss. Abstracts International
An examination and analysis of the contributions of teachers, performers, and choreographers to the development of jazz dance from 1950 to 1971. Twenty subjects are identified and interviewed concerning terminology, definitions, performance, training, and the function and purpose of jazz dance in American entertainment. It is found that jazz developed from dance halls to classes and concerts in schools, universities, and theatres all over America and is one of America's contributions to the arts.
See also: History

Styles: Modern

Beiswanger, Barbara Alice, Ph.D. (1944)
New York University, New York
The ideational sources of the modern dance in America as expressed in the works of two leading exponents, Isadora Duncan and Ruth St. Denis
Available from: New York University
Abstract not available.
See also: History

Brusstar, Lorna Terry, Ph. D. (1978)
Texas Woman's University, Texas
Designing and constructing costumes for modern dance
218 pp. 40/01-A, 03   ORDER NO. 791,5867
Available from: Diss. Abstract International
This study provides instructive materials for the college student, instructor, or choreographer in designing and constructing costumes for modern dance. It covers basic design skills, costume sketching, use of color, fabric selection, fitting, drafting patterns, dyeing, and redesigning tights and leotards.
See also: Choreography and Performance

Fitzgerald, Lynne E, Ed. D. (1984)
Temple University, Philadelphia
Breath: Principles derived from Eastern and Western literature and suggestions for its use in modern dance
153 pp. 45/07-A, 2038   ORDER NO. 841,9812
Available from: Diss. Abstracts International
This study derives breath principles and makes suggestions for the use of these in modern dance. A survey of eastern and western literature identifies the understandings and uses of breath in the somatic disciplines of Hatha Yoga, T'ai Ch'i Ch'uan, Karate, Bioenergetics, and the Alexander Technique. Three breath relationships are presented: breath-energy, breath-body, and breath-movement. Breath principles are used as a basis for suggestions for modern dance so that a full level of expression in dance is restored.
See also: Science

Kerr, Julie Ann, Ed. D. (1990)
Temple University, Pennsylvania
Parallels of African-based movement traits and aesthetic principles in selected examples of American modern dance
274 pp. 51/08-A, 2549   ORDER NO. 91-00298
Available from: Diss. Abstract International
This study provides a perspective on the interrelatedness between West African dance and American modern dance. Historical developments and anthropological theory provide the basis for illuminating the parallels between the dance forms. It is suggested that modern dance history be reexamined in terms of its movement vocabulary and aesthetic criteria.
See also: Ethnology and Anthropology

Little, Araminta Anne, Ph.D. (1966)
University of Southern California, California
Concepts related to the development of creativity in modern dance
215 pp.   ORDER NO. 66-5486
Available from: Diss. Abstracts International
This study investigates specific concepts pertaining to the creative person, process, product, and environment in modern dance. Subjects are college women in beginning modern dance classes who experience two different learning environments—freedom and conformity. It is found that creativity can be developed in modern dance in terms of the person, process, and product; but that the nature and extent of the development is dependent on the environment. The results are used to determine creative potential and to formulate high and low groups for composition work.

Lundahl, Vera L, Ph. D. (1983)
Texas Woman's University, Texas
Compositional form in modern dance and modern art

190 pp. 45/02-A, 326   ORDER NO. 840,9211
Available from: Diss. Abstracts International
A comparison of the attributes of compositional form in modern dance and modern art works from 1900 to 1983 to determine their interrelatedness. Photographs of art pieces from modern sculpture, painting, and modern dance are compared and analyzed in terms of line/shape, rhythm, light, and dynamics. Interrelationships are identified and the common denominator in artistic philosohphy is seemed to be related to the expression of the inner self.
See also: Theory and Philosophy, History, Related Arts: Visual

Moss, Susan F, Ph.D. (1988)
New York University, New York
Spinning through the weltanschauung: The effects of the Nazi regime on the German modern dance

378 pp. 50/01-A,   ORDER NO. 8910641
Available from: Diss. Abstracts International
This study probes the position of modern dance in Nazi Germany by examining the cultural trends that contributed to its popularity. Interviews with dancers who worked or studied in Germany during the twenties and thirties are used to corroborate information found in the literature of this period. It presents evidence of the political influence on modern dancers and the ambivalent relationship between modern trends in the arts and National Socialistic ideology.
See also: History

Van Dyke, Jan Ellen, Ed. D. (1989)
University of North Carolina, North Carolina
Modern dance in a postmodern world
239 pp. 50/11-A, 3472   ORDER NO. 900,8334
Available from: Diss. Abstracts International
This study defines a modern dance point of view through the work of early, seminal dance artists and then describes ways in which important social forces have shaped the form in the years since 1965. Special attention is paid to the polices of the National Endowment for the Arts for its influence on the art, including its impact on other sources of funding and on the organization of dance companies.
See also: Administration

Wheeler, Mark Frederick, Ph. D. (1984)
Ohio State University, Ohio
Surface to essence: Appropriation of the Orient by modern dance
320 pp. 45/06-A, 1836   ORDER NO. 841,9033
Available from: Diss. Abstracts International
A historical and philosophical study of the influence of the Orient on the evolution of modern dance from Isoadora Duncan's naturalsim to the circle dances of Deborah Hay and contemporary modern dance and ballet of the 1980's. Major choreographers and dancers who contributed to the West's increased understanding of the East include Ruth St Denis, Martha Graham, Merce Cunningham, and Erick Hawkins.
See also: History, Theory and Philosophy

Styles: Social

Calabria, Frank Michael, Ph.D. (1956)
New York University, New York
Sociometric group structure and improvement of social dancing skill in recreation groups
266 pp.   ORDER NO. AAC0020275
Available from: LD 3907
This study examines how giving different sanctions for interaction affect the group structure and improvement of social dancing skill of group members in three groups—a Psyche group, a Socio group, and a Control group.

The groups make sociometric choices and their social dancing skills are evaluated by judges using a social dancing skills rating scale. Quantitative and qualitative findings are related to a new frame of performance, sociokinesis, and movement in the social processing of recreation groups.
See also: Psychology and Therapy

Fellom, Martie, Ph. D. (1985)
New York University, New York
The Skirt Dance: A dance fad of the 1890's
253 pp. 47/01-A, 21   ORDER NO. 860,4051
Available from: Diss. Abstracts International
A chronicle of the development of the Skirt Dance which originated at the Gaiety Theatre in London from the 1870's through to the turn of the century. It describes the originator, John D'Auban, the steps of the dance, the costume, Gaiety Dancing, and the dancing careers of selected Skirt Dancers. It concludes with a discussion of the dance as a fad in the ballroom, drawing room, and dancing academies.
See also: History

Malnig, Julie M, Ph. D. (1987)
New York University, New York
Exhibition ballroom dance and popular entertainment
365 pp. 48/07-A, 1586   ORDER NO. 8722767
Available from: Diss. Abstracts International
This study examines the influential role played by exhibition ballroom dance teams in the cabaret, vaudeville, and the musical theatre of the teens and early twenties. These peredominantly male-female teams transformed contemporary social dances into theatrical and often flamboyant presentations. The study explores the background, changing patterns, new styles, techniques, and the professional development of the teams and concludes with a discussion of the decline of exhibition ballroom dance as a performance speciality.

Reichart, Sarah Bennett, Ph. D. (1984)
City University of New York, New York
The influence of eighteenth-century social dance on the Viennese classical style
415 pp. 45/11-A, 3236   ORDER NO. 850,1166
Available from: Diss. Abstracts International

This study demonstrates how elements of popular social dances of the eighteenth century (polonaise, menuet, French contredances, and English and German country dances) are incorporated into the art of music of the Viennese classical composers. It shows that this practice was pervasive and confirms intentionality on the part of the composer. The writings of dancing masters, theorists, composers, and performers are consulted to verify the use of dances as a compositional framework and to affirm that composers aimed to please.
See also: History, Music and Rhythm

Vedder, Clyde B, Ph.D. (1947)
University of Southern California, California
An analysis of the taxi-dance hall as a social institution with special reference to Los Angeles and Detroit
193 pp.
Available from: University of Southern California
Abstract not available.

Styles: Social (Square)

Oswalt, Helen Athera, Ed. D. (1976)
University of Arkansas, Arkansas
The relationship of specific aptitudes to ability in square dance
57 pp. 37/05-A, 2723   ORDER NO. 79-26,389
Available from: Diss. Abstracts International
A study of the multiplicity of the skills needed to square dance. Special aptitudes considered are the ability to follow directions, to recognize spatial relationships, to respond quickly and accurately, and to recognize rhythmic pattern. Correlations are made between males and females and between the aptitudes themselves.

Winslow, David John, Ph. D. (1972)
University of Pennsylvania, Pennsylvania
The rural square dance in the Northeastern United States: A continuity of tradition
312 pp. 33/05-A, 2262   ORDER NO. 72-25,688
Available from: Diss. Abstracts International
The continuity of the rural square dancing tradition is examined in Durkheim's terms of

the cohesive, revitalizing, and euphoric functions of ritual. The square dance was and is a complex social situation which becomes more simplified and understandable when viewed in terms of ritual tradition, function, and meaning.
See also: Ethnology and Anthropology

Zasloff, Ira, Ed.D. (1944)
New York University, New York
Manual of square dancing
191 pp.
Available from: New York University
This study collects, classifies, and integrates square dance materials and arranges them into a manual. The calls for the dances are arranged in a double page spread so that by reading across, one finds the calls, the procedures, and the visual aids in the form of photographs of figures demonstrating the patterns and movements. There is a glossary of calls and synonymous calls coupled and an index to cross-check all material in the manual.
See also: Education

Styles: Tap

Willis, Cheryl M, Ed.D. (1991)
Temple University, Pennsylvania
Tap dance: Memories and issues of African-American women who performed between 1930 and 1950
Available from: Temple University
This study identifies selected African-American women rhythm tap dancers who lived or performed from the 1930's to the 1950's. The research focuses on the lives of these women as entertainers, their role and contributions in the dance form, and the aesthetic of tap dance. Brief biographies are included and the study traces the history of tap dance and parallels it with the African-American fight for equality in the United States. Gender issues are addressed and the study concludes by delineating the decline and resurgence of tap dance.
See also: Biography, History

Technology and Film

Brooks, Virginia Loring, Ph.D. (1981)
Columbia University, New York
The art and craft of filming dance as a Documentary
173 pp. 42/06-A, 2335   ORDER NO. 812,5258
Available from: Diss. Abstracts International
An analysis of the principles of film-making and visual perception that aid the documentation of the performance and choreography of dance. An attempt is made to isolate the specific aspects of the choreography and performance that must be preserved to perceive the dance in a similar way to a live performance. The study suggest ways the film-maker can compensate for differences between live dance and film and then analyzes some examples of problems and successes in transposing stage choreograpies to the screen.
See also: Choreography and Performance

Burton, Carolyn, Ed. D. (1977)
University of Georgia, Georgia
Influence of instruction media on attitudes of modern dance students toward movement
131 pp. 38/11-A, 6599   ORDER NO. 780,5986
Available from: Diss. Abstracts International
A study of the influence of instructional media on the attitudes of modern dance students towards movement. This method is compared with traditional lecture demonstrations. Neither method is found to significantly influence attitudinal changes.
See also: Psychology and Therapy, Styles: Modern

Butzel, Marcia, Ph. D. (1985)
University of Iowa, Iowa
Movement as cinematic narration: The concept and practice of choreography in film
363 pp. 46/06-A, 1423   ORDER NO. 851,8810
Available from: Diss. Abstracts International
This is a theoretical and critical study of concepts and practices of cinematic movement as choreography. Movement is redefined as choreographic ecriture and is considered in relation both to the authorial stratagems and the cultural practices that inflect film history. The

study considers the predominant notions about cinematic movement, the status of subject's mobility, and the practice of choreography as a source for understanding spectator's relationship to film images.
See also: Choreography and Performance

Charness, Caset, Ph. D. (1977)
New York University, New York
Hollywood Cine-Dance: A description of the interrelationship of camerawork and choreography in films by Stanley Donen and Gene Kelly
163 pp. 38/10-A, 5760   ORDER NO. 780,3006
Available from: Diss. Abstracts International
An examination of the interrelationship between camera and dancer in the creation of dance for the commercial film musical screen. An historical overview of the Hollywood choreographer's craft precedes the study itself, which demonstrates that not until the collaboration of Stanley Donen and Gene Kelly was the Hollywood cine-dance born.
See also: Choreography and Performance

Cobb, Hazel Louanne, Ph. D. (1977)
Texas Woman's University, Texas
A delineation of three major sources of artistic output on the production of dance art films
207 pp. 38/09-A, 5096   ORDER NO. 780,1750
Available from: Diss. Abstracts International
A description of the relationship among threee major sources of creative output during the production of dance art films: the film maker, the choreographer, and the camera operator. These roles are defined, differentiated, and compared. Each is experienced differently and can be delineated in terms of a choreographic point of view, approach, and method.
See also: Choreography and Performance.

Ellis, Margaret, Ph.D. (1973)
University of Iowa, Iowa
Film Series: Movement education for young children
138 pp. 35/02-A, 868   ORDER NO. 74-16,615
Available from: Diss. Abstracts International
This study describes the construction and production of a series of two movie films about selected aspects of movement education for kindergarten children. An evaluation of the films by teachers indicate that they were effec-

tive teaching devises. The films are titled "Moving and Learning" and "Guiding Movement Experiences".
See also: Children, Education

Gargaro, Kenneth Vance, Ph. D. (1979)
University of Pittsburgh, Pennsylvania
The work of Bob Fosse and the choreographer-directors in the translation of musicals to the screen
219 pp. 41/01-A, 24   ORDER NO. 80-15,303
Available from: Diss. Abstracts International
This study explores the relationship of musical theatre and film as exemplified by Bob Fosse's successful attempts to make the tansition from one medium to the other. Fosse's personal approach is discussed as he sets the standard to which all musical adaptions are compared. The inquiry concludes that it is possible to translate a musical to the screen and retain theatrical vitality.
See also: Styles: Jazz, Choreography and Performance

Lorber, Richard, Ed. D. (1977)
Columbia University Teachers College, New York
Videodance. (Dancing presented on T.V)
173 pp. 38/01-A, 6   ORDER NO. 77-14,739
Available from: Diss. Abstracts International
An exploration of the problems and aesthetic possibilities in the areas of television translation of pre-existing dance and experimental collaboration in the creation of hybrid videodance. After a synoptic overview, the study explores the expressive potential for choreographers and visual artists and then discusses the work of Doris Chase, Jeffrey Bush, and Amy Greenfield. A critical analysis of dance on television from the 1940's to the "Dance in America" television series is included.
See also: Choreography and Performance

Mozafarian, Darius Masoud, Ph. D. (1974)
University of Southern California, California
A creative synthesis of dance and video-electronics: An exploratory investigation
223 pp. 35/04-A, 2037   ORDER NO. 74-21,493
Available from: Diss. Abstracts International
An investigation of the possibility of creatively synthesizing dance and video. Included is a list of criteria and a subsequent production of a videodance tape. An evaluation is conducted, the results of which indicate that the tape is a relatively successful creative synthesis of the two media.

Norwood, Louanne Cobb, Ph. D. (1977)
Texas Woman's University, Texas
A delineation of tree major sources of artistic output in the production of dance art films
207 pp.
Available from: Texas Woman's University Abstract not Available.

Penney, Phyllis Annette, Ed.D. (1981)
University of North Carolina at Greensboro, North Carolina
Ballet and modern dance on television in the decade of the 70's
221 pp. 42/12-A, 4962   ORDER NO. 821,0367
Available from: Diss. Abstracts International
A descriptive chronology of dance programs aired on commercial, public and cable television networks during the 1970's followed by a characterization of the form and content of dance programs of this period. The chronology reveals continuity, innovation, and collaboration, culminating in a new art form—video-dance.

Theory and Philosophy

Alter, Judith Lenore Berkenbilt, Ed. D. (1980)
Harvard University, Massachusetts
An examination of the methods and problems of dance theory written between 1930 and 1971
234 pp. 40/12-A, 6045   ORDER NO. 801,3895
Available from: Diss. Abstracts International
An analysis of the adequacy of the content and method of comprehensive dance theory written by dance theorists and aestheticians between 1930 and 1971. The analysis includes an examination of the choice and clarity of the terms used to explain dance and a recognition that dance theorists John Martin, Elizabeth Seldon and Margaret H' Doubler are influenced by aestheticians such as Collingwood, Langer, and Nelson Goodman. A Framework of Topics for Dance is formulated for the purpose of analyzing the relevant theoretical literature.

Bamossy, Gary Joseph, Ph. D. (1983)
University of Utah, Utah
An investigation of aesthetic judgement ability and art patronage behavior by adolescents
266 pp. 44/02-A, 1188   ORDER NO. 831,9366
Available from: Diss. Abstracts International
This research examines sociological and psychological factors influencing the development of aesthetic judgement skills and attitudes towards the arts of painting and dance, patronage intentions and actual patronage behavior of adolescents. A model to study the aquisition of aesthetic judgement and patronage behavior is proposed and tested. Results suggest that social class and gender are the key determinates of arts related experiences.
See also: Psychology and Therapy

Bloch, Alice, Ed.D. (1991)

Temple University, Pennsylvania
Isadora Duncan and Vaslav Nijinsky: Dancing on the brink
Available from: Temple University
An examination of the art and lives of Isadora Duncan and Vaslav Nijinski as a means of exploring dance as facilitator and indicator of the role of the body in cultural transformation. The artists are chosen because they are recognized as revolutionaries and part of the revitalization of the art of dance in the early twentieth century. They are seen as intrinsic to understanding how dance manifests and influences the cultural construction and individual experience of the body.
See also: Biography

Blumenfeld-Jones, Donald S, Ed. D. (1990)

University of North Carolina at Greensboro, North Carolina
Body pleasure, language and world: A framework for the critical analysis of dance education
206 pp.
Available from: University of North Carolina at Greensboro
A philosophical analysis of the language of dance education and the relation between language and body understanding. Language is related to the formation of consciousness and is categorized as metaphorical. The dance education texts of Margaret H'Doubler and Alma Hawkins are analyzed and a position is taken that we learn to become bodies. The author's dance experience of becoming a dance body, negotiating meanings with teachers, choreographers, and audiences, is described.
See also: Education

Braxton, Jean Patricia Bailey, Ed. D. (1984)

University of North Carolina, North Carolina
Movement experience in modern dance: A phenomenological inquiry
110 pp. 45/05-A, 1332   ORDER NO. 841,7879
Available from: Diss. Abstracts International
The movement phenomenon in modern dance is studied from the viewpoint of experience using phenomenology as the research approach. The study focuses on how students make meaning out of the dance movement experience. Six common themes emerge-kinesthetic awareness, feelings, sense of self, concentration, use of imagery, and direction. The study also reveals that reflection is important to a dancer's understanding of dance.
See also: Styles: Modern

Duffy, Alice Marie, Ph. D. (1972)

University of Southern California, California
Projection in dance
113 pp. 33/02-A, 604   ORDER NO. 72-21,666
Available from: Diss. Abstracts International
A description of the phenomenon of projection of dance as art as experienced subjectively by an audience member. This study involves the clarification and identification of projection in relational modes such as sequentiality, spontaneity, reciprocity, and cumulativeness. The essence of the projection experience is construed as the generation of change.

Foster, Susan Leigh, Ph. D. (1981)

University of California at Santa Cruz, California
Reading dancing: Gestures towards a semiotics of dance
252 pp. 43/06-A, 1729   ORDER NO. 822,6316
Available from: Diss. Abstracts International
Using methodologies adapted from structuralist and post-structuralist criticism, this study develops a theory of dance literacy based on an analysis of dance movement as sign. Four paradigms for choreographic organization in Western theatre dance are presented. Corresponding to these paradigms are four distinct roles for choreographer and dancer, and four sets of responsibilities for the dance viewer. Reading is presented as a technique for examining dance as a construction of signs.
See also: Choreography and Performance

Fowler, Sarah B, Ph. D. (1987)

Temple University, Pennsylvania
Unspeakable practices: Meaning and kinesis in dance
212 pp. 48/04-A, 938   ORDER NO. 871,6372
Available from: Diss. Abstracts International
This study shows how kinesthetic understanding can bring dancers, choreographers, and critics to a point of intersection where they can experience and discuss dance in terms of

its kinesthetic basis. The analysis draws upon the case study of Alexander Technique and the philosophical work of Maurice Merleau-Ponty.
See also: Psychology and Therapy

Franko, Mark, Ph. D. (1981)
Columbia University, New York
An intertextual model for the interaction of dancer and spectator in the Renaissance
122 pp. 42/09-A, 4022   ORDER NO. 820,4482
Available from: Diss. Abstracts International
This study discusses the theoretical link between dance and silent oratory, claiming that the ends of oratorical action are the same as those of the dance. It also demonstrates that dance and social behavior are not discontinuous during the Renaissance and examines the poses and movement of the basse dance to illustrate the interrelationship. Speech, silence, and audience interaction are also discussed within the context of Aristotle's extralinguistic rhetorical proofs.
See also: History

Friesen, Joanna, Ph.D. (1977)
Florida State University, Florida
A comparative analysis of "Othello" and "The Moor's Pavanne:" An Aristotelian approach to dances based on dramatic literature
269 pp. 38/12-A, 7026   ORDER NO. 780,8949
Available from: Diss. Abstracts International
An examination of Aristotle's theory of tragedy as a critical instrument for analyzing dances based on dramatic literature. The study concludes that this theory is appropriate and helps identify the factors of clarity and success in a dance based on dramatic literature. "Othello" and "The Moor's Pavane" are used as illustrations.
See also: Related Arts: Theatre

Gibbons, Ruth Elizabeth Goodling, Ph. D. (1989)
Texas Woman's University, Texas
A prismatic approach to the analysis if style in dance
237 pp. 50/11-A, 3390   ORDER NO. 900,8519
Available from: Diss. Abstracts International
This study describes a theoretical framework and conceptual model for the definition of style

in Western theatrical dance and accounts for the various components that contribute to the unique character of a dance event. A three-dimensional model is applied to an analysis of Jose Limon's "The Moor's Pavane".
See also: Choreography and Performance

Herthel, Thomas Barnes, Ph.D (1966)
Cornell University, New York
John Martin, dance critic: A study of his critical method in the dance as theatre art
320 pp. 27/05-A, 1464   ORDER NO. 66-10,254
Available from: Diss. Abstracts International
This study analyzes the critical principles of John Martin, the first professional dance critic. An examination of his critical method reveals insight into the total area of theatre as well as into the art of the dance. It focuses on the choreographic aspect of Western heritage ballet, modern dance, and German expressional dance. His critical method is based on the elements of form, substance, and content and the notion that theatre dance is subject to the principles of theatre art.
See also: Biography, Choreography and Performance

Hitchcock, Ned II, Ph. D. (1973)
Case Western Reserve, Ohio
Dancing ground: An approach to the criticism of the modern dance
104 pp. 34/01-A, 446   ORDER NO. 73-16,131
Available from: Diss. Abstracts International
This study develops a critical approach to the discussion of modern dance by relating three areas of concern to modern dancers—technique, theatricality, and aspirations—to the process of mythical thinking. The critical approach is influenced by the works of Martha Graham and Eric Hawkins.
See also: Styles: Modern, Choreography and Performance

Hottendorf, Diane, Ph. D. (1976)
University of Southern California, California
Criticism in the art of dance: An analysis of John Martin's reviews in the "New York Times", 1928–1962
37/09-A, 5442
Available from: Diss. Abstracts International

This study analyzes and compares the content of the Sunday feature articles, written by John Martin, from 1928–1962, when he was dance critic for the "New York Times." Martin, it is found, maintains a relatively consistent pattern of behavior concerning the primary critical functions he performs—reporting, educating, judging, and crusading.

Howe, Dianne Sheldon, Ph. D. (1985)
University of Wisconsin at Madison, Wisconsin
Manifestations of the German expressionist aesthetic as presented in drama and art in the dance and writings of Mary Wigman
244 pp. 46/07-A, 1762   ORDER NO. 852,0216
Available from: Diss. Abstracts International
This investigation clarifies the relationship between Mary Wigman and German Expressionism by examining the similarities of Wigman's work and philosophy as explained in her writings and as observed in film to the German expressionist aesthetic in drama and art. It includes the precursors to expressionism, a biographical sketch of Wigman, definitions of Expressionism, and a thorough examination of Wigman's works.
See also: Biography

Humphrey, Nicolas S, Ph. D. (1987)
John Hopkins University, Maryland
Heinrich Heine and Friedrich Nietzsche: Dance as metaphor and rhetorical imagery
401 pp. 47/12-A, 4401   ORDER NO. 870,7261
Available from: Diss. Abstracts International
This study addresses dance as metaphor and rhetorical imagery in nine selected works of Heinrich Heine and Friedrich Neitzsche. Through the dancing characters in their works, these writers fuse style and content to create unique forms of non-verbal communication. This study describes dance as an emblem by explaining the evolution of the metaphors and examining the physical rhetoric of dance.
See also: Related Arts: Literature

Johnson, Nancy Diers, Ed .D. (1981)
University of North Carolina at Greensboro, North Carolina
Two perceptions of the purposes, aesthetic concepts and background for writing dance criticism according to selected literature and Washington, D.C. dance critics
124 pp. 42/03-A, 1046   ORDER NO. 811,8776
Available from: Diss. Abstracts International
A description of the components of dance criticism, the aesthetic concepts guiding the viewing of dance performances, and certain aspects of education, training or experience needed to write dance criticism. Data is derived from a search of literature and from focused interviews of recognized dance critics. A pilot study tests the effectiveness of the interview schedule and format and a synopsis of the information obtained is the basis for the conclusions.

Kaprelian, Mary Haberkorn, Ph.D. (1969)
University of Wisconsin at Madison, Wisconsin
A comparison of two aesthetic theories as they apply to modern dance
173 pp. 31/03-A, 1164   ORDER NO. 70,3574
Available from: Diss. Abstracts Internaional
This study examines the art of dance as a medium for expression and communication in the light of a critical comparison and evaluation of two popular aesthetic theories—formalism and expressionism. It is found that both theories support the idea that the dance art is an expression of feeling, but there is disagreement among aestheticians regarding dance as a medium for communication.
See also: Styles; Modern

Kim, Malborg, Ph. D. (1986)
University of Wisconsin at Madison, Wisconsin
On expression and its artistic meaning in dance
214 pp. 47/09-A, 3356   ORDER NO. 862,1912
Available from: Diss. Abstracts International
In this study, movement is regarded as the medium of artistic expression in order to discern how its expressiveness is achieved and with which mechanisms meaningful dance expression is made possible. It is shown how

certain theories of dance (expression theory of John Martin and Margaret H'Doubler) share the same hypotheses and flaws as the expression theory of art. A general discussion on the nature of aesthetic and scientific theories is presented and a movement-oriented theory of dance is proposed.

Koritz, Amy E, Ph. D. (1988)
University of North Carolina, North Carolina
Gendering bodies, performing art: Theatrical dancing and the performance aesthetics of Wilde, Shaw and Yeats
169 pp. 50/03-A, 691   ORDER NO. 891,442
Available from: Diss. Abstracts International
This study integrates literary, critical, and theatrical treatments of dance within a feminist and materialsitic theoretical framework. The discussion analyses how and why writers Wilde, Shaw, and Yeats were engaged along with the dancers, in theorizing and enacting new performance practices at the turn of the century.
See also: Related Arts: Literature, History

Lazarus, J. A. Abbiechild, Ph. D. (1987)
Texas Woman's University, Texas
Contemporary dance and a feminist aesthetic
211 pp. 48/10-A, 2647   ORDER NO. 872,9666
Available from: Diss. Abstracts International
This study describes an organismic model of the conceptual framework of a feminist aesthetic for contemporary dance. The aesthetic reflects the underlying ways of thinking/perceiving/being inherent in the futuristic view of feminism and the creative process of dance making. The model reflects the belief that dance making and dance learning provide an ideal site for the expression of feminist ideology and as such can serve as a pedagogical as well as an art making aesthetic.

Levi, Bruce Alan, Ph. D. (1978)
Duquesne University, Iowa
The coherence of gestures in improvisational dance: An empirical exploratory study informed by Merleau-Ponty's phenomenological ontology
420 pp. 39/04-B, 1935   ORDER NO. 781,8565

Available from: Diss. Abstracts International
A description and analysis of the coherence of gestures in the dances of couples improvising to different musical segments. Merleau-Ponty's ontology for interpreting intercorporeality is employed and described and the significance of findings for research in nonverbal communication is also discussed.

Lively-Berger, Rosalind Calvert, Ed. D. (1983)
University of North Carolina at Greensboro, North Carolina
Relationships among interpretations of modern dance and cultural background
150 pp. 44/03-A, 612   ORDER NO. 831,5646
Available from: Diss. Abstracts International
An examination of the perceptions of three different dance stimuli by three cultural groups. A semantic differential serves as the technique for interpreting the perceptions of filmed presentations of modern dances by a group of Africans, Americans, and Asians. Results show that factors relating to individuals' perceptions of modern dance are not easily explained by culture, gender, education, experience, or title.

Maletic, Vera, Ph. D. (1980)
Ohio State University, Ohio
On the aisthetic and aesthetic dimensions of the dance: A methodology for researching dance style
200 pp. 41/10-A, 4211   ORDER NO. 810,7364
Available from: Diss. Abstracts International
A multidisciplinary investigation of dance style focusing on dance as a theatre art. Choreographic styles of Twyla Tharp and Dan Wagoner serve to exemplify the methodology. Findings show the significance of choreographic style as being more fundamental than is generally recognized and as representing several interlinked dimensions—aisthetic and aesthetic.
See also: Choreography and Performance

Mathieu, Louise, D.A. (1984)
New York University, New York
A phenomenological investigation of improvisation in music and dance
267 pp. 46/01-A, 14   ORDER NO. 850,5461
Available from: Diss. Abstracts International
A phenomenological analysis of the holistic nature of the process of improvisation of

selected dancers and musicians as soloists and as participants in music-dance duos. Each type of improvisation is described in its gestalt. Aspects of the process are clarified by Aron Gurwitsch's analysis of the field of consciousness and John Dewey's essential qualities of experience are revealed. The procedure shows that although spontaneous and immediate, the process of improvisation can be articulated.
See also: Music and Rhythm

Mead, Bernard Franklin, Jr, Ph. D. (1972)
University of Illinois at Urbana-Champaign, Illinois
A content analysis of modern dance values with application to recreation
155 pp. 34/02-B, 745   ORDER NO. 73-17,322
Available from: Diss. Abstracts International
An investigation of the nature of the fundamental differences in philosophical approach as reflected in the values of modern dance within higher education between 1930 and 1970 and the values of modern dance to recreation. The investigation concluded that modern dance be included in recreation programs.
See also: Styles: Modern

Phillips, Daniel Alvord, Ed. D. (1974)
University of North Carolina at Greensboro, North Carolina
The transposition of literary and rhetorical constructs to dance theory and choreography
185 pp. 35/02-A, 971   ORDER NO. 74-17,967
Available from: Diss. Abstracts International
An exploration of selected literary and rhetorical constructs as philosophical models for describing the aesthetic nature of dance, techniques of choreography, and the theory of choreography. The study is illustrated through Labanotation and pantomimic descriptions.
See also: Choreography and Performance

Powell, Rita Kirk, Ph. D. (1976)
Texas Woman's University, Texas
Cultural patterns as revealed by the content of selected dance magazines
203 pp. 37/07-A, 4215   ORDER NO. 77-759
Available from: Diss. Abstracts International
This study determines the relationship between content of selected dance magazines and certain cultural patterns indicated in the literature of social history. The magazines differ in emphasis but all of them reflect social and historical trends. magazines analysed are "Dance Digest," "Dance Magazine," "Dance News," and "Dance Observer."
See also: History

Powell, Suzanne Marilyn, Ph.D. (1969)
University of Southern California, California
Meaning in a dance form
119 pp. 30/07-A, 2836   ORDER NO. 70-361
Available from: Diss. Abstracts International
This investigation explores the potential of graphic representaiton as a way of calling attention to certain aspects of the 'total experience' of performing a specific folk dance. After studying students who had learned a polka, it is concluded that personal attempts to symbolize ideas and feelings into graphic forms is a potential meaningful experience which can serve to clarify, enrich, and intensify understandings or meanings found in other areas of human experience, and in particular the experience of dancing.
See also: Styles: Folk

Rio, Janice Andrea, Ph. D. (1981)
University of Nebraska- Lincoln, Nebraska
Contemporary aesthetic theory applied to dance as a performing art
198 pp. 42/03-A, 1186   ORDER NO. 811,8066
Available from: Diss. Abstracts International
This study discusses recent development in analytical philosophy that have made it possible to sketch a systematic account of dance as a performing art. Within this analytical framework, the logical nature of the criteria governing the use of the notion of dancing is worked out. Dance is also discussed as a language and it is argued that dance is a symbol system of a special art.

Sheets, Maxine L, Ph. D. (1963)
University of Wisconsin at Madison, Wisconsin
The phenomenology of dance
221 pp. 24/04-A, 1559   ORDER NO. 63-7674
Available from: Diss. Abstracts International
This descriptive study questions "What is dance?" and leads to implications for education in dance based on phenomenological analysis.

It explicates the nature of the illusion of force created by dance and includes the isolation and explanation of the phenomenological structures of time and space, the qualities of movement, the symbolic expressions, and the notions of abstraction and dynamics.

Sherlock, Joyce Inglis, Ph. D. (1988)
University of London, United Kingdom
The cultural production of dance in Britain, with particular reference to Ballet Rambert and Christopher Bruce's "Ghost Dances"
468 pp. 49/05-A, 981   ORDER NO. 82174
Available from: Diss. Abstracts International
An examination of the relationship of culture and ideology in dance study by critiquing British approaches from the perspective of cultural studies and postmodern culture. Procedures emphasize ethnographic approaches in a case-study of Ballet Rambert and Christopher Bruces' "Ghost Dances". Through a theoretical analysis of the relationship of culture and ideology it is recognised that theatre dance is a focus of study for cultural studies.
See also: Ethnology and Anthropology

Stevens-Jefcoate, Christine M, Ph. D. (1977)
University of Wisconsin at Madison, Wisconsin
Toward a structuralist approach to symbols in dance
206 pp. 38/11-A, 6370   ORDER NO. 780,2989
Available from: Diss. Abstracts International
This work presents an objective methodology for identifying and classifying dance symbols and it demonstrates the use of this methodology by applying it to two dances choreographed by Martha Graham—"Night Journey" and "Appalachian Spring." The study dissects certain observable dance symbols from the choreographic structure of the dances and classifies them according to a structuralist format. It also formulates questions and definitions which specify the structural requirements governing each symbol.
See also: Choreography and Performance

Taylor, Margaret Jane, Ph.D. (1989)
University of Alberta, Canada
Implicit knowledge of movement intelligence
50/12-A, 3889   ORDER NO. 056,7190
Available from: Diss. Abstracts International
This study analyzes declarative knowledge of skilled behavior by comparing the knowledges of library users, physical education majors, novice jazz dancers, and expert jazz dancers. The study finds that all groups believe that skilled behavior is characterized by grace, confidence, coordination, and rhythmical movement. Factor analysis and clustering techniques isolate the procedural knowledge component in the skilled data, whereas the metacognitive and affective domains interact.
See also: Styles: Jazz

Van Camp, Julie Charlotte, Ph. D. (1982)
Temple University, Philadelphia
Philosophical problems of dance criticism
288 pp. 42/12-A, 5153   ORDER NO. 82-10564
Available from: Diss. Abstracts International
This study addresses several philosophical problems concerning the object of criticism in dance. It identifies and analyzes such concerns as adequate definitions of dance, the primary and secondary media status of dance, notational systems, standards, and perceivability. The discussion maintains that basic to philosophical accuracy is understanding the art form as it is actually practiced and appreciated recognizing the unique use of human bodies as instruments.

Wallock, Susan Frieder, Ph. D. (1977)
United States International University/ School of Performing Arts, California
Dance/movement therapy: A survey of philosophy and practice
125 pp. 29–11B, 5598   ORDER NO. 790,9640
Available from: Diss. Abstracts International
An examination of the philosophy and practice of people working in the field of dance/movement therapy. Allowing for differences among the subjects, it is concluded that there are core commonalities, such as working holistically, beginning at the individual's level of

trust, and believing that changes at the movement level can produce changes in the psyche.
See also: Psychology and therapy

Welsh, Deborah Jane, Ed. D. (1984)
Syracuse University, New York
Symbolic expression in dance experience: Individuation and the sacred in three forms of dance
201 pp. 45/11-A, 3302   ORDER NO. 850,0774
Available from: Diss. Abstracts International
This study describes a theory of symbolic expression that includes the dimension of dance called grace, that is personally meaningful and unifies the dancer's energy from both inner psychic and outward worldly perspectives. There are two aspects to the theory—Carl Jung's individuation process and Mircea Eliade's theory of sacredness. The role of dance in the symbolic process is presented as evoking symbolism, enacting it, or being the symbol itself. The study shows that dance as symbolic expression leads toward unification, personal power, and grace.
See also: Psychology and Therapy

Williams, Drid, Ph. D. (1975)
Oxford University, England
The role of movement in selected symbolic systems
Available from: Oxford University
Abstract not available

Worthy, Terry Ellen, Ph. D. (1977)
Texas Woman's University, Texas
The creative thesis: Criteria for procedural development and evaluation
123 pp. 38/10-A, 5768   ORDER NO. 7801784
Available from: Diss. Abstracts International
The develpment of procedural criteria for producing, evaluating, and recording the creative dance thesis. Criteria for evaluating the choregraphic merit are rated essential, important, or desirable and four written evaluation instruments are constructed and presented.
See also: Choreography and Performance

Index by Author

Abrahams, Ruth Karen, 3
Acer, Charlotte Chase, 20
Adinku, William Ofotsu, 20
Adler, Reba Ann, 3
Akenson, James Edward, 20
Albig, Pegeen Horth, 46
Alcide, Marie-Jose, 34
Allanbrook, Wye Jamison, 75
Allen, Beverly Joyce, 63
Allen, Helen M, 21
Allen, William T., 81
Allison, Patrica Robinette, 63
Alter, Judith Lenore Berkenbilt, 91
Alves-Masters, Judy, 63
Amenta, Rosalyn Marie, 34
Andreasen, Lois E., 3
Andrews, Gladys, 21
Anthony, James Raymond, 54
Arnold, Nellie Doreen Webb, 8
Arnold, Stepanie Kevin, 10
Asai, Susan Miyo, 34
Ashton, Martha May Bush, 34
Atakpu, Benedict Ozengbe, 34
Ayob, Salmah, 21
Bacon, Camille Howard, 81
Baker, Mary Susan, 21
Ball, Wesley Allen, 21
Bamossy, Gary Joseph, 91
Bandem, I Made, 35
Banes, Sally R, 10
Barber, Beverly Anne Hillsman, 4
Barclay, Thomas Brian, 46
Barker, Barbara Mackin, 4
Barry, Thais Grace, 22
Bartee, Neale King, 54
Beal, Rayma Kirkpatrick, 63
Bealle, John Rufus, 35
Beck, Jill, 10
Becker, Theodore Jay, 78
Begho, Felix O, 85
Beiswanger, Barbara Alice, 86
Benison, Betty Bryant, 22
Benson, Norman Arthur, 54
Berg, Shelly Celia, 11
Bernstein, Penny Lewis, 63
Berrol, Cynthia Florence, 63
Bethune, Robert William, 76
Beveridge, Sandra Kay, 8
Bible-Federbush, Deborah Ann, 1
Blank, Judith, 35
Blatt, Arthur, 54

Bloch, Alice, 92
Bloom, Michael Paul, 35
Blumenfeld-Jones, Donald S, 92
Blumenthal, Paul Steven, 11
Boarman, Alice Marie, 64
Bonali, Gloria Ann, 4
Boorman, Joyce Lilian, 8
Boswell, Betty, Boni, 64
Bowman, Betty Ann, 22
Brandman, Russella, 46
Brauer, Lena, 22
Braxton, Jean Patricia Bailey, 92
Breazeale, Helene, 22
Brehm, Mary Ann, 22
Brennan, Mary Alice, 64
Brockmeyer, Grethchen A, 23
Brooks Schmitz, Nancy, 4
Brooks, Lynn Matluck, 46
Brooks, Virginia Loring, 89
Brown, Glenda Jean, 81
Brown, Ollie Mae Thomas, 9
Browne, Thomas J, 23
Browning, Gloria Seaman, 64
Brunoski, Elizabeth J, 4
Brusstar, Lorna Terry, 86
Buckley, Suzanne Shelton, 5
Buckman, Susan Donna, 46
Burdick, Dolores M. Plunk, 23
Burris, Maureen Smith, 78
Burton, Carolyn, 89
Bushey, Richard James, 1
Butzel, Marcia, 89
Byrum, Mary Carolyn, 11
Cabezas, Richard Edward, 23
Calabria, Frank Michael, 87
Calhoun, Miriam Eudora, 23
Callahan, Alice Anne, 35
Campbell, C. Jean Bailey, 77
Canty, Dean Robert, 54
Capy, Mara Myrtle, 64
Carlson, Richard George, 35
Carriere, Diane Louise, 11
Carter, Frances Helen, 64
Cashion, Susan Valerie, 35
Casten, Carole M. Sokolow, 1
Challender, James Winston, 11
Chambers, Vinton Blaine, 78
Charness, Caset, 90
Chatfield, Steven John, 78
Chazin-Bennohum, Judith, 81
Chin, Donna Lisa, 24

Chodorow, Joan, 65
Christopher, Luella Sue, 81
Chumbley, Joyce, 46
Clark, Sharon Leigh, 46
Clemente, Karen, 1
Clifford, Jacqueline Anne, 24
Cobb, Hazel Louanne, 90
Cocuzza, Ginnine, 5
Cohen, Barbara Naomi, 12
Cole, Ivy Lee, 65
Colley, Thomas, 47
Conroy, Mary, 24
Corey, Frederick Charles, 12
Costonis, Maureen Needham, 47
Cowan, Jane Kerin, 36
Cowan, Karen Lautenbach, 24
Cox, Rosann McLaughlin, 55
Craig, Jenifer Pashkowski, 47
Cravath, Paul Russel, 36
Crawford, John Richardson, 24
Croghan, Leland, 47
Culberston, Anne E., 47
Daniel, Yvonne Laverne Payne, 36
Daugherty, Diane, 12
Davis, Floyd Herman, Jr, 72
Davis, Marion Lorene, 77
De Guzman, Joseph Acosta, 79
De Metz, Ouida Kaye, 48
Deangelis, Edith Gladys Theresa, 36
Debold, Conrad II, 81
Delamater, Jerome Herbert, 48
Dennhardt, Gregory Chris, 12
Deny, Sharron Louise Kerr, 5
Detwiler, Frederick Emrey Jr, 36
Dibbell-Hope, Sandy, 65
Diller, Vivian Felice, 65
Disanto-Rose, Mary, 25
Dittmar, Ana M, 36
Dixon-Stowell, Brenda M, 5
Dobbin, Jay D, 37
Dorward, E. Marion, 25
Driscoll, Kathleen, 12
Duffy, Alice Marie, 92
Duke, Jerry Childress, 37
Dunn, Deborah Gail, 37
Dunner, Leslie Byron, 55
Duvall, Richard Paul, 25
Edwards, Charles Malcolm, 78
Eler, Barbara Jean, 65
Ellis, Margaret, 90
Emery, Leonore Lynne Fauley, 48
Engelhard, Doris Louise, 55
Ensign, Cynthia Jane Peterson, 55
Esses, Maurice I, 48
Evans, Jeffrey Ernest, 13

Federico, Ronald Charles, 82
Fellom, Martie, 88
Fenton, Wiiliam N, 37
Fischer, Barry, 13
Fitt, Sally Sevey, 79
Fitzgerald, Lynne E, 86
Fortunato, Joanne Alba, 85
Foster, Susan Leigh, 92
Fowler, Sarah B, 92
Fox, Jacqueline Elizabeth, 65
Franke, Johannah Schwarz, 25
Franken, Marjorie Ann, 37
Franko, Mark, 93
Freedman, Diane C, 38
Friesen, Joanna, 93
Fuller, Pamela Elizabeth, 79
Fusillo, Lisa Jean, 13
Gallemore, Sandra L., 25
Garafola, Lynn, 82
Gargaro, Kenneth Vance, 90
Garwood, Ronald Edward, 82
Gaus, Dorothy Shipley, 38
Gentes, Mary Josephine, 38
Gerbes, Angelika Renate, 48
Gibbons, Ruth Elizabeth Goodling, 93
Gintautiene, Kristina, 82
Glann, Janice Graham, 49
Glasow, E. Thomas, 82
Godowns, James Stephens, 55
Goldfield, Emily Dawson, 26
Goodrick, Terry Suzanne, 66
Googooian, Martha G, 26
Gordon, Sarah Ellen, 73
Gottheim, Vivien I, 38
Gray, Judith A, 5
Green, Eleanor Ruth, 66
Greenfield, Sarah Curtice, 61
Gregory, Robin Winifred, 61
Griffin, Vivian Joy, 66
Griffith, Betty Rose, 49
Gustafson, Sandra Elizabeth, 13
Gutierrez, Ireneo (Neo) Jr, 6
Gwynn, Eleanor W. Faucette, 13
Hagood, Thomas Kerry, 1
Halstead, Carol Elizabeth Decker, 66
Hanna, Judith Lynne, 38
Hansell, Kathleen Kuzmick, 49
Hansen, Martha Alice, 6
Hansen, Robert Craig, 82
Hanstein, Penelope, 14
Harding, Frances, 38
Hargrave, Susan Lee, 14
Hatch, Frank White, 66
Hatton, Gaylen A, 55
Hauck, Shirley A, 39

Hays, Joan Camille Francis, 79
Hazzard-Gordon, Katrina Yovonne, 39
Hearth, Dale Lynn, 2
Heausler, Nancy Lea, 26
Helpern, Alice J, 14
Herthel, Thomas Barnes, 93
Heth, Charlotte Ann Wilson, 39
Hinckley, Priscilla Baird, 26
Hindman, Anne Andrews, 49
Hinitz, Blythe Simone Farb, 9
Hirsch, Agnes A, 26
Hitchcock, Ned II, 93
Hodson, Millicent Kaye, 14
Hoehn, William Todd, 55
Hoffer, Diane Lynn, 83
Holcomb, James Marion, 67
Holloway, Jane Howell, 56
Hood, Robley, Munger, 14
Hoover, Carolyn Faye, 26
Horwitz, Dawn Lille, 49
Hottendorf, Diane, 93
Howe, Dianne Sheldon, 94
Hughes, Sarah Mahler, 56
Humphrey, Nicolas S, 94
Ingram, Anne Gayle, 27
Ito, Sachiyo, 39
Jay, Danielle Mary, 27
Jeffries, Catherine Wilson, 27
Jenkins, Jane R, 50
Jette, Nadine Marie, 67
Johnson, Cynthia June, 73
Johnson, Nancy Diers, 94
Johnson, Norman W., Jr, 77
Johnson, Ray, 67
Johnston, Elizabeth Carrington, 83
Kaeppler, Adrienne Lois, 39
Kaloyanides, Michael George, 56
Kaprelian, Mary Haberkorn, 94
Kaslow, Florence Whiteman, 67
Kassing, Gayle Irma, 50
Kasson, Cheryl G, 9
Kavaler, Susan Ivy, 67
Keali, 'Inohomoku, Joann Wheeler, 40
Kearns, Kathryn Fisher, 27
Keefer, Julia L, 6
Kehoe, Alice Beck, 40
Kerr, Julie Ann, 86
Kilpatrick, David Bruce, 56
Kim, Deukshin, 40
Kim, Malborg, 94
Kim, Theresa Ki-Ja, 40
Kimber, Robert James, 40
Klem, Yonah, 67
Kmen, Henry Arnold, 50
Koritz, Amy E, 95

Krance, Charles Andrew, 73
Kuo, Yu-Chun, 57
La Pointe, Janice McCaleb, 83
Lally, Kathleen Ann, 2
Larson, LeRoy Wilbur, 57
Lastrucci, Carlo Lawrence, 57
Latham, Jacqueline Quinn Moore, 6
Lawson, Mary Elizabeth, 40
Lazarus, J. A. Abbiechild, 95
Lee, Marie Smith, 28
Lee, Meewon, 40
Lee, Sun-ock, 14
Lehman, Rhea H, 83
Lekis, Lisa, 41
Lepczyk, Billie Frances, 61
Leshock, Malvina M., 57
Lessard, Elizabeth C, 79
Leventhal, Marcia Binnie, 67
Levi, Bruce Alan, 95
Levy, Francine Joan, 68
Lewis, Ellistine Perkins, 41
Lindner, Erna Caplow, 68
Lindquist, Barbara Anne, 2
Lindsey, Mort, 83
Little, Araminta Anne, 86
Lively-Berger, Rosalind Calvert, 95
Lloyd, Marcia Lou, 28
Lorber, Richard, 90
Lord, Madeleine Charlotte, 28
Lundahl, Vera L, 87
Lunt, Joanne Margaret, 28
Mace, Carroll Edward, 41
MacPherson, William Alan, 57
Madden, Dorothy Gifford, 15
Majzels, Claudine, 76
Maletic, Vera, 95
Malnig, Julie M, 88
Mandelbaum, Jean, 9
Mandin, Lucille Marie, 15
Manning, Susan Allene, 15
Marcow, Vivien Joy, 68
Marek, Patrica Anabel, 68
Mariani, Myriam Evelyse, 61
Marsh, Carol, 50
Martin, Jennifer Kaye Lowe, 50
Martin, Randy, 15
Martin, Vicki Lee, 15
Martinez-Hunter, Sanjuanita, 51
Maschio, Geraldine Ann, 77
Mathieu, Louise, 95
McConnell Anne, 51
McConnell, Judith Ann, 68
McCutchen, Mary Gene, 28
McKinney, Barbara Joan, 73
McQuillan, Melissa Ann, 76

McVoy, James Earl, Jr, 57
Mead, Bernard Franklin, Jr, 96
Meckel, Mary V, 41
Mehraban, Ho-sein Shirazi Zadeh, 57
Mehrhof, Joella Hendricks, 2
Melcer, Fannie Helen, 28
Merrill, Stina Margareta, 15
Miles, James Baker, 68
Miller, Raphael Francis, 16
Mills, Antonia Curtze, 41
Minton, Sandra Cerny, 29
Mirabella, Bella Maryanne, 73
Mishler, Craig Wallace, 42
Mitchell, Lillian Leonora, 6
Moe, Lawrence Henry, 58
Montague, Mary Ella, 69
Monty, Paul Eugene, 51
Morrow, Robert Russel, 58
Moses, Nancy Heise, 61
Moss, Susan F, 87
Mozafarian, Darius Masoud, 91
Murphy, Timothy Fredric, 69
Murray, Patricia Ann, 69
Muxworthy Feige, Dian Margaret, 29
Nadon-Gabrion, Catherine Anne, 29
Napoli, Joanne, 73
Nasaruddin, Mohamed Chouse, 42
Neal, Nelson Douglas, 29
Nelson, Susan Adele Lee, 16
Neser, Gwendolyn, 16
Ness, Sally Ann Allen, 42
Nichols, Lucille Marie, 80
Nickolich, Barbara Estelle, 16
Nixon, Jessica Eliza, 30
Norwood, Louanne Cobb, 91
Nosse, Carl Eugene, 84
Novack, Cynthia Jean, 42
O'Donnell, Mary Patricia, 30
O'Neill, Donna Kathlyn, Vansant, 62
Oglesby, Carole Ann, 69
Olander, Kathleen Rae, 30
Olson, Kevin, 80
Oshuns, Margaret Gwen, 69
Oswalt, Helen Athera, 88
Overby, Lynnette Young, 16
Owen, Jerry Michael, 58
Palmiotto, Carol Elaine, 84
Pantaleoni, Hewitt, 42
Pappalardo, Margaret Doyle, 80
Parker, Ellen, 2
Paulson, Pamela, Nan, 3
Payne-Carter, David, 6
Penney, Phyllis Annette, 91
Pepin, M. Natalie, 58
Perkins, Janet Blair, 51

Peters, Jonathan Alexander Samuel, 42
Peterson, Daniel, 76
Phillips, Daniel Alvord, 96
Phillips, Partricia Ann, 51
Plastino, Janice Gudde, 80
Pond, Marden Jensen, 58
Popkin, Sheryl S, 16
Powell, J Robin, 69
Powell, Rita Kirk, 96
Powell, Suzanne Marilyn, 96
Preston-Dunlop, Valerie Morthland, 62
Prevots-Wallen, Naima, 17
Primus, Pearl, 42
Propper, Herbert, 17
Pruett, Diane Milhan, 58
Puretz, Susan Luskin, 70
Putnam, Mark Glenn, 58
Pyron, Mary Virginia, 74
Rae, Caral Yvonne, 17
Ramirez, Emma Hocking, 30
Ramsay, Margaret Hupp, 51
Raskind, Lisa Bonoff, 84
Rausch, Carlos, 59
Ravarour, Adrian Hill, 17
Ray, Ollie Mae, 7
Reichart, Sarah Bennett, 88
Richards, Sylvia Pelt, 7
Richardson, James Alexander, Jr, 80
Ries, Frank W. D, 84
Riis, Thomas Laurence, 52
Riley, Alan, 30
Rinzler, Paul E., 59
Rio, Janice Andrea, 96
Rivers, Olivia Skipper, 43
Robbins, Bonnie, 70
Rock, Judith, 52
Roman, Adylia Rose, 30
Roos, Gertruida Woutrina, 30
Rose, Albirda Jean Landry Charles, 31
Roswell, Peggy McGuire, 31
Rubin, Martin Lewis, 17
Russell, Tilden A., 59
Ruyter, Nancy Lee, 52
Sagolla, Lisa Jo, 17
Saleh, Magda Ahmed Abdel Ghaffar, 43
Salvati, Julianne Mia, 74
Sande, David Joseph, 9
Sanders, Gary Elvin, 31
Sandoval, Marina Consuelo, 43
Santos, Ramon Pagayon, 59
Scarborough, Cindy, 17
Schaefer, George E, 18
Schlundt, Christena Lindborg, 7
Schneider, Friedrech Johann, 70
Schnoenhof, Madeleine, 31

Schoettler, Eugenia, 52
Schubert, Deborah David, 31
Schuman, Barbara Jean, 3
Schwartz, Vera Simon, 70
Seidel, Andrea Mantell, 18
Sgroi, Angela, 31
Shackelford, George Thomas Madison, 76
Shafranski, Paulette Evelyn, 18
Shaw, Sylvia Jean, 70
Sheehy, Daniel Edward, 59
Sheerwood, Sandra Mason, 74
Sheets, Maxine L, 96
Shell, Caroline Goodrich, 84
Shelley, Paula Diane, 74
Sherlock, Joyce Inglis, 97
Siegel, Elaine Vivian, 71
Silva, Maristela De Moura, 32
Silver, Judith A, 71
Skye, Ferial Deer, 71
Sloan, Ronna Elaine, 7
Sloss, Joan Nora, 71
Smith, A William, 62
Smith, Dorman Jesse, 32
Smith, Ronald Richard, 43
Smith, Sylvia Alexis, 32
Snyder, Diana Marie, 18
Soares, Janet Mansfield, 7
Sparkis, Sylvia Traska, 43
Sparrow, Patricia, 18
Sperber, Martin, 19
Stampp, Michele Susan, 62
Stanton, Lilian, 74
Steinke, Gary Lee, 19
Stevens-Jefcoate, Christine M, 97
Stewart, John Dean, 60
Stinson, Susan W, 32
Straits, Sue Ann, 32
Strickland, William Franklin, 74
Strobel, Katherine Brown, 44
Summers, Louis Jeriel, 19
Sutlive, Josephine Laffiteau, 10
Sweet, Jill Drayson, 44
Sweigard, Lulu E, 80
Swift, Mary Grace, 84
Sydor, Elizabeth Ernst, 60
Tate, Patricia Coleman, 60
Taylor, Margaret Jane, 97
Taylor, Willie Lee, 71
Thomas, William Radford, III, 33
Thomson, Susan Jean, 44
Trexler, Alice Elizabeth, 19
Trigg, Marilyn Gertude, 72
Trujillo, Lorenzo Alan, 72

Tucker, Iantha Elizabeth Lake, 52
Turner, Eula Douglas, 7
Turner, Louise Kreher, 19
Twillie, Gwendolyn Brown, 33
Vallance, Janette Margaret, 10
Vallillo, Stephen M, 8
Valverde, Carmen Edna, 33
Van Camp, Julie Charlotte, 97
Van Dyke, Jan Ellen, 87
Van Hoy, Karen Lee Anderson, 33
Vashi, Nataraj G, 74
Vedder, Clyde B, 88
Venson, Gloria Mathis, 72
Vickers, Clinton John, 75
Volland, Anita, 44
Wagner, Ann Louise, 53
Wagner, Charlotte A, 53
Wallock, Susan Frieder, 97
Walsh, John J, 85
Walther, Suzanne, 20
Warner, Mary-Jane Evans, 53
Weaver, Wilhelmina Clark, 44
Weeks, Sandra Rivers, 8
Welsh, Deborah Jane, 98
Welton, John Lee, 75
West, Jeanne M, 75
Westfall, Suzanne Ruth, 53
Wheeler, Mark Frederick, 87
White, Judith Simpson, 75
White-Dixon, Melanye P, 33
Whiteman, Erlyne F., 3
Whitman, James Kerry, 60
Wiesner, Theodora, 34
Wild, Stephen Aubury, 45
Wiles, Patricia Joyce Wade, 85
Williams, Drid, 98
Willis, Cheryl M, 89
Wilson, John Michael, 77
Wilson, Kristine Lee, 84
Wilson, Timothy Robert, 72
Winchell, Richard Marvin, 60
Winslow, David John, 88
Witherell, Anne Louise, 53
Wong, Peter Kim-Hung, 45
Woodbury, Virginia Garton, 85
Worthy, Terry Ellen, 98
Wortman, Mary Alice, 45
Wrazen, Louise Josepha, 60
Wynne, Shirley Spackman, 53
Youngerman, Suzanne, 45
Yousof, Ghulam-Sarwar, 45
Yun Chang Sik, 75
Zasloff, Ira, 89
Zupp, Nancy Thornhill, 20

Index by Abstract Title

Adapted dance for mentally retarded children: An experimental study, 64

Adult amateur dancers: A field study of their learning, 31

Aesthetic education: Interdisciplinary and the interrelated arts approach based on the ANISA model (Activities in movement, music, and language arts), 29

"Always at Sea": Selected traditions of Martha's Vineyard presented in dance, 15

The Alwin Nikolais artist-in-residence program at the University of Wisconsin-Madison: An ethnography of dance curriculum-in-use, 32

The American careers of Rita Sangalli, Giuseppina Morlacchi and Maria Bonfanti: Nineteenth century ballerinas, 4

American folklore revival: A study of an old-time music and dance community, 35

The American Indian culture and its relationship to dance and games, 36

An analysis and comparison of the choreographic process of Alwin Nikolais, Murray Lois, and Phyllis Lamhut, 20

An analysis of attitudes and definitions by selected teachers and pupils toward dance in general and dance in the classroom, 66

An analysis of management competencies as viewed by selected dance administrators in dance programs in higher education in the United States, 3

Analysis of "Orion, a Ballet", 57

An analysis of professional conceptions of modern dance education as reflected in "Journal of Physical Education and Recreation" and in "Dance Magazine". Articles from January 1965 to December 1979, 26

An analysis of relationships between experiences in correlated courses in art, music, and modern dance and certain behavioral changes related to aesthetic experience, 68

Analysis of selected factors related to the element of space in movement creativity, 67

Analysis of the dance sequences in Busby Berkeley's films; "Forty Second Street": "Footlight's Parade"; and "Gold Diggers" of 1935, 19

An analysis of the taxi-dance hall as a social institution with special reference to Los Angeles and Detroit, 88

An analysis of three non-objective choreographic techniques, 11

Ang putting waling- waling: A musico-dance drama in three acts: Story, libretto and music (original composition, musical (volumes I and II), 59

The Ann Hutchinson School at work, 31

Anne Schley Duggan: Portrait of a dance educator, 8

An anthropological study of masks as teaching aids in the enculturation of Mano children, 42

The anthropology of dance ritual: Nigeria's Ubakala Nkwa Di Iche Iche, 38

Anxiety and energy expenditure in modern dance, 80

Anyone can dance: A survey and analysis of Swahili Ngoma, past and present, 37

An approach to human movement for the stage, 77

The art and craft of filming dance as a Documentary, 89

Art and enterprise in Diahilev's Ballets Russes. (Volums I and II), 82

Art in the dance: A study of the use of the fine arts in Anthony Powell's "A dance to the music of time", 74

The art of dance in the USSR: A study of politics, ideology, and culture, 84

The arts in Polynesia—A study of the function and meaning of art forms in the pre-contact Pacific, 44

Assessment of attitude change and position shift in fourth graders after participation in modern dance, 29

The assessment of dance movement satisfaction of elementary age children participating in a creative dance instructional program, 31

An assessment of the functions of dance in the broadway musical: 1940/41–1968/69, 49

The assessment of the inter-rater agreement and validity of observation techniques for the identification of neuromuscular excitation patterns, 79

"Atiba's a Comin": The rise of social dance formations in Afro-American culture, 39

Atrox: The composition, performance and analysis of a chamber composition for abstract choreography, 60

Attitudes of Canadians of Ukrainian descent toward Ukrainian dance, 70

Ballet and modern dance on television in the decade of the 70's, 91

Ballet as a special case of dance: Implications for program development, 85

Ballet as an occupation, 82

Ballet comes to America, 1792–1842: French contributions to the establishment of theatical dance in New Orleans and Philadelphia, 47

The ballet dancer: In-depth psychobiographical case studies, 65

"Ballet: 'La Belle Dame Sans Merci' ", 81

The ballet music of Constant Lambert: A study of collaboration in music and dance, 56

Ballet of the Jesuit in Italy, Germany, and France, 85

Ballet: 'The Lottery', 18

The Ballets Suedois: Modernism and the painterly stage, 14

The bawdy politic: Strips of culture and the culture of strip, 35

The Beaver Indian prophet dance and related movements among North American Indians, 41

A behavioral cybernetic interpretation of dance and dance culture, 66

Bella Lewitzky: A description of her methods and views on performance and choreography, 5

Bilateral asymmetry in the alignment of the skeletal framework of the human body, 80

A biographical study of the lives and contributions of two selected contempory black male dance artists-Arther Mitchell and Alvin Ailey—in the idioms of ballet and modern dance, respectively, 6

Biographies of selected leaders in tap dance, 7

A biography of Charles Weidman with emphasis upon his professional career and his contributions to the field of dance, 7

A biography of Walter Terry with emphasis upon his professional career and his contributions to the field of dance, 3

Biomechanical analysis of the classical grand plié and two stylistic variations, 79

Biomechanical quantification of specific ballet movements using tri-axial cinematography, 80

Birth of a ballet: August Bournoville's "A Folk Tale," 1854, 83

"The Black Crook": Ballet in the gilded age (1866–1876), 82

Black dance continuum: Reflections on the heritage connection between African dance and Afro-American jazz dance, 85

Black dance in the United States from 1619 to 1970, 48

Black musical theatre in New York, 1890–1915, 52

Bob Fosse: An analytic-critical study, 7

Body awareness: The kinetic awareness work of Elaine Summers, 69

Body pleasure, language and world: A framework for the critical analysis of dance education, 92

Body politic: The dances of Mary Wigman, 15

Boris Volkoff: Dancer, teacher, choreographer, 6

Breath: Principles derived from Eastern and Western literature and suggestions for its use in modern dance, 86

"B'resheet"—a ballet inspired by the commentaries of Rashi. (Original composition), 58

Career patterns of 1961–1965 graduates of performing dance curricula in selected colleges and universities, 25

Change in social dance song style at Allegany Reservation, 1962-1973: The Rabbit Dance (volumes I and II), 38

The changes in composition, function, and aesthetic criteria as a result of acculturation found in five traditional dances of the Eastern band of Cherokee Indians in North Carolina, 43

Changing self-esteem of women through Middle Eastern dance, 63

The charms of compliassance: The dance in England in the early eighteenth century, 53

Children expressing emotions in dance: A phenomenological study, 9

The choreographic devices: Their nature and function as related to the principle of opposition, 18

A choreographic experiment with mixed means for the purpose of communicating through the act of theatre, 13

The choreographic innovations of Vaslav Nijinsky: Towards a dance-theatre, 14

The choreographic intent as analysed by three audiences, 18

Choreographic models using a group process: Analysis and production, 16

Choreography in the American musical, 1960–1969: The dramatic functions of dance, 17

A cine-dance work: "Progression", 15

A clarification of the concept of focus in the performing art of dance, 11

The classical ballet dancer: A psyco-social analysis of the dance personality profile, 83

Clog dance of the Appalachian mountain region of the United States of America, 37

The coherence of gestures in improvisational dance: An empirical exploratory study informed by Merleau-Ponty's phenomenological ontology, 95

A collection of dance music of Europe: 1200–1600 transcribed and arranged for school instrumental ensembles, 58

Collegial conversation: A search for meaning in children's creative dance., 10

Commentary on creative dance in elementary schools with filmed anecdotes, 28

A comparative analysis of "Othello" and "The Moor's Pavanne:" An Aristotelian approach to dances based on dramatic literature, 93

A comparison of organizational principles used by the choreographer, composer and painter which incorporates dance as an educational focus, 24

A comparison of the attention span of hyperactive and nonhyperactive children while performing to live and recorded dance instructions, 9

A comparison of the effects of dance and physical education on the self-concept of selected disadvantaged girls, 70

A comparison of the novice and experienced dancers' imaginary ability with respect to their performance on two body awareness tasks, 16

A comparison of two aesthetic theories as they apply to modern dance, 94

The composition, performance and analysis of an original musical work, "The Seven Ages of Man": A chamber ballet based on text by William Shakespeare, 83

Compositional form in modern dance and modern art, 87

The concept of Machismo in the poetry, music, and dance of the Gaucho of the Rio De La Plata, 45

The concepts and practices of elementary pointe technique level students, 84

Concepts related to the development of creativity in modern dance, 86

Contemporary accounts of dance from the American West in the nineteenth century, 47

Contemporary aesthetic theory applied to dance as a performing art, 96

Contemporary dance and a feminist aesthetic, 95

A content analysis of modern dance values with application to recreation, 96

Continuity and change within a social institution: The role of the taxi-dancer, 41

Continuity and creativity in Tiv theatre, 38

A contrastive study of movement style in dance through the Laban perspective, 61

The contribution of beginning modern dance to cardiovascular fitness in college women, 79

The contribution of French court dance to performance of the Couperin organ masses, 55

The contributions of selected Broadway musical theatre choreographers: Connolly, Rasch, Balanchine, Holm, and Alton, 16

Country Western dance: Analysis, description, and illustrated instructional materials, 32

Creation and performance of six original works by six choreographers: Danced by one soloist enahanced by video introductions for analysis of audience perceptions, 18

Creative dance for lchildren: Materials and methods for the first three grades, 30

Creative movement: A analysis of methods used by experts, 30

A creative synthesis of dance and video-electronics: An exploratory investigation, 91

The creative thesis: Criteria for procedural development and evaluation, 98

Crime, curriculum and the performing arts: A challenge for inner city schools to consider integrated language, music, drama and dance experiments as compensatory curriculum for at-risk urban minorities in Elementary school (Volumes I and II), 20

A critical and historical analysis of dance as a code of the Hollywood musical, 48

Criticism in the art of dance: An analysis of John Martin's reviews in the "New York Times", 1928–1962, 93

Cultural influences on dance in the T'ang dynasty and the movement characteristics of a dance of the period, 45

Cultural patterns as revealed by the content of selected dance magazines, 96

The cultural production of dance in Britain, with particular reference to Ballet Rambert and Christopher Bruce's "Ghost Dances", 97

The current status of dance education in Wisconsin and developmental influences, 24

Curricular activities of the secondary school modern dance teacher, 24

Dance and instrumental "differences" in Spain during the seventeenth and eighteenth centuries, 48

Dance and jazz elements in the piano music of Maurice Ravel, 58

Dance and movement therapies: A study in theory and applicability, 67

Dance and music of the Desa performing arts of Malaysia, 42

Dance as a cutural trait of some cutural groups of the Inca empire at the time of the Spanish conquest, 44

Dance as communication code in Romanian courtship and marriage rituals, 38

Dance as expression in Mozart opera, 75

Dance as recreation: A comparison of college students' perceived values in dancing, 33

Dance commentary: An original suite of fourteen dances based upon the evolution of dance through the ages of man, 17

The dance compositions of Edgar Degas, 76

The dance direction of Ned Wayburn: Selected topics in musical staging, 1901–1923, 12

The dance direction of Seymour Felix on Broadway and in Hollywood from 1918 through 1953, 3

Dance education in American schools: 1925 to 1935, 28

The dance factory: A collegiate dance company as a artistic enterprise, 16

Dance for the hearing-impaired in the United States, 30

Dance in a sightless world: A phenomenology, 65

Dance in Denver's pioneer theatres: 1859–1871, 46

Dance in Sanskirt literature from Panini to Bharata Muni, 74

The dance in the art of Pieter Bruegel the elder, 76

Dance in the public schools: Implementing state policies and curricular guidelines for dance in education—a nationwide study, 1

Dance injuries: An audio-slide presentation, 79

The dance motif in Zola's "L'Assommoir", 73

Dance music in printed Italian lute tablatures from 1507 to 1611, 58

A dance of Senghor, Achebe, Soyinka, and African cultural history, 42

The dance of Shiva, 60

"The Dance of the Seven Veils": A historical and descriptive analysis, 60

Dance on the St. Louis stage: 1850 1870, 50

Dance ritual and cultural values in a Mexican village: Festival of Santo Santiago, 35

Dance therapy for the special child: An integrative treatment model, 67

Dance therapy: Foundations and organization of theory and practice, 68

Dance therapy with a nonverbal, autistic child: A documentation of process, 65

Dance therapy with adult day hospital patients, 68

Dance/movement as active imagination: Origins, theory, practice, 65

Dance/movement therapy: A survey of philosophy and practice, 97

The dancer from the dance: Meaning and creating in modern dance, 13

The dances of the processing of Seville in Spain's golden age, 46

Dancing ground: An approach to the criticism of the modern dance, 93

Dancing in the dark: The life and times of Margot Webb in Aframerican vaudeville of the swing era, 5

A delineation of three major sources of artistic output on the production of dance art films, 90

A delineation of tree major sources of artistic output in the production of dance art films, 91

A description of children's verbal responses to a modern dance work in grades kindergarten through six, 10

Descriptive analysis of fifteenth-century Italian dance and related concepts found in Antonio Cornazano's dance threatise "Libro Dell 'Arte Del Danzare" (citta del vaticano, Biblioteca apostolica Vaticana, Codice Capponiano 203) and in the dance treatise of Domenico Da Piacenza, Cornazano's teacher, "De Arte Saltandi et Choreas Ducendi", 62

Designing and constructing costumes for modern dance, 86

Development and evaluation of a teacher behavior instructional unit for eliciting creative movement performance, 23

The development of a refined movement analysis and it's relationship to motor creativity among grade two children, 62

Development of creative dance for children in the United States: 1903–1973, 26

The development of creative movement within early childhood education, 1920 to 1970, 9

The development of dance in Mexico: 1325–1910, 51

A developmental project for advanced dance-movement therapists in Israel: An intercultural experiment, 64

The developmentof a theoretical position on conducting using principles of body movement as explicated by Rudolf Laban, 54

The differences between dance programs allied with physical education departments and fine arts departments in American colleges and universities, 1

Differential effects of a comparative advance organizer on performance, attitudes and practice in learning a dance skill, 27

The director-choreographer in the American musical theatre, 12

Divine dancer: The life and work of Ruth St. Denis, 5

A documentation of the ethnic dance traditions of the Arab Republic of Egypt, 43

"Do'en dee dance": Description and analysis of the jombee dance of Montserrat, West Indies, 37

The dramaturgical functions of song, dance and music in the comedies of John Dryden, 72

The E. Azalia Hackley memorial collection of Negro music, dance, and drama: A catalogue of selected Afro-American materials, 41

Earth in flower: An historical and descriptive study of the classical dance drama of Cambodia, 36

The earth mysticism of the Native American tribal peoples with special reference to the circle symbol and the Sioux Sun Dance rite, 34

"The Ebony and Ivory Horse": Ballet for orchestra. (Musical score and essay), 57

The education of professional dancers: In inquiry into their secondary school experiences, 23

Educational criticism: Perceptions of values, criticism, and appreciation as aesthetic education across arts disciplines, 25

Educative dance: Fundamentals and practice, 30

e.e. cummings dramatic imagination: A study of three plays and a ballet, 74

The effect of a dance/movement activity program on the successful adjustment of aging in the active/independent older adult, 63

Effect of creative dance classes on the learning of spatial concepts and the ability to analyze spatial pathways in dance video by third and fourth grade students, 25

The effect of creative movement and contact improvisation experiences on self-awareness, 72

The effect of dance/movement on the self-concept of developmentally handicapped fourth and fifth grade students, 63

The effect of Kabuki training on the western performances of Western acting students, 76

The effect of movement exploration and mime on body-image, self-concept, and body-coordination of seventh grade children, 70

The effectiveness of a narrated dance/pantomime program in communicating selected basic health concepts of third graders, 26

The effectiveness of ballroom dance instruction on the self-concept and mobility of blind adults, 71

The effectiveness of movement strategies in reducing physically aggressive behaviors in five to twelve year old children hospitalized for severe conduct disorders, 70

The effects of a cognitive-affective structured arts curriculum upon the visual perceptual skills of pre-school disadvantaged children using a visual training approach, 32

Effects of a dance program on the creativity and movement behavior of pre-school handicapped children, 27

The effects of a data based dance skills program on the motor skill performance and self-concept of moderately handicapped students, 31

The effects of a Hispanic ethnic dance curriculum upon high school students' self concept and academic performance, 72

The effects of a semester of modern dance on the cardiovascular fitness and body composition of college women, 79

The effects of a six-week aerobic dance and folk dance program vs. the effects of a six-week aerobic jogging program on the cardiovascular efficiency and percent of body fat in postpubescent girls, 78

The effects of creative dance movement on development of a specific cognitive skill (spelling) in primary students, 31

The effects of creative dance on the school readiness of five year old children, 33

The effects of dance experiences upon observable behaviors of women prisoners, 69

The effects of dance /movement as a learning medium on the acquisition of selected word analysis concepts and the development of creativity of kindergaten and second grade children, 26

The effects of dance movement instruction on spatial awareness in elementary visually impaired students, and self-concept in secondary visually impaired students, 24

The effects of dance on selected physiological variables, 78

The effects of dance therapy on mentally retarded children, 67

The effects of dancing and relaxation sessions on stress levels of senior citizens, 67

The effects of discotheque dancing on selected physiological and psychological parameters of college students, 80

The effects of folk dancing upon reaction time and movement time of senior citizens, 64

The effects of modern dance and music on body image and self concept in college women, 67

The effects of movement notation on the performance, cognitions, and attitudes of beginning ballet students at the college level, 61

Effects of movement training on body awareness, self-concept, and antisocial behavior in forensic psychiatric patients, 68

The effects of several types of teaching cues on postural alignment of beginning modern dancers: A cinematographic analysis, 29

The effects of time related modern educational dance programs on the self-concept of fourth, fifth and sixth-grade girls in a Southern urban city, 72

The effects of two movement remediation programs on selected measures of perceptual-motor ability, academic achievement, and behavior on first grade children manifesting learning and perceptual-motor problems, 63

The effects of varying amounts of creative modern dance activities on creative-thinking ability and self concept, 72

Eleanor Metheny: Teacher scholar, 7

Embodiments: The social construction of gender in dance-events in a northern Greek town, 36

The emergence of social structure in a modern dance company: A case study, 12

Energy flow choreography: Principles of energy transformation and transcendental dance, 17

The English dancing master, 1660–1728: His role at court, in society, and on the public stage, 50

The English masque and the French court ballet, 1581–1640, 83

The entertainment of a noble patron: Early tudor household revels, 53

Erick Hawkins, modern dancer: History, theory, technique, and performance, 6

Ethnography of rumba: Dance and social change in contemporary Cuba, 36

Eve of Sant John's Day: A work in words and images based on an aesthetic inquiry into the dramatic-dance "Bumba-Meu-Boi" in San Luis of Maranhao, Brazil, 38

The evolution of jazz dance from folk origins to concert stage, 46

The evolution of Martha Graham's dance technique, 14

The evolvement of "Yimoko III": Zen dance choreography, 14

An examination of purpose concepts in creative dance for children, 21

An examination of the effects of range, frequency and duration of movement on rhythmic synchronization, 55

An examination of the methods and problems of dance theory written between 1930 and 1971, 91

Exhibition ballroom dance and popular entertainment, 88

Experiencing oneself in dance: A phenomenological study of centeredness, relatedness and projection, 71

Expert determination of knowledge and skills essential to the elementary classroom teacher for the instruction of creative dance, 28

An exploratory study of creative movement as a means of increasing positive self-concept, personal, and social adjustment of selected seventh grade students, 69

Expressive movement and psychopathology: An exploratory study, 62

Extinction and reconstruction of Aleut music and dance, 39

Extraversion—Introversion and the use of locomotor space in modern dance, 69

Facial decoration in Kathakali dance-drama, 12

"Femina Ludens" compared to exemplary games: A structural analysis of an avant-garde-derived process dance, 19

Film Series: Movement education for young children, 90

Folk dance as a staged attraction in Yugoslavia: A study of an evolving tradition, 43

Folk music of Fars Province, Iran: A section of children's games, folk songs, and dances, 57

The form of content: The dance-drama of Kurt Jooss, 20

The formulation of charted verbilizations in the study of human movement, 61

French court dance in England, 1706–1740: A study of the sources, 50

From a chorus line to "A Chorus Line": The emergence of dance in the American musical theatre, 52

From the "Sun Dance" to the "Ghost Dance": A social and intellectual history of the Lakotas, 1868 to 1890, 35

Function and style in Pontic dance music, 56

The function of the choreographer in the development of the conceptual musical: An examination of the work of Jerome Robbins, Bob Fosse, and Michael Bennett on Broadway between 1944 and 1981, 11

Gavottes and Bouquets: A comparative study of changes in dance style between 1700 and 1850, 53

Gendering bodies, performing art: Theatrical dancing and the performance aesthetics of Wilde, Shaw and Yeats, 95

George M. Cohan, Director (American Musical Comedy), 8

The Ghost Dance religion in Saskatchewan: A functional analysis, 40

The "Goralski" of the Polish Highlanders: Old World musical tradition from a New World perspective, 60

Gottfried Taubert on social and theatrical dance of the early eighteenth-century, 48

Gower Champion and the American musical theatre, 6

Graham's dance "Steps in the Street" and selected early technique: Principles for reconstructing choreography from videotape, 13

Grand Union (1970–1976), an improvisational performance group, 51

The great dance: A study of Eliot's use of the dance metaphor in the Four Quartets, 73

Greek votive reliefs to Pan and the nymphs, 78

Gregory Bateson and Waldorf education: Gestures in the dance variations on an aesthetic epistemological theme, 29

A guide to selected traditional dances of the Bendel State of Nigeria, 34

Guides for creative experiences in dance for the teacher in the self-contained classroom in the elementary school, 30

Gwich in Athapaskan music and dance: An ethnography and ethnohistory, 42

"Hahoe pyolsin-kut": The oldest extant Korean mask-dance theatre, 40

Harriette Ann Gray: Her life and her career as a dancer, choreographer, and teacher 1913–1968, 4

Heinrich Heine and Friedrich Nietzsche: Dance as metaphor and rhetorical imagery, 94

Hemisphericity and its relationship to athletics, art, dance and achievement: A study among grade twelve students, 23

Hemisphericity in athletes and dancers, 66

Hinduism through village dance drama: Narrative image and ritual process in South India's Terukkuttu and Yaksagana ritual theaters, 38

An historical account of the United States tours of the Royal Ballet of Great Britain from 1949–1970, 84

A historical study of the Society of Stage Directors and Choreographers through 1973, 47

A history of the Federal Dance Theatre of the Works Progress Administration, 1935–1939, 2

A history of the Robert Joffrey Ballet (Vols I and II), 46

The Hollywood Bowl and Los Angeles dance, 1926–1941: Performance theory and practice, 17

Hollywood Cine-Dance: A description of the interrelationship of camerawork and choreography in films by Stanley Donen and Gene Kelly, 90

An ideal model and flexible undergraduate dance major curriculum for two-year and four-year state-supported colleges and universities, 22

The ideational sources of the modern dance in America as expressed in the works of two leading exponents, Isadora Duncan and Ruth St. Denis, 86

Image into symbol: The evolution of the dance in the poetry and drama of W. B. Yeats, 75

Images of dancing in sixteenth-century English poetry, 73

Images of movement and dance in ancient Greek art: A qualitative approach, 51

Imagination and children: Implications for a theory of imagination in children's learnings, 8

Implicit knowledge of movement intelligence, 97

Improvisation in the performing arts: Music, dance and theatre, 19

Improvisations for modern dance: Implications for dance education, 22

The influence of Eastern thought in the dance of Erick Hawkins, 16

The influence of eighteenth-century social dance on the Viennese classical style, 88

Influence of instruction media on attitudes of modern dance students toward movement, 89

Influence of perceived aspects of parental and peer expectancies, warmth, and authority, on self-identification as active and competent movement performers, 69

The influence of the alpha rhythm during mental practice while acquiring a specific tap skill, 64

"The I'N-Lon-Schka" (playground-of-the-eldest son) the June ceremonial dance of the Osages: A study in American Indian arts, 35

Inquiry and art in elementary social study: Modern dance and social study in conjunction, 20

An instrument to measure the creative dance attitudes of grade five children, 63

Interpretive movement: A training approach for performers of literature, 75

An interrelated arts approach to awareness of selected composition components in art, music, and dance, 8

The interrelatedness of dance with music and art through a study of form as a unifying concept, 24

The interrelationships and effects of creative dance on the physical self-esteem, body image and problem solving of grade four children, 30

An intertextual model for the interaction of dancer and spectator in the Renaissance, 93

Investigation into the relationship between creative ability in dance, field independence, and creativity, 64

An investigation of aesthetic judgement ability and art patronage behavior by adolescents, 91

An investigation of the practices of selected Manhattan-based corporations and private foundations in assessing the eligibility of performing arts groups for funding, 2

An invitation to dance: The gentle art of teaching, 15

Isadora Duncan: A literary inquiry into the somatic foundations of her art, life, and ideology during the early years 1900–1914, 6

Isadora Duncan and Vaslav Nijinsky: Dancing on the brink, 92

An isotonic universal gym weight training program for dancers to increase strength, dispel myths, and increase subjective and objective dance technique, 80

The itinerant dancing and music masters of eighteenth century America, 54

Jean Cocteau and the ballet, 84

John Martin, dance critic: A study of his critical method in the dance as theatre art, 93

Judson Dance Theatre: Democracy's body 1962–1964, 10

"Kamyonguk": The mask-dance theater of Korea (t'alch'um, sandae, okwangdae), 40

The Kelantan Mak Yong dance theatre. A study of performance structure, 45

A key determinant of dance style: The structural use of the dance instrument as illustrated by the choreography of Katherine Dunham's "Rites de Passage", 13

Kinetic and kinematic parameters of landing impact forces in the dance jump and leap, 78

"Layers", an original composition for wind ensemble based on African rhythm, 59

"Le sacre du printemps": a comparative study of seven versions of the ballet, 11

Learning experiences in selected aspects of a dance movement sequence, 22

"A Legend of the Andes": Ballet in one act, 59

Leonide Massine: Choreographic genius with a collaborative spirit, 13

"Let me Dance before You": The education role of performance in a West African children's masquerade, 26

The life and art of Uday Shankar, 3

Lighting design for modern dance: Preferences of men and women, 15

Livrets of ballet and pantomimes during the French Revolution, 81

Louis Horst: Musician in a dancer's world, 7

Louis Pecour's 1700 "Recueil de Dances", 53

Luisa Triana: Biography of a Spanish dancer, 6

A magical flight: A study of religious symbolism in the romantic ballet, 84

Major influences affecting the development of jazz dance, 1950–1971, 85

Manifestations of the German expressionist aesthetic as presented in drama and art in the dance and writings of Mary Wigman, 94

Manual of square dancing, 89

Margaret H'Doubler's approach to dance education and her influence on two dance educators, 22

Marion Cuyjet: Visionary of dance education in black Philadelphia, 33

Marketing the performance arts: The Joffrey Ballet's twenty-fifth anniversary season., 2

Meaning in a dance form, 96

The meaning of the dancer in the poetry of William Butler Yeats, 73

"Medicine Wheel:" A ritual dance drama inspired by plains Indian myths and symbols, 18

Metrical and tonal stability in the dance music of the Fitzwilliam Virginal book, 60

Michel Fokine in America, 1919–1942, 49

Minuet, scherzando, and scherzo: The dance movement in transition, 1781–1825, 59

"The mirror of our selves": A psychoanalytic study in dance-movement therapy, 71

The modern dance as dramatic theatre (A comparison of selected elements), 77

Modern dance in a postmodern world, 87

Modes of aesthetic experience in the ballet de cour, 1581–1650, 81

Moliere, Lully, and the comedy-ballet, 82

Moliere's 'comedies-ballets', 82

Movement and world view: Applying Laban movement analysis and Magoroh Maruyama's paradigms to the Comanche dance and lifestyle data in three Tewa Pueblos, 43

Movement as cinematic narration: The concept and practice of choreography in film, 89

The movement effort quality profiles of children in a nursery school, 9

Movement experience in modern dance: A phenomenological inquiry, 92

Moving toward health: A study of the use of dance-movement therapy in the psychological adaption to breast cancer, 65

Music and dance at the John C. Campbell Folk School in Brasstown, North Carolina, 1925–1985, 47

Music and dance in their social and cultural nexus, 45

Music and drama in N Omai of northern Japan, 34

Music for a choreographic narrative and a supporting study: Composing for theatrical dance. (Volumes I and II). (Original score), 58

Music for dance. (original composition), 60

The music of Cretan dances, a study of the musical structures of Cretan dance forms as performed in the Irakleion Provinces of Crete, 56

The music of the English country dance, 1651–1728: With indexes of the printed sources, 57

Musical accompaniment for dance: Preference of males and females at four educational levels, 55

Musical education through rhythmical activity for elementary and junior high school teachers: A handbook for professional schools for teachers, 25

The myth of the Western Frontier in American dance and drama: 1930–1943, 49

A natural philosophy of movement style for theatre performers, 77

The nature of the embodiment of choreutic units in contemporary choreography, 62

The new poetry of William Carlos Williams: Poetic uses of music and dance, 74

New York burlesque: 1840–1870: A study in theatrical self-criticism, 47

Nijinsky's "New Dance": Rediscovery of ritual design in "Sacre du Printemps", 14

Nikolais dance theater: A total art work, 16

Notation systems for transcribing verbal and nonverbal behavior in adult education research: Linguistics (phonetics and phonemics), paralinguistics, proxemics, the micro analysis of the organized flow of behavior, haptics, dance notations, and kinesics, 61

On expression and its artistic meaning in dance, 94

On the aisthetic and aesthetic dimensions of the dance: A methodology for researching dance style, 95

On the nature of art making in dance: An artistic process skills model for the teaching of choreography, 14

Opera and ballet at the Regio Ducai Teatro of Milan, 1771–1776: A musical and social history, 49

The opera-ballet of Andre Campra: A study of the first period French opera-ballet, 54

The opera-ballet: Opera as literature (Portions of text in French), 51

The organizational sociology of dance: An analysis, comparison and environmental description of primary organizations advocating dance in higher education., 1

The origin and development of ethnic Caribbean dance and music, 41

Origins of traditional Okinawan dance, 39

P. T. Barnum: a work for dancers, musicians and electronic tape (Original Composition), 11

Painters and the ballet, 1917–1926: An aspect of the relationship between art and theatre, 76

"Parade" and "Le Spectacle Interieur": The role of Jean Cocteau in an avant-garde ballet, 81

Parallels of African-based movement traits and aesthetic principles in selected examples of American modern dance, 86

Part I—Mute rhetoric dance in Shakespeare and Marston. Part II—The Machine in the Garden: The theme of work in 'Tess of the D'Urbervilles'. Part III—Art and imagination in Edith Wharton's 'The House of Mirth', 73

Passionate learning: The process of educating the creative arts therapist, 68

Pearl Primus—in search of her roots: 1943–1970, 4

Performance requirements held by artistic directors of professional modern dance companies, 1

Performance space as sacred space in Aranda Corroboree—An interpretation of the organization and use of space as a dramatic element in the performance of selected Aborignal ritual in central Australia, 40

Period movement style and the waltz: A choreo-kinetic model for actor training, 77

A phenomenological investigation of improvisation in music and dance, 95

The phenomenology of dance, 96

A philosophical, historical, and cultural analysis of the American square dance (volumes I and II), 51

Philosophical problems of dance criticism, 97

A philosophical study of qualitative movement: Implications for early childhood music programs, 21

A physiologic and aesthetic cross-sectional analysis of modern dancers, 78

Pirouettes with bayonets: Classical ballet metamorphosed as dance-drama and its usage in the People's Republic of China as a tool of political . . . , 81

The placement of the dance program within the college and university in relation to the congruence of goals across three administrative structures, 3

A plan for programming sequential integrated dance and rhythmic activities for the elementary school level utilizing the medium of television, 22

A portrayal of the Brazilian Samba dance with the use of Labananalysis as a tool for movement analysis, 61

The preparation of a manual for the teaching of dance composition through the use of folk dance materials, 34

Principles and techniques of choreography: A study of five choreographers from 1983, 10

Principles for the establishment and conduct of programs in dance for senior high school girls, 23

Principles for the use of stylized movement during the interpretation and performance of literature based on Martha Graham's use of classical tragedy in modern dance, 12

A prismatic approach to the analysis if style in dance, 93

A procedure for systematically describing teacher-student verbal and nonverbal interaction in the teaching of choreography, 28

The professional dance musician, 57

A profile of Catherine Littlefield, a pioneer of American ballet, 4

A profile of women leaders in physical education, sport, athletics and dance organizations and a study of role models and mentors of the leaders, 3

A program of proposed study of five integrated arts including visual art, music, drama literature, and creative dance designed specifically for both future elementary teachers and elementary students, 33

Projection in dance, 92

A psychobiographical study of Vaslav Nijinsky, 4

Reading bodily action from the operatic score: A new approach to the operatic criticism domain with reference to Gaim Carlo Menotti's "The Telephone", 76

Reading dancing: Gestures towards a semiotics of dance, 92

Recommendations for professional preparation in dance for the public schools of Missouri, 23

Reflections and visions: A hermeneutic study of dangers and possibilities in dance education, 32

Reformers and visionaries: The Americanization of the art of dance, 52

The relationship among motor creativity, movement satisfaction, and the utilization of certain movement factors of second grade children, 8

The relationship between Shamanic ritual and the Korean masked dance-drama: The journey motif to chaos/darkness/void, 40

The relationship of dimensions of Jungian psychological type of college major, either physical education or dance, and preferred approach to teaching human movement, 70

The relationship of specific aptitudes to ability in square dance, 88

Relationships among interpretations of modern dance and cultural background, 95

The rhythm of Atsia dance drumming among the Anlo (Eve) of Anyako, 42

Rhythmic responses of normal elementary school children: An investigation of the developmental differences in the rhythmic response of the normal child when rhythmic stimulii is utilized as contrasted with music stimulii, 54

"Richard Cory" (original ballet), 84

"Ring": Concerto for dance and music. (Original composition), 57

The rise of the director/choreographer in the American musical theatre, 19

Rock dance in the United States, 1960–1970: Its origins, forms and patterns, 46

The role of Afro-Americans in dance in the United States from slavery through 1983: A slide presentation, 52

The role of movement in selected symbolic systems, 98

The role of Ruth St. Denis in the history of American dance: 1906–1922, 7

The role of the dance and dance lyrics in the Spanish comedia of the early eighteenth century, 46

Rudolf Laban's theory of modern educational dance: Implications for program development in elementary school, 32

The rural square dance in the Northeastern United States: A continuity of tradition, 88

Scandinavian-American folk dance music of the Norwegians in Minnesota, 57

Scenic and costume design for the Ballet Russes between 1909 and 1929, 82

Seeds of desire: The common ground of performance and politics, 15

Selected kinesthetic and psychological differences between the highly skilled in dance and in sports, 64

The Seneca Eagle dance: A study of personality expression in ritual, 37

Sensitivity to choreographic styles in dance as related to age, experience, and cognitive differences, 66

Seraikela Chhau dance and the creation of authority: From princely state to democracy, 44

Serena, Ruth St. Denis, and the evolution of belly dance in America (1876–1976), 51

Seventeenth-century dance characteristics in the organ masses of Francois Couperin (1668–1733), 56

Shakespeare into dance: The ballet of "Romeo and Juliet", 81

"Shaking is no Foolish Play": An anthropological perspective on the American shakers-person, time, space, and dance-ritual, 45

Sharing the dance: An ethnography of contact improvisation, 42

Shelley and the dance: A study of "Queen Mab," "Alastor," "Prometheus Unbound," and "The Triumph of Life", 75

The significance of dance in sixteenth century courtesy literature, 53

Singing and dancing in New Orleans: A social history of the birth and growth of ball and opera, 1791–1841, 50

The 'Sinulog' dancing of Cebu city, Philippines: A semiotic analysis, 42

The Skirt Dance: A dance fad of the 1890's, 88

Social dance in North Carolina before the twentieth century—an overview, 50

Social interaction in a drama dance group of hospitalized schizophrenics, 65

Societal influences on the programmes of modern dance in American colleges and universities: 1918–1945, 1

The society of Los Congos of Panama: An ethnological study of the music and dance-theatre of an Afro-Panamanian group, 43

Sociometric group structure and improvement of social dancing skill in recreation groups, 87

The Son Jarocho: The history, style, and repertory of a changing Mexican musical tradition, 59

Song and dance as an approach to teacher preparation in music for primary classroom teachers, 55

Space/symbol: The spatial concepts in selected dances of Martha Graham, 17

Spinning through the weltanschauung: The effects of the Nazi regime on the German modern dance, 87

Staging dance in higher education: A study to help teachers with theater experience in the presentation of dance programs in higher education, 28

A status study of dance and dance curricula in selected American colleges and universities with bases for establishing a department of dance, 33

Status survey of the mediated instructional materials used for dance in the area of higher education, 21

The stomp dance music of the Oklahoma Cherokee: A study of contempory practice with special reference to the Illinois District Council Ground. (volumes I & II), 39

The story of the Chou Dance of the former Mayurbhanj State, Orissa, 35

Stravinsky and dance: A conductor's study of "Renard", 55

Structure in motion: The influence of morphology, experience, and the ballet bar on verticality of alignment in the performance of the plié, 80

The structure of Tongan dance, 39

The student teaching experience: Perceptions of student teachers, cooperating teachers, and university supervisors, 25

The study and analysis of selected dance forms in the keyboard music of the Baroque period: A pedagogical guide for elementary pianists in college, 56

The study of arts directed programs in the Kent Intermediate School District, 1987–1988, 2

A study of creative expression courses in music and dance in selected liberal arts colleges, 26

A study of "Job, a Masque for Dancing" by Ralph Vaughan Williams, 85

A study of the effectiveness of teaching folk dancing by television to third and fourth grade children, 21

A study of the effects of dance education on stress in college-age American Indian women, 71

A study of the pasodobles of Pascual Marquina; including a brief history of the Spanish pasodoble and specific analysis of the performance practices of pasodobles from three established categories (volumes I and II), 54

A study of the relationship of an in-service program in music and movement to opportunities for creativity in selected Kindergartens, 9

A study of the relationship of Isadora Duncan to the musical composers and mentors who influenced her musical selection for choreography, 58

A study of the stability of perception for two extreme perceptual types, the visual and haptic, in relation to learning dance movements, 66

A study to describe and relate experiences for the use of teachers interested in guiding children in creative rhythmic movement, 21

The Sun Dance of the Oglala: A case study in religion, ritual, and ethnics, 36

"Sundry measures": Dance in Renaissance comedy, 74

Surface to essence: Appropriation of the Orient by modern dance, 87

A survey of arts education in programs in California public elementary schools, 30

A survey of student evaluations of teacher/course effectiveness within dance technique courses and the development of new instrumentation, 31

Symbolic expression in dance experience: Individuation and the sacred in three forms of dance, 98

Tap dance: Memories and issues of African-American women who performed between 1930 and 1950, 89

Teaching approaches in modern dance, 22

Teaching dance as a career, 27

The teaching of dance: A characterization of dance teacher behaviors in techniques and choreography classes at the University level, 28

Teaching the dance: Nietzsche as educator, 69

The television direction of a video-tape of original choreovideo dance: An analysis of selected spatial and design elements for choreographing television dance for presentation via video-tape, 19

Terpsichore at Louis Le Grand: Baroque dance on a Jesuit stage in Paris, 52

Tersichore in the night: Dance patterns and motifs in 'Voyage Au Bout De La Nuit', 73

Tewa ceremonial performances: The effects of tourism on an ancient Pueblo Indian dance and music tradition, 44

The theater of Angna Enters: American dance-mime, 5

Theatre as a verb: The theatre art of Martha Graham, 1923–1958, 18

A theatre of spatial poetry: A study of the Modern Dance drama as it concretizes twentieth-century visions of gesture, 10

Theatrical and dramatic elements of Haitian Voodoo, 34

Theatrical narrative dance in England: 1747–1775, 53

Theoretical foundation of dance in higher education in the United States 1933–1965, 49

Theory and methods for the anthropological study of dance, 40

Therapeutic aspects of folk dance: Self concept, body concept, ethnic distancing and social distancing, 71

Therapeutic Dance/Movement for Older Adults, 68

Three formats for the dance for winds, percussion, and six string instruments, 58

Three Quiché dance-dramas of Rabinal, Guatemula, 41

To want to dance: A biography of Margaret H'Doubler, 5

Topeng Pajegan: The mask dance of Bali (Indonesia), 37

Toward a general theory of body psychotherapy based on the theories of Reichian and dance-movement therapies, 67

Toward a structuralist approach to symbols in dance, 97

Toward an implicit theory of dance-movement therapy, 63

Towards the national theatre concept: A model for the development of dance education within the Ghanaian University system, 20

'Toxcatl' Ballet, 55

Tradition, change, and meaning in Kiribati performance: An ethnography of music and dance in a Micronesian society, 40

A tradition of spectacle: Busby Berkeley on stage and screen, 17

The traditional dances of the Cumberland Plateau, 44

Traditional Yugoslav dance in a changing society, 36

The tragic theatre: The "No" and Yeat's dance plays, 75

The transposition of literary and rhetorical constructs to dance theory and choreography, 96

Two perceptions of the purposes, aesthetic concepts and background for writing dance criticism according to selected literature and Washington, D.C. dance critics, 94

Unspeakable practices: Meaning and kinesis in dance, 92

The use of dance in Jacobean drama to develop character, 74

The uses of dance in the English language theatres of New Orleans prior to the Civil War, 1806–1861, 48

Utilization of funds and perceptions of corporate funding resources for university dance performance programs, 2

Videodance. (Dancing presented on T.V), 90

Virtue and virtuosity: America's vision of the romantic ballet, 1827–1840, 83

Visual information processing: Eye movements and success in replication of beginner and advance modern dancers, 27

W. B. Yeats and his "Sweet Dancer", 74

Wayang Wong in contemporary Bali, 35

William Yeats and the dancer: A history of Yeat's work with dance theatre, 75

The work of Bob Fosse and the choreographer-directors in the translation of musicals to the screen, 90

The world of Moliere's comedy-ballets, 46

Yakshagana Badagatittu Bayalata: A South Indian dance drama, 34

The Ziegfeld Follies: Form, content, and significance of an American revue, 77